SOGGY SNEAKERS

Guide to Oregon Rivers

WILLAMETTE KAYAK AND CANOE CLUB

SECOND EDITION

First Printing - February 1986
Second Printing - May 1986
Third Printing - July 1988
Fourth Printing - March 1990

ACKNOWLEDGMENTS

As the length of the book grows, so does the list of people to whom we are indebted for getting it into print.

First we acknowledge the authors, without whose contribution the book would not be possible, and the loyal readers, who did not give up on us through the delays that always seem to accompany projects running on volunteer labor.

The editors of the Second Edition can fully appreciate the enormous contribution made by the creators of the First Edition, who got The Soggy Sneakers off the ground and into print before the days of word processors. Bill Ostrand provided the first push; Ron Mattson, Gene Ice, George Ice and Rob Blickensderfer gave up personal publishing goals; Kim Hummer, Dan Valens, T. R. Torgersen, Ellen Oliver, Richard Hand, and Lance Stein carried the manuscripts through the process of typing, editing, typesetting and printing.

Gary Adams, President of the WKCC 1983-1985, provided the inspiration for the Second Edition, and kept it rolling through the initial stages. Rob Blickensderfer, Laurie Pavey, and John Westall edited the initial set of new write-ups and took care of the typing. Gary Adams and Laurie Pavey managed the editorial correspondence with the authors and fended off those with the question, "...what have you done to my write-up?" Rich Brainerd produced all of the maps and became the resident expert in deciphering shuttle descriptions. Dan Valens read the entire book one more time, checking for accuracy. Steve Holland obtained the data on gauge heights and river flow. Naomi Zielinski and Tee Taylor proofread the manuscript. Brian Tooley is acknowledged for his work on river classification, and Richard Hand for typesetting.

Three people should be recognized for service above and beyond the call of duty. Laurie Pavey did more than her share of typing, editing, and volunteering to take care of whatever needed to be done. Lance Stein, a veteran of the First Edition, contributed his talents in many ways: printing consultant, business manager, and typesetter for the maps. John Westall is acknowledged for his endurance, as one of the original editors, and the one into whose lap the manuscript fell when it was time to tie all of the loose ends together and send it off to press.

Cover Photo . . . . *OWYHEE RIVER* . . . . Rick Starr

This book may be purchased by sending $9.00 plus $1.00 for shipping and handling to: WKCC, P.O. Box 1062, Corvallis, OR, 97339.

ISBN 0-9616257-0-8

FOREWORD TO THE FIRST EDITION

The Soggy Sneakers Guide to Oregon Rivers has as many beginnings as the state has rivers. Willamette Kayak and Canoe Club (WKCC) members have been keeping notes and collecting trip reports for many years. Some had the idea of publishing; some merely wanted to aid their friends in trip planning. Periodically, individual trip reports had been written by club members for publication in the club newsletter. Bill Ostrand brought these numerous beginnings together. After gathering all previous trip reports Bill discovered that he needed much more information to compile an adequate guide book. He next approached George Ice, Gene Ice, and Ron Mattson who graciously turned over all of their material to the club project. Rob Blickensderfer offered his notes and assistance and our guide to Oregon rivers had begun.

Word of this ambitious effort soon had club members volunteering for various committees and duties. The call went out to paddling partners throughout the state. Trip reports on rivers near and far began to arrive.

As the reports became available a technical review committee checked each for accuracy. Trip reports were sometimes sent back to authors for clarification. The report was next sent to an editorial committee who unified the text. The book soon became much more work than any of us dreamed. Like most other committee projects, deadlines were missed by months. Gradually, individual trip reports merged into river drainage systems and finally into chapters. The Soggy Sneakers Guide to Oregon Rivers became a reality.

Since most of the authors described their favorite runs, many superlatives and much of the author's enthusiasm is reflected in each report. So join in the author's excitement and rest assured that the river trip you're planning for next weekend is on the "best river in the state."

Lance Stein
President WKCC 1980

Bill Ostrand
President WKCC 1979

FOREWORD TO THE SECOND EDITION

The Second Edition of the Soggy Sneakers Guide to Oregon Rivers began life in the Summer of 1984, as the supply of the First Edition, Third Printing began to dwindle. Gary Adams, President of the WKCC 1984-1985, and Lance Stein, who was president when the First Edition was published, began discussing with club members ideas for revisions of the book; soon there were so many "great ideas" that it became clear that an all new Second Edition was the answer. An editorial committee was formed, and the call for new write-ups went out. More than one hundred new write-ups were submitted, including an entire chapter on surf kayaking on the Oregon Coast. The Soggy Sneakers more than doubled in size from the First Edition to the Second Edition.

The editorial policy for the Second Edition was similar to that of the First Edition. The attempt was made to edit the articles for clarity and consistency, while allowing the myriad of styles of the many different authors to shine through. The result is a book that's not only the most complete guide to Oregon Rivers, but also very interesting reading, even if you aren't going boating!

John Westall, 1986

STATE MAP WITH CHAPTER DIVISIONS

TABLE OF CONTENTS

Chapter 1: Surf Kayaking on the Oregon Coast

Chapter 2: North Coast Rivers

Chapter 3: South Coast Rivers

Chapter 4: Southern Oregon Rivers and the Smith River, California

Chapter 5: Upper Willamette and McKenzie Drainages

Chapter 6. Willamette River and Western Tributaries

Chapter 7. Eastern Tributaries in the Mid-Willamette Valley

Chapter 8. Lower Willamette Valley and Columbia Gorge Drainages

HOW TO USE THIS BOOK

SCOPE OF THE BOOK: The descriptions reflect the character of a river under a particular set of conditions. A river's character can change dramatically in the course of a day, a season, or a year. While this book is a guide to the rivers and what to expect, it must in no way be regarded as the exact description of what you will find on a particular day. Further information on boating safety is given at the end of this section. It is recommended that you read this carefully and understand the risks that you accept when you go out on a river.

The river descriptions are organized by major drainages. Sections within one river are arranged from upstream to downstream. Surfing locations are ordered from north to south. All rivers reported in this book were run by the author. The river descriptions are presented in the following format:

HEADING: river name, section, and author of the report.

CLASS: The class designations given in this book indicate the class of the majority of the run, according to the American Whitewater Affiliation International Scale of River Difficulty, which is reprinted below. If only one or two spots are more difficult than the majority of the run, parentheses are used, e.g., South Santiam as 4(6) or Lower McKenzie as 1(2). The letter "T" is used after the number designation to indicate that a run is predominantly technical in nature, and the letter "P" is used in to indicate that at least one portage is mandatory.

Class 1. Moving water with a few riffles and small waves. Few or no obstructions.

Class 2. Easy rapids with waves up to 3 feet, and wide clear channels that are obvious without scouting. Some maneuvering is required.

Class 3. Rapids with high, irregular waves often capable of swamping an open canoe. Narrow passages that often require complex maneuvering. May require scouting from shore.

Class 4. Long difficult rapids with constricted passages that often require precise maneuvering in very turbulent waters. Scouting from shore is often necessary, and conditions make rescue difficult. Generally not possible for open canoes. Boaters in covered canoes and kayaks should be able to Eskimo roll.

Class 5. Extremely difficult, long, and very violent rapids with highly congested routes which nearly always must be scouted from shore. Rescue conditions are difficult and there is significant hazard to life in event of a mishap. Ability to Eskimo roll is essential for kayaks and canoes.

Class 6. Difficulties of class 5 carried to the extreme of navigability. Nearly impossible and very dangerous. For teams of experts only, after close study and with all precautions taken.

If the water temperature is below 50 degrees F, the AWA states that the river should be considered one class more difficult than normal.

Still water and class 1 are sometimes subdivided according to water speed:

Class A. Standing or slow flowing water, not more than 2.5 mph.

Class B. Current between 2.5 and 4.5 mph, but backpaddling can effectively neutralize the speed.

Class C. Current more than 4.5 mph, but backpaddling cannot neutralize the speed of the current. Simple obstacles may occur that require a certain amount of boat control.

GRADIENT: The average gradient of the section, reported in feet of elevation change per mile of river length. The letters "PD" are used to indicate that a run is primarily "pool-drop" in nature. Most of the elevation change on such a run occurs over relatively steep sections, which are separated by relatively level stretches. The letter "C" is used to indicate that a run is primarily "continuous" in nature. The elevation change on such a run is relatively uniform over the length of the section.

MILES: Length of run.

CHARACTER: The most significant topographic, geographic, and/or scenic features of the river run are described in a few words. This subjective designation has been made by the author of the description or by the editors. It may include key words relating to accessibility, climate, man-made features or other uses of the area.

SEASON: The time of year that a river can normally be run is related to the weather and the source of the river. West of the Cascade Range, it rains more or less continuously from November through May, and is dry from typically June or July through September or October. East of the Cascade Range, conditions are mostly dry and desert-like throughout the year, although significant snowfall accumulates in mountainous regions during the winter months. The classifications according to weather and source of water are:

ALL YEAR - There is adequate water for boating year-round. The sources of these rivers are generally dam controlled. Examples: North Santiam, Metolius, the lower Deschutes, Rogue.

DAM CONTROLLED - The flow of these rivers is controlled by dams or irrigation diversions, but there is no requirement for minimum flow. Water may be shut off or reduced below runnable flows by the controlling agency. Examples: the upper Deschutes runs, and the Middle Santiam between the dams.

RAINY - These rivers reach runnable levels after several days of rain. Many of the rivers of western Oregon are in this group. Examples: Coquille, Siletz, Wilson, Molalla, Calapooia.

SNOWMELT - These rivers generally receive the bulk of their water from melting snow in the spring and early summer. Such rivers are at high elevations or in Eastern Oregon. Examples: White Salmon, John Day, Owyhee.

RAINY/SNOWMELT - These rivers receive their water both from rain and from snow. They will be runnable after a few days of good rain and into early summer because of melting snowpack. Examples: Breitenbush, Sandy, Quartzville Creek.

DESCRIPTION: This section includes both a general description of the character of the river and a more detailed account of rapids and landmarks that are found on the run. Unless otherwise indicated, "right" and "left" are used with respect to an observer looking downstream (river right and river left). Books are referenced by the author's name and the publication date; complete information on the books is found in Appendix D.

DIFFICULTIES: In this section the most difficult rapids are described, and some suggestions are made about how they can be approached. Other hazards such as sweepers, weirs, dams, and portages are described.

SHUTTLE: Directions to the river, primary and optional put-ins and take-outs, and directions on running the shuttle are described here. For surfing descriptions this section is referred to as "access." A description of maps that are useful to boaters is given in Appendix E.

GAUGE: In this section is described how to obtain information on flow, what the author regards as "high" and "low", and what optimum flows are. Further information is available in the appendices: Appendix A contains a list of agencies, with addresses and phone numbers, from which flow information can be obtained; Appendix B gives a table correlating gauge readings in ft to river flows in cfs; and Appendix C contains a list of newspapers which report river stages. These tables are correct in 1985, but the correlations may change over the course of time as riverbed shapes change.

WATERMARKS: For longer runs, much of the description of highlights is given in terms of watermarks and river mileages. Watermarks are also useful on longer runs for determining location on the river.

MAPS: The maps in this book show the rivers, the locations of put-ins and take-outs, and major landmarks. Roads are not shown. It is intended that a state road map be used with the maps in the book and the shuttle descriptions. Further information on maps is given in Appendix E. Sections of rivers that are described in the book are designated by a broad line.

RIVER SAFETY
By T.R. Torgersen

People run rivers for different reasons; some seek a relaxing aesthetic experience, others seek adventure or challenge. Many seek a combination of the two. For whatever reasons you choose to boat, your river running experience will be more fun, and more rewarding if done safely. On any river, even innocently small ones, the price of ignorance or carelessness can be anything from lost or damaged equipment to personal injury or the loss of human life.

A large part of safe boating lies in identifying potential dangers. Prevention is the key; not just reacting to a hazardous situation already in motion. Recognizing potential hazards requires experience. Boating clubs offer the novice a way to acquire that experience and learn boating safety other than by trial and error. Clubs normally have people who teach boating and are willing to share their experience and instill safe boating practices. Many clubs provide instruction in boat handling. Another way of learning boating skills and safety is through classes offered by City Parks and Recreation Departments, Community Colleges, the Red Cross, or YMCA.

The basic risks in river running are derived from the temperature of the water and the air, the water volume, and the character of the river channel and obstructions. In the Safety Code of the American Whitewater Affiliation (reprinted with permission following this article) the hazards associated with these features are mentioned. Many of the books in the bibliography discuss personal safety, party rescue techniques, and safety equipment. Most libraries have a selection of boating books that address various aspects of river safety.

WHITEWATER SAFETY CODE
AMERICAN WHITEWATER AFFILIATION
Personal Preparedness and Responsibility

1. Be a competent swimmer with ability to handle yourself underwater.
2. WEAR a lifejacket.
3. Keep your craft under control. Control must be good enough at all times to stop or reach shore before you reach any danger. Do not enter a rapid unless you are reasonably sure you can safely navigate it or swim the entire rapid in event of capsize.
4. Be aware of river hazards and avoid them. Following are the most frequent killers.

A. High water. The river's power and danger, and the difficulty of rescue increase tremendously as the flow rate increases. It is often misleading to judge river level at the put-in. Look at a narrow, critical passage. Could a sudden rise from sun on a snow pack, rain or a dam release occur on your trip?

B. Cold. Cold quickly robs one's will and ability to save oneself. Dress to protect yourself from cold water and weather extremes. When the water temperature is less than 50 degrees F., a diver's wetsuit is essential for safety in event of an upset. Next best is wool clothing under a windproof outer garment such as a splash-proof nylon shell; in this case one should also carry matches and a complete change of clothes in a waterproof package. If after prolonged exposure, a person experiences uncontrollable shaking or has difficulty talking and moving, he must be warmed immediately, by whatever means available.

C. Strainers: brush, fallen trees, bridge pilings, or anything else which allows river current to sweep through but pins boat and boater against the obstacle. The water pressure on anything trapped in this way is overwhelming, and there may be little or no whitewater to warn of danger.

D. Weirs, reversals, and souse holes. The water drops over an obstacle then curls back on itself in a stationary wave, as is often seen at weirs and dams. The surface water is actually going upstream, and this action will

trap any floating object between the drop and the wave. Once trapped, a swimmer's only hope is to dive below the surface where current is flowing downstream, or try to swim out the end of the wave.
5. Boating alone is not recommended. The preferred minimum is three craft.
6. Have a frank knowledge of your boating ability. Don't attempt waters beyond this ability. Learn paddling skills and teamwork, if in a multiple-manned craft, to match the river you plan to boat.
7. Be in good physical condition consistent with the difficulties that may be expected.
8. Be practiced in escape from an overturned craft, in self-rescue, in rescue, and in ARTIFICIAL RESPIRATION. Know first aid.
9. The Eskimo roll should be mastered by kayakers and canoers planning to run large rivers and/or rivers with continuous rapids where a swimmer would have trouble reaching shore.
10. Wear a crash helmet where an upset is likely. This is essential in a kayak or covered canoe.
11. Be suitably equipped. Wear shoes that will protect your feet during a bad swim or a walk for help, yet will not interfere with swimming (tennis shoes recommended). Carry a knife and waterproof matches. If you need eyeglasses, tie them on and carry a spare pair. Do not wear bulky clothing that will interfere with your swimming when water-logged.

Boat and Equipment Preparedness
1. Test new and unfamiliar equipment before relying on it for difficult runs.
2. Be sure craft is in good repair before starting a trip. Eliminate sharp projections that could cause injury during a swim.
3. Inflatable craft should have MULTIPLE AIR CHAMBERS and should be test inflated before starting a trip.
4. Have strong adequately sized paddles or oars for controlling the craft and carry sufficient spares for the length of the trip.
5. Install flotation devices in non-inflatable craft, securely fixed, and designed to displace as much water from the craft as possible.
6. Be certain there is absolutely nothing to cause entanglement when coming free from an upset craft, i.e., a spray skirt that won't release or tangle around legs; life jacket buckles, or clothing that might snag; canoe seats that lock on shoe heels; foot braces that fail or allow feet to jam under them; flexible decks that collapse on boater's legs when a kayak is trapped by water pressure; baggage that dangles in an upset; loose rope in the craft, or badly secured bow and stern lines.
7. Provide ropes to allow you to hold onto your craft in case of upset, and so that it may be rescued. Following are the recommended methods:
A. Kayaks and covered canoes should have 6-inch diameter grab loops of 1/4 inch rope attached to bow and stern. A stern painter 7 or 8 feet long is optional and may be used if properly secured to prevent entanglement.
B. Open canoes should have bow and stern lines (painters) securely attached consisting of 8 to 10 feet of 1/4 or 3/8 inch rope. These lines must be secured in such a way that they will not come loose accidentally and entangle the boaters during a swim, yet they must be ready for immediate use during an emergency. Attached balls, floats and knots are NOT recommended.
C. Rafts and dories should have taut perimeter grab lines threaded through the loops usually provided.
8. Respect rules for craft capacity and know how these capacities should be reduced for whitewater use. (Life raft ratings must generally be halved.)
9. Carry appropriate repair materials: tape (heating duct tape) for short trips, complete repair kit for wilderness trips.
10. Car top racks must be strong and positively attached to the vehicle, and each boat must be tied to each rack. In addition, each end of each

boat should be tied to car bumper. Suction cup racks are poor. The entire arrangement should be able to withstand all but the most violent vehicle accident.

Leader's Preparedness and Responsibility

1. River conditions. Have a reasonable knowledge of the difficult parts of the run, or if an exploratory trip, examine maps to estimate the feasibility of the run. Be aware of possible rapid changes in river level and how these changes can affect the difficulty of the run. If important, determine approximate flow rate or level. If trip involves important tidal currents, secure tide information.

2. Participants. Inform participants of expected river conditions and determine if the prospective boaters are qualified for the trip. All decisions should be based on group safety and comfort. Difficult decisions on the participation of marginal boaters must be based on total group strength.

3. Equipment. Plan so that all necessary group equipment is present on the trip; 50 to 100 foot throwing rope, first aid kit with fresh and adequate supplies, extra paddles, repair materials, and survival equipment if appropriate. Check equipment as necessary at the put-in, especially life jackets, boat flotation, and any items that could prevent complete escape from the boat in case of an upset.

4. Organization. Remind each member of individual responsibility in keeping group compact and intact between leader and sweep (capable rear boater). If group is too large, divide into smaller groups, each of appropriate boating strength, and designate group leaders and sweeps.

5. Float plan. If trip is into a wilderness area, or for an extended period, your plans should be filed with appropriate authorities or left with someone who will contact them after a certain time. Establishment of checkpoints along the way at which civilization could be contacted if necessary should be considered. Knowing location of possible help could speed rescue in any case.

In Case of an Upset

1. Evacuate your boat immediately if there is imminent danger of being trapped against logs, brush, or any other form of strainer.

2. Recover with an Eskimo roll if possible.

3. If you swim, hold onto your craft. It has much flotation and is easy for rescuers to spot. Get to the upstream end so craft cannot crush you against obstacles.

4. Release your craft if this improves your safety. If rescue is not imminent and water is numbing cold, or if worse rapids follow, then strike out for the nearest shore.

5. When swimming rocky rapids, use backstroke with legs downstream and feet near the surface. If your foot wedges on the bottom, fast water will push you under and hold you there. Get to slow or very shallow water before trying to stand or walk. Look ahead. Avoid possible entrapment situations: rock wedges, fissures, strainers, brush, logs, weirs, reversals, and souse holes. Watch for eddies and slackwater so that you can be ready to use these when you approach. Use every opportunity to work your way toward shore.

6. If others spill, GO AFTER THE BOATER. Rescue boats and equipment only if this can be done safely.

RIVER ETIQUETTE

By Kim Hummer

Etiquette on the river means treating other people as you would like to be treated, and keeping the environment as clean and natural as you would like to find it on your future trip. Landowners' rights, paddling and rowing etiquette, and camping conservation should be recognized and practiced. Private landowners have rights to the middle of the river adjacent to their land on rivers which are not designated navigable by the State of Oregon or the United States Army Corps of Engineers. Many of the rivers in this book are not "navigable" within the narrow river rights definition. The North Santiam River, for example, is not a "navigable" river. While free passage on an unnavigable river is assured, access to and use of the river banks can be withheld by private landowners. Landowners justifiably complain about mistreatment; beer cans, garbage, fishing tackle, fish guts, sandwich wrappers, and toilet paper are strewn over their land. Several California rivers have effectively been closed to boating because disgruntled landowners have closed the access. Keep Oregon rivers and river banks clean so the private landowners won't close us out too. Carry out not only the beer cans or other garbage that you bring in, but also any garbage that you may find along the way. Do not let Oregon rivers be closed.

Paddling and rowing etiquette involves all river craft. Kayakers who stop at surfing waves should be aware of and yield to other crafts paddling downstream. Rafters and drifters should be alert for smaller boats. Be courteous on the river.

Camping conservation is important. On long trips in fragile river environments, carry and use a fire pan if you have campfires. Pack out the excess coals and ashes. For less impact on the wilderness use a gas stove.

Pack out your camping garbage, including bottle caps, cigarette butts, burnt aluminum foil, and orange peels. Buried human waste decomposes within 2 to 3 weeks but toilet paper may last a year or longer, so pack out the toilet paper or burn it in your campfire. Do not bury it.

You river runners who are independent and enjoy wilderness, accept your responsibility.

RIVER PRESERVATION

By Rick Bader

While you read these lines efforts are underway to destroy most, if not all, of the whitewater rivers described. Like the snail darter and the humpback whale, free-flowing rivers are endangered, threatened to fall prey to interests supposedly acting in the name of progress. Powerful federal organizations, headed by the Army Corps of Engineers and the Water and Power Resources Service (WPRS), formerly the Bureau of Reclamation, and strongly supported by large agricultural and power interests, are damming our rivers and streams at an alarming rate. Placid, man-made lakes are left where a rich, riparian ecosystem previously existed. Rivers require centuries to carve streambeds; man only seconds to shut flood gates to completely wash out these beds.

River conservation is a must if we are to save these special places. The battle record for those working to save rivers shows many bitter defeats, some significant victories, and much work still to be done. Perhaps the biggest victory came in 1968, when Congress passed the Wild and Scenic Rivers Act, and protected parts of eight different rivers, including the Rogue River in Oregon. Since then others have been added and many are currently being studied for inclusion. In Oregon, the Illinois and the Owyhee are now included and the North Umpqua is being considered. The rate at which rivers have been protected under this act has unfortunately been slow, but the act does provide conservationists with a legal means of fighting organizations such as the Army Corps of Engineers and the WPRS.

As those who derive considerable pleasure from playing in whitewater, we have a responsibility to become active in preserving rivers. As individuals, and as groups, we should keep aware of river issues locally and nationally, and should work to save rivers whenever possible. Every letter helps.

The issue is more than a conflict between agriculture and power on one side, and whitewater recreation on the other. The issue is CONSERVATION. New dams will, for a limited period of time, perpetuate a facade of unlimited water and encourage wasteful agricultural methods and electrical power use. The solution is to make more efficient use of the local water, not to make more water available from other watersheds. Water use has been notoriously wasteful in this country. If future generations are to have free-flowing rivers, this waste must stop. We must act now to change our values.

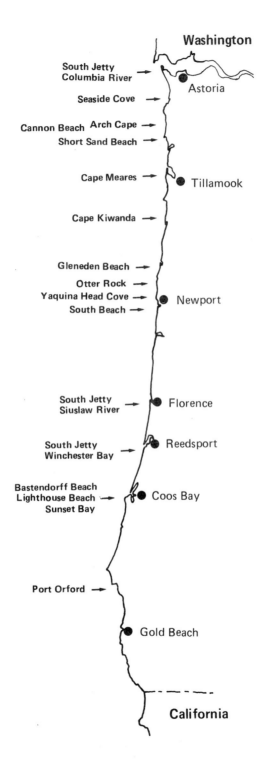

Washington

South Jetty Columbia River →

Astoria

Seaside Cove →

Cannon Beach Arch Cape →
Short Sand Beach →

Cape Meares →

Tillamook

Cape Kiwanda →

Gleneden Beach →
Otter Rock →
Yaquina Head Cove →
South Beach →

Newport

South Jetty Siuslaw River →

Florence

South Jetty Winchester Bay →

Reedsport

Bastendorff Beach
Lighthouse Beach →
Sunset Bay

Coos Bay

Port Orford →

Gold Beach

California

Chapter 1. Surf Kayaking on the Oregon Coast

SURF KAYAKING

Curt Peterson, Rick Starr, and Dale Mosby

Riding ocean waves in kayak, surf shoe, or surf ski is a thrilling form of whitewater boating which requires knowledge of ocean conditions, strong swimming skills, and suitable equipment. Rugged headlands, expansive beaches, and direct exposure to north Pacific ocean swells make the Oregon Coast one of the most spectacular surfing areas in North America.

However, these same factors can produce hazardous ocean conditions that are both subtle and unique to the Pacific Northwest. The following sections outline some safety tips for kayak surfing along the Oregon Coast. In addition to reading these sections, we strongly suggest that boaters unfamiliar with the ocean arrange initial trips with experienced wave riders.

Waves. Irregular ocean seas that form at sea by storm winds are transformed into smooth ocean swells as they travel away from the storm center. Swells approaching shore typically begin to shoal (drag on the bottom) in water depths one and one-quarter times the swell height, as measured from crest to trough. Steep beaches produce steep plunging breakers with wave crests that plunge from top to bottom. Flatter beaches produce spilling breakers with wave crests that gradually tumble down the wave face. Swell size, wind conditions, and tidal height also control wave shape. These conditions can vary dramatically within a few hours.

Small spilling breakers in the 2-4 ft height range are ideal for beginning surf kayakers. Plunging breakers in the 6-8 ft height range can rip paddles from boaters' hands and pop spray skirts, forcing even the most skilled boater to swim for shore. Since larger waves break in deeper water, they also break farther from shore, leading surfers to greatly underestimate their size. For this reason, it is prudent to start surfing close to shore, and then to move out gradually to the larger surf as true wave size is confirmed. Such an approach also ensures that surfers will observe the infrequent sets of very large waves called "clean-up sets" before they commit themselves to a thorough cleaning!

Beaches, Reefs, and Points: The Breaks. In their search for waves, surfers usually concentrate their efforts on beaches with offshore sandbars and reefs, as well as on points such as headlands and harbor jetties. These features cause swells to refract, or bend toward shore, and produce waves that break right or left along the shore, giving surfers longer rides.

However, these features also create a variety of nearshore currents which are intensified during conditions of large surf. The least hazardous "current" is the undertow, which is not really a current at all, but just the backwash of a wave surge on a steep beach face. The backwash dissipates its force a few yards seaward of the beach face, and is of little concern to the experienced swimmer.

By contrast, true nearshore currents can attain sustained flow velocities of several knots, or twice the speed of a swimmer. During conditions of large surf these currents can extend across the width of the surf zone up to a half mile offshore. Nearshore currents are generated by shoaling waves which push water inshore of the breaker zone. Escaping water flows parallel to the shore in longshore currents, and then heads back out to sea in rip currents, through gaps between offshore sandbars or reefs. Particularly strong rip currents occur alongside headlands and jetties, as these seaward projections effectively divert longshore currents out to sea.

Nearshore currents cover broad areas and can be difficult to recognize in the turbulent surf zone. Rip currents heading out to sea can sometimes be identified by choppy surface water, turbid zones, or streaks of sea foam. Surfers and swimmers in the surf zone should keep an eye on fixed points on shore to establish whether they are drifting in a nearshore current. To get out of a nearshore current, a person should swim or paddle perpendicular to the direction of current flow. In large surf, it might take twenty minutes or longer to swim out of a rip current and into shore. In extreme cases where an open water rescue by other boaters is not possible, a tiring or chilled swimmer should leave the boat and head for shore. Waves and wind will eventually put the boat ashore.

Sticks and Skins: The Equipment. Eskimos spent thousands of years developing the ultimate, all-purpose surf vehicle--little else need be said about the kayak. Flotation bags, support walls, and grabloops are necessary additions to decked boats used in the high energy surf zone. Boaters should use helmets and wear belted life jackets that can't be pulled up over their shoulders by turbulent waves. Most important, a full wetsuit, or watertight drysuit, is essential for safe boating in cold coastal waters where large surf can force boaters to take long swims. For winter kayak surfing, a hood and booties are worthwhile additions to the full wetsuit or drysuit.

Paddling Out and Dropping In: The Etiquette. To avoid collisions in congested surf zones, surfers should paddle out to the breaker zone off to the side of other surfers who are catching and riding waves. The surfer who is closest to the breaking part of the wave has the right-of-way over others riding the wave face. Other surfers trying to catch the wave should back off to avoid dropping in on the surfer who is already in position. Finally, something should be said about wave-sharing. Unlike the favorite play wave on the local river run, there isn't a well ordered line up of boaters waiting to catch waves out in the surf zone, so all boaters must make a conscious effort to share waves and to avoid catching waves that might propel them into other surfers.

Good waves, Mates!

SELECTED SURF KAYAKING LOCATIONS ALONG THE OREGON COAST
Curt Peterson

North Coast
COLUMBIA RIVER SOUTH JETTY

Description: The area just south of the Columbia River south jetty marks the northernmost surfing location on the Oregon coast and provides some of the longest rides to be had on Oregon waves. Like most other south jetty breaks, the Columbia River south jetty produces slow, mushy wave peaks during high tide with 2-4 ft swells approaching from the west-northwest. An increase in swell height (to 4-6 ft) and a drop in tide level can result in the spilling breaker zone moving farther seaward with longer walls lining up to the south and shorter wave shoulders dying into the rip current channel against the south jetty. Larger swells (6-8 ft) force the breaker zone more than a mile offshore, driving hazardous longshore currents and rip currents against the jetty.

Hazards: Moderate to large swells from the west-southwest drive strong longshore currents northward which turn and flow seaward along the south jetty.

Access: Beach access is easily found northwest of Fort Stevens, off US 101. Follow the road signs to Columbia River South Jetty. Surf conditions can be scouted from the observation stand adjacent to the south jetty parking lot.

SEASIDE COVE

Description: The cove and point breaks just south of Seaside lie on the northern flank of Tillamook Headland and thus are protected from direct exposure to large winter swells that approach shore from the southwest. As the big swells wrap around the point and break over the rocky bottom, surfers test their skills on some of the largest waves (12 + ft) ridden in Oregon.

However, smaller winter swells (6-8 ft) and westerly summer swells (4-6 ft) travel farther shoreward before shoaling in Seaside Cove. At medium to low tide these spilling breakers form long walls, breaking from south to north. Understandably, the cove is a popular spot for board riders, leading to a congested surf zone and competition for waves.

Hazards: The cove waves are noted for substantial punch, and clean-up sets are frequent. In addition, a rocky bottom and potential long swims can make Seaside Cove a poor choice for inexperienced surfers.

Access: Take one of several coastal access roads immediately south of Seaside to reach the beach. Turning south at the beach, drive one to two miles on the frontage road while looking for parking and trails to the beach. Surf conditions can be scouted from along the road and the cobble beach berm.

CANNON BEACH AND ARCH CAPE

Description: Several beach breaks can be found between Cannon Beach and Arch Cape, two small coastal communities separated by about five miles. A series of small headlands and offshore sea stacks protect offshore sandbars from direct exposure to ocean swells, while offshore bar irregularities produce spilling breakers with short wall sections. Well formed beach breaks can be found at Cannon Beach and Arch Cape areas during most tide levels and during westerly swell conditions of 2-6 ft. Strong onshore winds in summer months can blow out surf at either area, so early morning conditions are preferable.

Hazards: Both Cannon Beach and Arch Cape beach breaks become un-rideable (close out) and form strong rip currents between offshore bars with swell conditions in excess of 6 ft.

Access: Beach breaks are easily located and scouted from beach access and frontage roads at Cannon Beach and Arch Cape, just off US 101.

SHORT SANDS BEACH

Description: This delightful beach is less than a mile in length but has some of the best summer surf on the north coast. The small pocket beach is protected from summer onshore winds by headlands to the north and south. Crescentic offshore sandbars create well formed wave peaks that break both north and south on medium tide with ocean swells of 2-6 ft. The waves commonly turn into plunging breakers at low tide and form spilling breakers during high tide, thus offering a variety of wave shapes throughout the day. The short length of this beach does not permit the development of strong nearshore currents, and the wide separation of wave peaks makes it easy to paddle out in small to moderate size surf. Short Sands Beach has proven to be a popular surfing beach for beginning and experienced surfers alike.

Hazards: You won't want to leave this tiny sandy beach and its forested headlands.

Access: Short Sands Beach is located in Oswald West State Park, between Arch Cape and Mazanita. From the Oswald West parking lot next to US 101, walk down a paved path about 0.5 mile to the beach. In the past, the Park Service has provided carts to transport gear down to camping sites by the beach.

CAPE MEARES
Description: A broad surf zone occurs immediately north of Cape Meares. Under the right conditions spilling breakers form long lines that alternately shoal and reform in several successions before finally collapsing on the cobbly beach face below the Cape. These breakers are often at their best during low tide with moderate ocean swells of 4 + ft. Strong onshore winds in summer months can blow out these delicate waves, so save this spot for those late spring and early fall outings. Due to the long paddle out and the gradually shoaling breakers, this spot is rarely surfed by board surfers, leaving the long gentle breakers to more mobile kayakers. Brief excursions around the Cape can spice up the afternoon when the surf is low.
Hazards: The long paddle out can lead to long swims for boaters with marginal rolls.
Access: To reach Cape Meares take the Three Capes Scenic route west of Tillamook and follow road signs to Cape Meares. In Cape Meares follow the beach front road south until it ends in a small parking area. Surf conditions can be scouted from either the parking area or the beach cobble berm.

CAPE KIWANDA
Description: Several beach breaks can be found just south of a tiny headland, Cape Kiwanda, during medium to low tide and during westerly to northwesterly ocean swells of 2-6 ft. Small spilling breakers form in the lee of the tiny headland, and a small sea stack forms near the end of the headland. Larger plunging breakers form farther south of Cape Kiwanda, but as a result of greater exposure to ocean swells and onshore winds, these breakers are more sensitive to swell and wind conditions. Summer weekends can be busy at Cape Kiwanda, as hang gliders are attracted to the wind swept bluffs on the north side of the headland, and fishermen launch their double ended dories in the south lee of the Cape.
Hazards: Beach breaks south of Cape Kiwanda become unrideable (close out) and generate strong nearshore currents during large winter surf.
Access: Cape Kiwanda forms the northern beachfront boundary of Pacific City, a coastal resort town several miles west of US 101 and about 15 miles north of Lincoln City. Surf conditions can be scouted from a parking lot just south of the Cape or from beach access roads to the south in Pacific City.

Central Coast
GLENEDEN BEACH
Description: Some of the fastest breaking waves on the central coast can be found at Gleneden Beach during medium to low tide with westerly swells of 4+ ft and offshore winds. Irregularities in offshore sandbars produce plunging breakers that peel to the north or south, often forming hollow wave faces. "Going for the tube" in a kayak is something like dropping sideways into a nasty river hole: guaranteed excitement and a probable thrashing in the end! Strong wave surges on steep beach faces, such as those at Gleneden Beach, make getting in and out of the surf zone difficult for a kayaker; bring a friend who doesn't mind getting wet feet to lend a hand.
Hazards: Beach breaks at Gleneden Beach become unrideable (close out) with ocean swells greater than 6 ft. Longshore currents and rip currents between offshore bars are well developed even in moderate surf conditions, but are greatly intensified by large winter surf.
Access: Gleneden Beach State Park is found by following road signs in Gleneden, a coastal community off US 101 about 7 miles south of Lincoln City. Surf conditions can be scouted from the parking lot at the State Park.

OTTER ROCK

Description: A beach break forms off sandbars to the south of Otter Rock, a small headland known for an unusual rock formation called the Devils Punch Bowl. The beach break is sheltered from winds and large surf by the headland and offshore reefs, resulting in rideable surf when other beach breaks are closing out. However, the headland is relatively short, permitting small summer swells to wrap around the point and shoal in the small cove just south of the headland. The spilling breakers formed in the cove are typically small but increase in size to the south, where offshore sandbars are more directly exposed to ocean swells. Rideable waves are formed over a wide range of conditions at Otter Rock, but rarely break with consistently good form.

Hazards: Large winter surf generates a moderately strong rip current that flows seaward along the headland.

Access: Take the Otter Rock exit off US 101 about 9 miles north of Newport and follow road signs to the Devils Punch Bowl. Wooden steps lead down to the beach from the parking lot, from which there is a good view of surf conditions in the small cove.

YAQUINA HEAD COVE

Description: Yaquina Head produces some of the most consistently rideable surf on the central coast. Westerly to northwesterly ocean swells of 2-8 ft wrap around the long headland and form spilling to plunging breakers in the cove south of the headland. As the ocean swells increase in size, or as the tide level drops, the breaker line moves farther offshore, and long walls line up to the south.

In moderate size surf, wave shoulders die into the rip channel along the south side of the headland. The rip channel offers an easy paddle out to the breaker zone. However, during conditions of larger ocean swells (6-8 ft), waves break across the rip channel and against the headland, making paddling out between sets very interesting.

During conditions of small summer swells (2-4 ft), small breakers offer short rides close to shore, with the gentle wave crests protected from onshore summer winds by the large headland. The trip out to the end of Yaquina Head, a distance of about a mile, often rewards boaters with close encounters with sea birds, seals and possibly even grey whales that frequent the Yaquina Head Marine Reserve.

Hazards: Large winter surf generates strong longshore currents which flow north and turn seaward at the headland, producing a strong rip current that flows several hundred yards seaward along the headland. Submerged rocks underlie the surf zone in the cove during high tide, but are avoidable by staying several hundred yards south of the headland.

Access: To find and scout Yaquina Head Cove, park in a paved lot just south of the Yaquina Headland off US 101, about 4 miles north of Newport. Follow a wide path a couple of hundred yards southwest to the beach.

YAQUINA BAY SOUTH JETTY TO SOUTH BEACH

Description: A series of beach breaks form between Yaquina Bay south jetty and South Beach State Park, about one mile south of the bay entrance. These beach breaks are formed over offshore sandbars separated by rip channels and are protected from direct exposure to northwest summer swells by the long jetty system that extends about 0.5 mile seaward off the beach. Spilling breakers shoal over a shallow sandbar immediately south of the south jetty during low tide with westerly swells of 4-6 ft. The breaks farther south of the jetty are more exposed to

ocean swells. Plunging breakers form at most tide levels with ocean swells of 2-6 ft, approaching from either the west or northwest. These breakers become unrideable (close out) when ocean swells exceed 6 ft. In addition, the unsheltered beach breaks are often blown out by summer onshore winds. Either arrive early for the morning glass off or wait for windless fall conditions.
Hazards: Many surfers have frightening stories of getting caught in the south jetty rip current during large winter surf. Large southwest swells drive longshore currents northward against the south jetty, forming a wide rip current that extends beyond the end of the jetty.
Access: Scout surf conditions from either the south jetty or the beach dunes at South Beach State Park. The south jetty is found by exiting off of US 101 immediately south of Yaquina Bay bridge at Newport and following road signs to the south jetty. To find the South Beach State Park access road, which leads to the beach parking lot, continue south on US 101 another mile beyond Yaquina Bay bridge.

SIUSLAW RIVER SOUTH JETTY
Description: A short beach break occurs just south of the Siuslaw River south jetty at medium tide with westerly ocean swells of 2-4 ft. The south jetty is presently (1985) being lengthened; this beach break might be able to handle larger ocean swells when jetty construction is completed. At present the south jetty break forms spilling breakers with short wall sections that are very susceptible to summer onshore winds.
Hazards: Like other Oregon jetty systems, a strong rip current flows seaward along the south jetty during conditions of large winter surf.
Access: A south jetty access road turns off US 101 immediately south of the Siuslaw Bay bridge just south of Florence. Take the road to the end of the spit and scout surf conditions from the south jetty.

South Coast
WINCHESTER BAY SOUTH JETTY
Description: Perhaps the finest jetty beach break to be found on the Oregon coast occurs south of the Winchester Bay south jetty. Westerly to northwesterly ocean swells of 2-6 ft reflect off the south jetty wall and form wave peaks that turn into long wall sections that break north and south. Lower tides and larger ocean swells produce top to bottom plunging breakers while higher tides and smaller surf result in spilling breakers with well formed shoulders. The high jetty wall deflects much of the onshore wind energy in summer months, but windless morning conditions are preferable. The height of the south jetty wall and the distance offshore to the breaker zone have led many experienced surfers to underestimate wave size. Scout the surf conditions carefully before paddling out to the breaker zone.
Hazards: Large fall and winter surf conditions generate strong nearshore currents well south of the jetty and a wide rip current that flows seaward along the south jetty.
Access: Turn off US 101 at Winchester Bay about 5 miles south of Reedsport and follow road signs to the harbor and then to the south jetty. Surf conditions can be scouted from the beach at the south jetty parking lot.

BASTENDORF BEACH
Description: Bastendorf Beach is situated between the Coos Bay south jetty and a small headland one mile south of the Bay mouth. The jetties and headland alternately protect either end of Bastendorf Beach from direct exposure to prevailing wind and ocean swells. This results in spilling

breakers south of the south jetty in summer months and larger plunging breakers north of the headland in stormy winter months. The beach breaks here are rideable over a wide variety of ocean swell and tide conditions, but paddling out is difficult in large winter surf when clean-up sets close out rip current lanes.

Hazards: Large ocean swells close out much of the central part of Bastendorf Beach with freight train walls that often break in only a few feet of water.

Access: Leave US 101 at North Bend or Coos Bay and head for Charleston where road signs point the way to Sunset Bay and Ocean Beaches. One mile south of Charleston pass the Coos Head Naval Facility turnoff and take the next right to Bastendorf Beach, following road signs to the beach front.

LIGHTHOUSE BEACH

Description: This popular surfing area is also a nice residential area. The waves at this beach are midway in intensity between Bastendorf and Sunset. It is probably the most popular beach in the Coos Bay area. Depending on conditions and distance from shore, the surf here will challenge everyone.

Hazards: None in particular.

Access: Proceed west from Charleston beyond the Bastendorf Beach turnoff. About 100 yards past milepost 11, just before Sunset Beach, turn right onto Dead End Road. Proceed about 100 yards and then park off the pavement. The dirt/mud trail on the right winds down to the beach.

SUNSET BAY

Description: Sunset Bay is a tiny cove that offers small waves when other breaks are closed out by large storm surf. The cove is only one quarter mile in diameter and is connected to the open ocean by a narrow strait only 300 yards across. The narrow entrance and shallow reefs offshore greatly reduce the size of ocean swells that can enter the cove, resulting in ideal beginner conditions of small spilling breakers during high tides. A small, sandy beach fronts the landward side of this delightful cove. Interesting rock formations and nearby tide pools are additional attractions.

Hazards: The interior of the cove is entirely protected from strong nearshore currents. However shallow reef areas at the cove entrance are directly exposed to powerful waves and strong nearshore currents during periods of large storm surf.

Access: Leave US 101 at North Bend or Coos Bay and head for Charleston. Follow road signs pointing the way to Sunset Bay Park and Campground, about three miles south of Charleston. Surf conditions can be scouted from the beach parking lot.

PORT ORFORD

Description: Long glassy walls characterize early morning waves that form offshore of steep beaches between Battle Rock and Humbug Mountain south of the tiny port of Port Orford. These classic summer beach breaks are protected from direct exposure to northwest ocean swells and onshore winds by Oregon's most westward land mass, Cape Blanco. Medium to low tides and moderate size ocean swells (4 + ft) produce spilling breakers that peel to the north and south. Wave size and steepness generally increase with increasing distance south of Battle Rock. After a morning of wave sliding, barter with returning fishermen for fresh fish at the Port Orford pier.

Hazards: Some of the beach breaks form over a shallow rocky bottom and become unrideable (close out) when ocean swells exceed 6 ft.

Access: The Port Orford beach breaks can be scouted from the Port Orford Waterfront or from US 101 to the south.

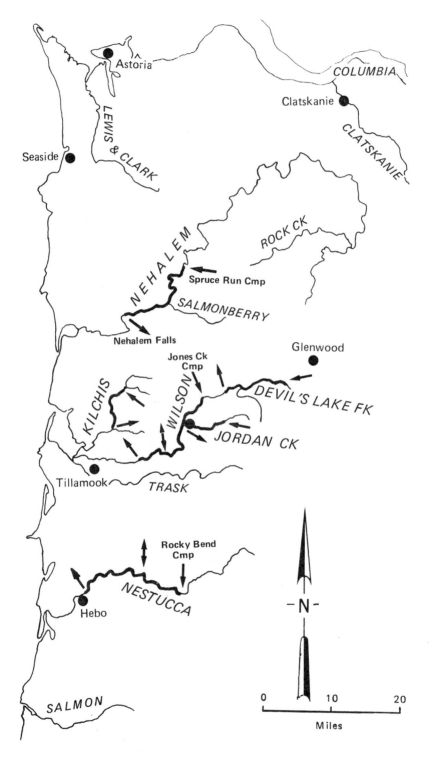

Astoria

COLUMBIA

Clatskanie

CLATSKANIE

LEWIS & CLARK

Seaside

NEHALEM

ROCK CK

Spruce Run Cmp

SALMONBERRY

Nehalem Falls

Glenwood

Jones Ck Cmp

KILCHIS

WILSON

DEVIL'S LAKE FK

JORDAN CK

Tillamook

TRASK

Rocky Bend Cmp

NESTUCCA

Hebo

-N-

SALMON

0   10   20

Miles

Chapter 2. North Coast Rivers

NEHALEM RIVER
Spruce Run Park to Nehalem Falls
Rob Blickensderfer

Class	Flow	Gradient	Miles	Character	Season
3	2000-8000	16 C	14	forest	rainy

Description: The Nehalem River flows westward from the northern Coast Range to the Pacific Ocean, and is among the largest rivers in the Coast Range. In earlier times many logs were floated down the Nehalem from the lush forests where they were cut. The terrain along the river is rugged with very few inhabitants, and the hills in places rise 1200 feet above the river. One freight train per day still makes the round trip from Portland to Tillamook on the coast, following a 1910 route along the Salmonberry and Nehalem Rivers.

Spruce Run Park, at the put-in, is a pleasant place with very few visitors during the winter and spring. Below the put-in, it is fairly straightforward for the first mile to Little Falls. At mile 7, the gradient increases and the river narrows in a long curve to the left through a gorge.

The next river mark is at mile 8 where the Salmonberry River enters from the left. A short distance farther is Salmonberry Drop, the largest rapids on this section.

Several more miles of good whitewater continue before reaching the take-out above Nehalem Falls in a small park by the same name. At moderate flows there are many play-spots in the river. At high water, the hydraulics become powerful, and many of the play-spots are washed out. Nehalem Falls (class 3 to 4 depending on water level) can be run as a finale.

Difficulties: Little Falls, a mile below the put-in, should be scouted at low water. It consists of several shelves of 2-4 ft drops. At 8000 cfs, it is hardly visible and can be run easily. The rapids can be seen from the road. Salmonberry Drop, a short distance below the confluence with the Salmonberry River, should definitely be scouted. This drop cannot be seen from the road, but can be recognized from the river by a large rock at least 10 feet high on the right at the head of the rapids. At 8000 cfs, some of the river flows to the right of the large rock. The main chute, at 5000 cfs and less, has a stopper-keeper that is much more vicious than it looks, and should be avoided.

Nehalem Falls, just below the normal take-out, can be run at flows of 5000 cfs and above, but scouting is required. Class 2 rapids lead into the main rapids and the run-out is fast. At low water it becomes unrunnable.

Shuttle: To reach the put-in take US 26, the Sunset Highway, to the Nehalem River, five miles west of the highway summit. About one mile farther west, turn south on a secondary road or proceed another mile west on US 26 to Elsie and take the road south. In either case, Spruce Run Park is about 6 miles beyond the turn-off. The same road becomes very rough and unpaved as it continues along the river to the take-out at Nehalem Falls Park. An alternate take-out for those who run Nehalem Falls is at the bridge, less than 0.5 mile downstream.

Gauge: Contact the River Forecast Center in Portland. The entire river is unregulated (1985). The gauge-flow conversion table is in Appendix B.

NORTH FORK KILCHIS RIVER
Headwaters to South Fork Kilchis River
Alex McNeily and Paul Norman

Class	Flow	Gradient	Miles	Character	Season
2 + (3)	300 800 +	45 PD-C	6.5	forest	rainy

Description: Beautiful clear green water, small waterfalls cascading in from steep banks, moss-laden trees, and few signs of civilization characterize this scenic coastal stream. It is a rainfall river, so catch it after a good rain or during the wet season.

The run begins with several class 2 drops pushing around blind corners, with an abundance of eddies to catch. There are nice play-spots and surfing waves in this section. Toward the middle of the run there are several 3-ft ledges. All of the obvious chutes are runnable, but be sure to check for logs in the drops before committing yourself. At about mile 3.5 the gradient increases and the river becomes more constricted. This section cannot be seen from the road but can be lined or portaged. There are two good class 3 rapids in here which can be run without scouting by eddy hopping. Soon the gradient eases and the river splits around several islands. At about mile 5 there is a tricky drop. Here the river narrows and pours over a basalt ledge. The route seems clear, but should be scouted. A large diagonal hole at the bottom loves to give the unwary open boater a twist (and often a swim). The remainder of the trip is a pleasant class 1 + to 2.

Difficulties: The ledge at about mile 5 should be scouted. Otherwise be sure to keep an eye out for logs. At high water this narrow run becomes a little more pushy, but new surfing spots appear, and the major rapids are no more difficult.

Shuttle: Take US 101 North from Tillamook to Kilchis River road. Drive upriver about 3 miles and turn right across the river. Continue on this road about 2 miles past the end of the pavement until it crosses a sizeable creek (South Fork Kilchis). The take-out is on the left just above the confluence of the S. Fork with the N. Fork Kilchis. It's advisable to walk to the river to ensure recognition of the take-out on the way down. To reach the put-in, drive another 6.5 miles up the bumpy pot-holed road to a fork. Take the small road left down towards the river. Follow this road as far as you dare. Lower your boat down the steep slope to the river.

Gauge: There is no known gauge. Generally when the Wilson River is over 5 ft, there will be enough water, but there is no consistent correlation. When the Wilson is too high to run, this stretch is a good alternative.

JORDAN CREEK
Headwaters to Wilson River
Alex McNeily and Paul Norman

Class	Flow	Gradient	Miles	Character	Season
3	150- 500	70 C	5	forest	rainy

Description: Anyone who has run the Wilson has driven by Jordan Creek. This tight technical creek can be run after a good rain or when the Wilson is over 7 feet. Lots of maneuvering and tight turns are required. The biggest hazard on our run was overhanging brush. Many of the drops are blind and rather precipitous, and possibly blocked by logs. About halfway through the run is a technical ledge drop of about 4 ft that goes left under a bridge and then over another 4-ft drop. The lower drop has two slots. The left slot might scrape a boat along the wall, so take the right one.

Take out at the confluence with the Wilson, or continue down the Wilson for a few more good rapids.

Difficulties: Overhanging brush and logs. The most technical rapid (about halfway through the run) is clearly visible and can be scouted from the road.

Shuttle: From Oregon 6, which runs along the Wilson River, proceed upstream along Jordan Creek on good gravel and dirt logging roads, crossing the creek several times and paralleling the entire run. Keep driving until there's not enough water to float a boat.

Gauge: Wilson River above 7 feet.

DEVIL'S LAKE FORK OF THE WILSON RIVER
Six Miles West of Glenwood
Chuck Stanley (adapted by K. Hummer)

Class	Flow	Gradient	Miles	Character	Season
4 T	400	117 C	7	forest	rainy

Description: The first section of the river is called The Flume, with good reason. The rapids alone would be class 2, but considering the narrowness of the river and the overhanging trees, it should be classed as 3. After about 1 mile a real class 3 rapids occurs. This rapids was named Tough Chuck by Richard Montgomery and Chuck Stanley, who took the first exploratory trip down the Devil's Lake Fork.

After Tough Chuck the river flattens out a bit, picks up a little water, and then enters a canyon. This is the good part! Here the river goes through a series of 4 to 5 rapids, each running into the next (no swimming allowed).

The rocks are sharp (blasted from the road above) and very numerous. This section is class 4. The biggest drop in the series is named The Big One; the rapids immediately following is The Little One. The rest of the river is similar to, but smaller than, the main Wilson (see the Jones Creek Forest Camp put-in description).

Difficulties: All of the difficult sections of this river can be seen and scouted from the road. Keep an eye out for trees and logs.

Shuttle: The put-in is about 6 miles west of Glenwood on Oregon 6, where the river is first sighted from the road. There is a sharp turn in the road, as it passes through a deep road cut. The actual put-in is about 0.2 mile from the road cut. The scree is class 2; ropes were needed to lower the boats to the river. The take-out is 7 miles below the put-in.

Gauge: This river rises and falls quickly. If the main Wilson is runnable or a bit high, this stretch is probably runnable.

WILSON RIVER
Jones Creek Forest Camp to Milepost 15
Kim Hummer

Class	Flow	Gradient	Miles	Character	Season
2 +	1000	35 PD	8	forest	rainy
3	2300				
4	7000				

Description: This section of the Wilson River is narrow, from 18 to 100 feet wide, and winds between basalt rock walls. At medium flow most rapids are pool-drop, and eddies directly below major rapids are turbulent with eddies of their own. The river curves frequently, pushing curling rapids off rock walls. Many small tributaries and cascading streams join the Wilson on this section, so the volume increases as the run progresses.

About 100 yards above the bridge at the put-in is a class 4 drop which a boater can carry to and run without warm-up. The usual put-in is directly under the bridge on the left. The first several miles have warm-up class 2 rapids. At about mile 2.5 an island divides the river. Either the left or the right channel can be run at 2300 cfs or above. When running the right channel stay far right; a rock strainer lies on the left side of the bottom drop in this channel. At low flows the right channel ends in an unrunnable rocky outfall.

Below the island, the river narrows into a gorge. This section is extremely turbulent at high water and excitingly turbulent with good drops at medium levels. Several log bridges cross the river at the beginning and end of the gorge section (at miles 3 and 4.8). After the second log bridge, Jordan Creek enters on the left. At medium levels, play-spots are common throughout the gorge and below. The take-out is on a rock ledge on the left, before a right bend in the river. Look for parked shuttle cars.

The Wilson is a popular winter steelhead fishing stream; boaters should attempt to minimize their contact with the many fishermen along this section. Do not play in their fishing holes!

Difficulties: This river can rise from a mild run to a hair-raiser within 3 to 4 hours, so beware of a fast run-off. The gorge section consists of several blind corners with no place to land or to scout from the river. Therefore, scout the gorge when driving the shuttle. Park at a pull-off on the river side at about 3.5 miles downstream of the put-in. Check for logs jamming the drops.

Shuttle: Oregon 6 parallels the Wilson River throughout this section. The put-in at Jones Creek Forest Camp is at milepost 23 on Oregon 6, 20 miles west of Glenwood. The road to the forest camp crosses the Wilson and is wide enough to accommodate parking. The take-out is opposite milepost 15 on Oregon 6. Park on a small right turnout overlooking a rocky ledge. The carry from the river is not too difficult.

Gauge: Contact the River Forecast Center in Portland for the flow of the Wilson River near Tillamook. Several daily papers report the gauge reading. See Appendix B for a correlation of gauge reading and flow.

WILSON RIVER
Milepost 15 to Boat Ramp
Lloyd Likens

Class	Flow	Gradient	Miles	Character	Season
2(3)	1500	26 PD	8	forest houses	rainy

Description: The river flows through some beautiful sunless canyons. Spectacular hues of green and yellow lichens cover the trees and rocks. There are several very large Sitka spruce and red maples. In the spring before the trees have foliage, young saplings and flowers can be seen growing from the thick moss on the tree limbs. The clean white bark of young alder trees is predominant.

This beauty can be enjoyed even by beginners while drifting in the glassy reflective pools and flatwater between the rapids. The highway, never more than 0.5 mile from the river, and the homes overlooking the river do not detract from the scenery. One does not realize that the drifting speed is between 4 and 7 mph until one looks through the crystal clear water at the various colored rocks on the bottom. This section is ideal for a beginner's second or third river trip and for other boaters wishing to sharpen their skills.

One class 3 rapids is located just before the second bridge crossing, approximately 2.5 miles below the put-in. It is clearly visible and can be easily scouted from or portaged on the right bank. The river narrows to a width of 6 feet, creating a fast chute with a large wave at the bottom. Below the wave the water is soft (aerated), with many boils rising from the deep river bottom. This provides excellent reactive bracing practice. There are no obstructions either in the chute or in the run-out This rapids is safe but should be scouted for proper alignment. About 1 mile downstream is a rock garden with room-size boulders scattered across the river. There is no particular difficulty with this rapids; it has a clear passage on the right. Other than the two listed rapids, the river is fast-flowing in many areas, with eddies for playing and maneuvering.

It is easy to miss the take-out. Look for the boat skid rails down the bank to the waters edge on the right.

Difficulties: Two rapids, as mentioned in the Description, are class 3.

Shuttle: The Wilson River Highway, Oregon 6, follows the river. From Portland, travel west on US 26 a few miles past North Plains and turn southwest towards Tillamook on Oregon 6. The put-in is at a small county park 13 miles past Lee's Camp, or if this landmark is missed, just 7 miles west of Jordan Creek Cafe. The take-out is a driftboat launch site 4 miles west of the county park on the left side of the road.

Gauge: Contact the River Forecast Center in Portland for the gauge reading near Tillamook. See Appendix B for a correlation of gauge reading and flow.

NESTUCCA RIVER
Rocky Bend Camp to Blaine
Rob Blickensderfer

Class	Flow	Gradient	Miles	Character	Season
3(4,5)T	1000	50 C	8	forest, hills	rainy

Description: This coastal river drops relentlessly through a lush scenic forest into a small valley where a few small farms are squeezed in. Some stretches are quite uniform in gradient, others are pool drop. Much of the river can be seen from the road.

Near the put-in at Rocky Bend Camp and at the two bridges above the camp, the gradient is nearly uniform, as can be seen from many places along the road. A mile below Rocky Bend Camp, after a curve to the right, the river drops into, over, and through a jumble of boulders, class 5. Immediately following is a class 4 rapids in which the river flows around some boulders and over a shelf. A fast rock garden then leads to a log bridge (partially collapsed in 1985) that is an alternate put-in. Enjoyable class 2 and 3 water continues for the remaining 6.6 miles to the take-out on river right.

Difficulties: The two rapids a mile below Rocky Bend Camp are by far the most difficult. The first is the worst. It has been run at high water (not by the author). At moderate water, it was deemed inadvisable to run, despite the arduous portage on the left. Immediately after putting back in, look for a place to land in order to scout the next rapids, class 4. The first of the two difficulties can be seen from the road where it is highest above the river and curves to the left when driving upstream.

Shuttle: The river may be reached from the coast on US 101 at the town of Beaver, about 16 miles south of Tillamook. At Beaver take the paved county road 858 east along the river. The take-out is 6.3 miles from Beaver near the community of Blaine. Look for a parking turn-out where the road is quite near the river. There is a large school-like house across the road nearby.

Continue upstream to the put-in, either at the log bridge, 6.6 miles upstream from the take-out, or at Rocky Bend Camp, 8 miles upstream. Alternate put-ins are at either of two bridges upstream from the camp. Alternately, the river may be reached from the Willamette Valley by driving west on the paved road out of Carleton. After 13 miles, pass Meadow Lake, the headwaters of the Nestucca River, and continue to the desired put-in.

Gauge: The gauge is located about 2 miles below Beaver. Contact the River Forecast Center in Portland. Several local newspapers list the gauge reading during the winter steelhead fishing season. A reading of 4 ft is too low; probably 6 ft or so is good.

NESTUCCA RIVER
Blaine to Hebo
Kathy Sercu

Class	Flow	Gradient	Miles	Character	Season
1-2	500-2000	25 PD	14	rolling hills rural	rainy

Description: This section of the Nestucca starts in the sparsely populated coastal mountains and continues through the rolling hills and dairy farms of Tillamook County. The first several miles below Blaine are the steepest. Between Blaine and Beaver there are numerous riffles and a couple of ledge drops. Below the confluence with Beaver Creek, just past the curving concrete bridge outside the town of Beaver, the river character changes. Here it becomes wider and flatter, yet it still contains riffles. The lower Nestucca River to the bay is described by Jones (1982).

All of the drops are short and can be easily scouted from a boat. Many can be viewed from the shuttle road. At low water technical maneuvering is required to avoid exposed rocks. Low levels also produce several good surfing spots with nearby eddies. Higher flows provide additional play-spots and make most of the drops more straightforward, but increase the difficulty of the ledge drops. Throughout the run the river splits into channels. All appear to be runnable if there is enough water and there are no log jams. Sweepers are present at several spots and extra caution should be taken at higher flows.

During certain times of the year fishermen abound. Remember to be courteous.

The run is suitable for open boaters with class 2 experience.

Difficulties: None in particular; rocks at low water.

Shuttle: US 101 and county road 858 follow the Nestucca River and make multiple crossings of it throughout this section. Many of the bridges on county road 858 have boat launches, thus allowing boaters to change the length and difficulty of the run.

The take-out for the entire run is located on US 101 one mile north of Hebo at the steel bridge. Turn east onto Evergreen Dr. at the south end of the bridge and park at the pullout. An alternate take-out is a wayside boat ramp on US 101 1.2 miles north of the steel bridge.

To reach the put-in, drive north on US 101 to Beaver and turn east on county road 858 toward Blaine. The Blaine put-in is 6.3 miles from Beaver at a wide pullout next to the river and across from a large school-like house. Blaine is 0.3 mile farther upstream.

Six bridges cross the river between Beaver and the Blaine put-in, offering alternate put-ins and take-outs. Mileage from Beaver to each bridge: 1: 0.3 miles; 2: 0.9 miles; 3: 1.5 miles; 4: 2.5 miles; 5: 3.6 miles; 6: 4.8 miles.

Gauge: Contact the River Forecast Center in Portland. Readings are published in local newspapers in the winter. A reading of 4.0 ft is about the minimum desirable level.

SILETZ RIVER
Elk Creek to Buck Creek
Lance Stein

Class	Flow	Gradient	Miles	Character	Season
2 +	1000	20 PD	5	forest	rainy
	and up			no road	

Description: The river canyon here is extremely beautiful, remote and unlogged. Once on the river, a boater has no contact with the road. The diversity of the rapids on this class 2 + run gives intermediate boaters the chance to experience some interesting paddling. There are short ledgedrops, fast constricted chutes and broad V-slicks leading to standing waves below.

This run begins anywhere one can get a boat to the river below the Falls. At the Falls the river squeezes through a basalt plug and plunges 70 ft within a few hundred yards. This awe inspiring section of the river is absolutely unrunnable, but fun to look at.

Therefore, this description begins 1 mile below the Falls, at Elk Creek. Boaters choosing to put in between the Falls and Elk Creek will find a class 5 put-in, and two rapids which are class 3 and class 4 at medium flows. Below Elk Creek the gradient drops and allows boaters to enjoy the plentiful play-spots, solitude and scenery. A bald eagle was once sighted along this stretch. Take out at the Buck Creek bridge.

Many boaters combine this run with parts of the next run (Buck Creek to Moonshine Park) for a longer day's paddle. There is a bridge above Silache Rapids (see next write-up) which is a possible take-out for those not yet ready for class 4 water.

Difficulties: The first two rapids are the trickiest. The remoteness of the river dictates caution since a broken paddle or boat would lead to a tough hike out.

Shuttle: From Logsden head north on USFS 307. About 10 miles upstream, the road crosses the river at the head of Silache Rapids. Two miles farther upstream, the road forks. The right fork leads to the take-out at Buck Creek. To reach the put-in, stay on the left fork and continue upstream. Follow this road for about 6 miles to the first and only place where the road meets the river, at Elk Creek bridge. This is the best put-in and avoids the bigger rapids upstream. To have a look at the Falls, continue up the road for one mile. A small road to the right leads to the Falls. At the head of the falls there is cable across the river, but there is no "last eddy" for unsuspecting boaters floating downstream to the Falls.

Gauge: Contact the River Forecast Center. A level of 5.5 ft provides adequate water. At 7.5 ft the rapids are faster and more plentiful, but no more difficult.

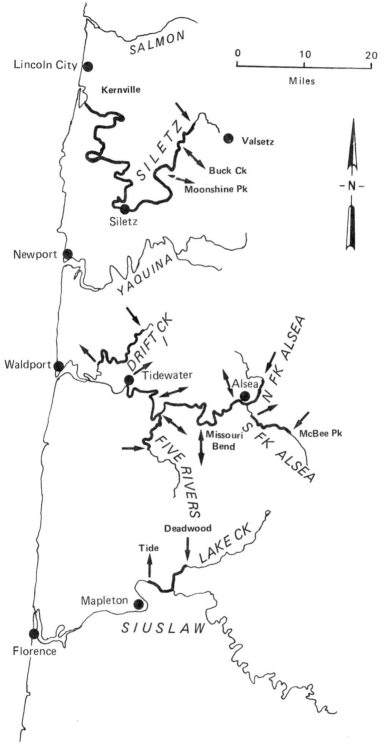

SALMON

Lincoln City

Kernville

SILETZ

Valsetz

Buck Ck

Moonshine Pk

Siletz

Newport

YAQUINA

DRIFT CK

Waldport

Tidewater

Alsea

N FK ALSEA

McBee Pk

Missouri
Bend

FIVE RIVERS

S FK ALSEA

Deadwood

LAKE CK

Tide

Mapleton

SIUSLAW

Florence

0   10   20

Miles

- N -

SILETZ RIVER
Buck Creek to Moonshine Park
Dan Selig and Kim Hummer

Class	Flow	Gradient	Miles	Character	Season
3(4)	1600	40 PD	7.5	second growth	rainy
4(5)	3500			canyon	

Description: Several possible put-ins vary the distance for this run from 3 to 12 miles. The put-in at Buck Creek provides about 2.5 miles of warm-up class 2 rapids before the most difficult stretch, Silache (Sil-a-che) Rapids. This first couple of miles include about five or six ledge-drop rapids, which have some very nice play-spots.

The bridge about 2.0 miles from the put-in marks the beginning of Silache. At low water, Silache is a class 4 rock garden; at very high water it is class 5 rapids with many huge hydraulics and holes. Silache Rapids can be divided into two parts. The upper part is an eddy-hopping route from the left to middle and back again. The second part can be run by taking the route scouted previously during the shuttle on the way to the put-in. The river frequently modifies the planned route, forcing the boater to make last minute navigation decisions.

Good surfing spots are plentiful on the section below Silache. The rapids again tend to be pool- and ledge-drop. Two locations should be noted. About 2 miles above the take-out, there is a gravel-pit area on the side of the road opposite the river. At this spot the river narrows into a rock-sided gorge, called the Lower Gorge. At the beginning of the Lower Gorge are several holes on the right. These holes can be challenged, or avoided by keeping left. The last hole is the biggest, but is not very noticeable from upstream.

The second location to note is about 1.5 miles from the take-out. Here the river is divided by a gravel island. The left channel has the most water; the right channel falls over a 4-ft rocky ledge into a pool.

The finale to the run is a group of beautiful surfing waves on the left of the island at the beginning of Moonshine Park. Although the boater may be tired out from the lovely play-spots upstream, energy can be found to surf these waves too. If there are any difficulties here, the boater will wash out at the sandy beach take-out. Below Moonshine Park the gradient decreases and the river is frequently drifted by steelhead fishermen.

Difficulties: The boater is encouraged to scout at the gravel pit about 2 miles upstream of the take-out, at Silache Rapids, at the boulder garden 5 miles above the take-out where the river looks extremely busy, and at any other bodacious rapids seen from the car. Be courteous to the many fishermen encountered on this river.

Shuttle: The shuttle road follows the river for this section. To get to this run from Logsden, take the road on the east side of the river marked (very small sign) "To Moonshine Park." The park will be on the left within about 5 miles. Take the left turn into the park. Toilets at this park are locked during the winter. To reach the put-ins, follow the gravel road which parallels the Siletz river and eventually reaches Valsetz. There are several optional put-ins. Silache Rapids can be avoided by putting in just below it. Those who want to get right down to business and face Silache directly can put in below the bridge 5 miles above Moonshine Park. The usual put-in for a 7.5 mile paddle is at Buck Creek. After the road crosses Buck Creek, take the right road which leads to a new bridge across the Siletz. A hairpin right turn will bring the boater to the put-in.

Gauge: The optimum flow for this run is about 5.4 to 6.5 feet on the Siletz gauge. The river at 7.4 is awe-inspiring at Silache; below 4.5 feet the river is scratchy. The flow information can be obtained from the River Forecast Center in Portland. Several daily papers carry the reading for the Siletz gauge. The gauge reading and flow are correlated in Appendix B.

DRIFT CREEK
Drift Creek Wilderness Area
Carl Landsness

Class	Flow	Gradient	Miles	Character	Season
2(3)	700	23 C	17	wilderness	rainy

Description: Drift Creek flows through one of the most remote regions of the Sluslaw National Forest, including the Drift Creek Wilderness Area. Except for farmland along the last 5 miles, there is little evidence of civilization on this run. The only known descent of this river was made by 9 WKCC members in February of 1984 after a few days of rain. The first 12 miles is a steady series of class 2- technical rock gardens with some playspots. At about mile 11 is a fairly straightforward class 3 drop. Shortly thereafter, the river flows under a private bridge at which the owners were unwilling to allow a take-out. The next take-out is at a bridge 5 flat miles downstream.

Difficulties: The shuttle. At high water low bridges may require a portage.

Shuttle: Be sure to bring a Siuslaw National Forest map and some patience. The shuttle takes 1 hour (each way) on gravel roads. The put-in is at a bridge about 1/2 mile downstream from the mouth of Meadow Creek. The shuttle generally follows USFS Roads 50 and 51. The take-out is where USFS Road 202 crosses the river about 3 miles above the confluence with the Alsea River.

Gauge: There is no gauge on this river. With the nearby Alsea at 5.5 ft and the Siletz at 5.3 ft, there was adequate flow in Drift Creek.

ALSEA RIVER
Introduction by Rob Blickensderfer

The Alsea River carries water from the crest of the Coast Range to the Pacific Ocean at Waldport. The source is near Marys Peak, the highest Coast Range peak in Oregon at 4,097 feet, the mouth forms Alsea Bay, known for its treacherous bar. The Alsea River is known primarily for winter steelhead fishing. Oregon 34 follows along the river for many miles. Driving this road from December through March, one will usually see fishermen striving to catch one of the 8 to 20 pound fish. Many fishermen use McKenzie boats for their 6 to 8 miles of drift fishing. Several fishermen's conservation organizations have been responsible for construction of the boat landings and also for cleaning up litter from the river banks every year.

The mainstream of the Alsea has very little whitewater, but it has a section that, in the spring, makes one of the best beginning kayaker's first trips. In the winter the mainstream usually runs quite full of both water and drift boats carrying fishermen. In the summer the river usually becomes too low to negotiate in anything but a swimsuit and innertube. On the other hand the South Fork offers an interesting whitewater run in the winter after a hard rain.

SOUTH FORK ALSEA RIVER
Hubert McBee Memorial Park to Rock Quarry Weir
Dan Valens

Class	Flow	Gradient	Miles	Character	Season
2	400	45 PD	6	forest	rainy
3	1000			logging	

Description: The South Fork of the Alsea is a narrow stream runnable only during or shortly after substantial rains. It runs through the scenic coniferous forests of the Coast Range, although recent logging and road building have encroached upon its beauty.

The upper 2 miles, down to the third concrete bridge, is a leisurely class 2 run with several small play-spots at higher water levels. Around the corner below the third bridge is a drop which is runnable on the right. This drop begins a half-mile stretch of fairly continuous rapids. This stretch is a technical class 2 at lower water and a good class 3 with chutes and twisting turns at higher flow. The last third of the run flattens out somewhat, but is punctuated by several ledges and nice play-spots.

Difficulties: Since the South Fork is a small seasonal stream, boaters must constantly be on the lookout for brush, low-hanging trees, and sweepers. The weir just below the take-out should be avoided. Although it may look as if there is a runnable channel on the left during higher water, large broken concrete blocks with exposed reinforcing rods may be encountered in the middle of the channel.

Shuttle: From the town of Alsea, located on Oregon 34 about 25 miles southwest of Corvallis, turn south on the paved road with a sign pointing toward Lobster Valley. One mile from Alsea, turn left on South Fork Road toward Alsea Falls. At 2.7 miles from Alsea the pavement ends; 0.2 miles farther is a weir across half of the river. The take-out is in the pool above the weir. Approximately 6.5 miles from Alsea, the road crosses the river. This is the bridge mentioned in the description as the third from the top, and is an optional put-in. The put-in at Hubert McBee Memorial Park is 8.7 miles from Alsea. This park may also be reached by driving east from Alpine.

Gauge: Flow information is not readily available for the South Fork, but the gauge reading on the main Alsea at Tidewater can be used for a close correlation. A gauge reading of 6.9 feet (which corresponds to about 400 cfs on the South Fork) is minimum for an acceptable run. Some good small play-spots will be found, but expect some bumping and scraping. A reading of 7.5 and above provides a delightful run. The upper gauge limit has not been established. The gauge reading can be obtained from the River Forecast Center in Portland. Several local papers also carry the gauge reading, but the time of the reading should be noted since the river level can change rapidly.

NORTH FORK ALSEA RIVER
North Fork Bridge to Public Boat Landing
Rob Blickensderfer

Class	Flow	Gradient	Miles	Character	Season
1	400-1500	15 C	5	wooded	rainy

Description: This is an enjoyable trip with attractive forest scenery, but without significant whitewater. About 0.2 miles below the put-in bridge, Crooked Creek enters from the left, adding about 25% more water. At the first bridge at mile 0.6 is Clemens County Park, a very pleasant place. After another 1.5 miles is a second bridge, and then a third bridge at mile 3.3 in the town of Alsea. After another 0.5 mile the South Fork of the Alsea enters from the left. One-half mile farther Mill Creek enters from the right and thence it is a short distance to the take-out at the public boat landing, which has toilets.

Difficulties: The class 1 rapids that can be seen from the bridge at the put-in is the most difficult on this stretch. A certain amount of rock dodging is required on the remainder of this section. Consequently, it is not recommended as a beginner's first trip.

Shuttle: The put-in is at the upstream side of a bridge that crosses the North Fork of the Alsea at milepost 43 on Oregon 34. This is 20 miles west of Corvallis. The take-out is Pink House Public Boat Landing at milepost 34.6.

Gauge: The River Forecast Center in Portland has information on the flow at Tidewater. The flow in the North Fork is about one third of that at Tidewater 8 to 12 hours later.

ALSEA RIVER
Pink House Public Boat Landing to Missouri Bend
Rob Blickensderfer

Class	Flow	Gradient	Miles	Character	Season
1	500-2000	7 PD	8	rural fishing	rainy

Description: This section offers an enjoyable drift, although most of it is near the highway. The small park at Missouri Bend is a very pleasant place.

Difficulties: There is very little whitewater on this section. The overhanging brush at high water and some rocks at low water give it the class 1 designation. There are several surfing waves at high water.

Shuttle: The put-in is on Oregon 34 at Pink House Public Boat Landing at milepost 34.6, which is 25 miles west of Corvallis and 2 miles west of the town of Alsea. The take-out is at Missouri Bend Park, milepost 30.8. An alternate take-out is at a bridge on a side road about 0.5 mile below Missouri Bend.

Gauge: Contact the River Forecast Center in Portland for the reading at Tidewater. See Appendix B for the gauge height to flow conversion.

ALSEA RIVER
Missouri Bend Park to Five Rivers
Rob Blickensderfer

Class	Flow	Gradient	Miles	Character	Season
1(2)	500	8 PD	12	rural	rainy
	2000			fishing	

Description: This section is a pleasant drift. It gets farther from the highway and gives more of a feeling of isolation than either the preceding or following sections. Just below the midpoint of the run, Fall Creek enters from the right.
Difficulties: With a few rocks to dodge and some overhanging brush, the trip is rated class 1. Some fairly long stretches of flat water must be paddled. About 1 mile above the take-out is a class 2 rapid that is fairly long, steep, and shallow. At high water it becomes bigger.
Shuttle: The put-in is about 33 miles west of Corvallis on Oregon 34 at Missouri Bend Park, milepost 30.8. The take-out is at an inconspicuous boat ramp 0.2 mile upstream from Five Rivers Junction. The ramp is at the upstream end of the old road from Five Rivers. An alternate take-out is 5 river miles above Five Rivers, where a bridge on a side road crosses the Alsea River.
Gauge: Contact the River Forecast Center in Portland for the reading at Tidewater.

ALSEA RIVER
Five Rivers to Rock Crusher or Hellion
Rob Blickensderfer

Class	Flow	Gradient	Miles	Character	Season
1(2)	500-	10 PD	5-6	rural	rainy
	2000			fishing	

Description: This section is perfect for novice kayakers on their first trip. It can also be good fun for an open canoeist's introduction to whitewater when the flow is near the ideal of 750 cfs. At flows above 1000 cfs the drops tend to wash out. Access via a boat ramp can be obtained at Blackberry Campground, a little over half way down.
   A combination of small waves, small eddies, and a few straightforward, fast chutes make this an ideal section for the beginner.
Difficulties: From small riffles at the beginning, this section gradually builds to some class 1 or 1+ chutes. The entrances to the chutes near the end are straightforward to an experienced leader. The last drop, the Rock Crusher, is at the take-out. If the alternate take-out one mile downstream is used, the Hellion Rapids will be run. This rapids is class 1+ at low flow and 2 at high water. Hellion has a tendency to push inexperienced boaters onto the rocks on the right.
Shuttle: The put-in at Five Rivers Boat Ramp at milepost 20.6 on Oregon 34 is 0.2 mile above Five Rivers Junction. This is about 43 miles west of Corvallis. An alternate put-in is the boat launch below Five Rivers. The take-out is at Rock Crusher Rapids, identified by the basalt cliff across the river. The parking area is below the highway at a sharp right curve (heading downstream) about 5 miles from Five Rivers. Look for the Basalt cliff. An alternate take-out is about 1 mile farther at Hellion Rapids, below Mike Bauer Park. This rapids can be seen from the road. Park near the rapids on the south shoulder of the road.
Gauge: Contact the River Forecast Center in Portland for the reading at Tidewater.

ALSEA RIVER
Hellion Rapids to Tidewater
Rob Blickensderfer

Class	Flow	Gradient	Miles	Character	Season
1	500-2000	6 PD	6	rural fishing	rainy

Description: Although the impact of civilization is seen much more on this section than on the above sections, the river is still pleasant. Several of the suspension foot bridges that cross the river are amusing. There are no significant rapids below Hellion and the river gradually flattens and slows as it approaches tidewater at the town of Tidewater.

After following the highway for about 3 miles, the river makes a large 3-mile horseshoe bend. Along the latter half of this bend a secondary road from Tidewater parallels the river. The high density of homesites along here limits access.

Shuttle: Follow Oregon 34.

Gauge: Contact the River Forecast Center in Portland for the Tidewater reading.

FIVE RIVERS
Bridge 10 miles above Oregon 34 to Alsea River
Steve Holland

Class	Flow	Gradient	Miles	Character	Season
1	600 +	12 PD	10	forest,houses	rainy

Description: Five Rivers is a tributary of the Alsea River, entering it about 20 miles west of the town of Alsea. The river meanders through alders and conifers typical of Coast Range forests, following a road much of the way. Several small ledges provide regular waves for effortless surfing. This stream is suitable for intermediate canoeists, but it is too shallow for pleasant boating except after heavy or sustained rains.

Difficulties: Brush and trees growing over the water's edge can be a problem. A 2-ft shelf about a mile below the put-in can be seen on the drive upstream.

Shuttle: A sign on Oregon 34 about 20 miles west of the town of Alsea marks the Five Rivers Junction. The take-out is on the right, just downstream of the confluence with the Alsea River. Drive to the put-in by crossing the bridge over the Alsea River and continuing upstream along Five Rivers. About 3 miles upstream, Lobster Creek and a side road enter from your left; bear right and continue upstream another 7 miles to a bridge where another stream and side road come in from your left. The put-in is under the bridge. A bicycle shuttle is practical.

Gauge: A gauge is located downstream of the mouth of Lobster Creek. A reading of 4.8 ft is a good level.

LAKE CREEK (SIUSLAW RIVER)
Deadwood Creek to Tide
George Ice

Class	Flow	Gradient	Miles	Character	Season
2 +	1600-8000	26 PD	7	rural	rainy
3(4)	10000-31000				

Description: This section of Lake Creek is an excellent winter run. A boater can usually expect a good trip immediately after or during a major storm. Lake Creek is named for Triangle Lake in the Oregon Coast Range. Emerging from the lake, the creek meanders a few hundred feet, turns a swift corner and drops over several unboatable falls into impassable log jams and unrunnable rapids. The traditional put-in for the run is 10 miles downstream from Triangle Lake, after Lake Creek becomes a swiftly flowing river with lots of waves and eddies. Putting in at Deadwood Creek at least gives the boater a chance to warm up for The Horn! Several boaters have often wondered whether a less ominously named put-in should be used.

The upper 2 to 3 miles of the run has several small holes, innumerable waves to play on, and wide-eyed fishermen who watch any boaters go by. After turning a corner, the boater is engulfed in a series of drops leading to The Horn. The Horn is a unique rapids, formed by a hard volcanic formation. The rapids starts with small waves and keeps building up to bigger waves and holes. The last set of gigantic waves forms below a monster rock that bisects the river. Scout the rapids from the road. When running the rapids, keep far left. Once in the rapids stay upright. A large wave near the bottom crashes down on boats and stands C-2's on end. Below The Horn, where the river bends right, is a significant shelf. It is easy on the right. The 4 mile run from The Horn to the take-out continues with big waves and holes. The last few miles are on the Siuslaw River. But when boats are dragged out near Big Ed's Market at Tide, the question is always the same: Did you run THE HORN?

Difficulties: The Horn should be scouted during the shuttle. Run the rapids on the left. About a mile above the take-out, where a small tributary comes into the river, is a manmade structure on the left bank of the Siuslaw. This structure, often submerged at higher flows, should be avoided.

Shuttle: This trip has the distinct advantage of a 1-hour drive from either Eugene or Corvallis. Trips usually begin where Deadwood Creek, a major tributary, enters Lake Creek. Just upstream from the confluence of Deadwood and Lake Creeks there is a pull-off on Oregon 36. Park here. Five miles downstream from Deadwood Creek, Lake Creek flows into the Siuslaw River. The take-out is at the small park in the "town" of Tide. This town's claim to fame is having one of the state's smallest liquor stores.

Gauge: The gauge reading or flow for the Siuslaw at Mapleton is given in several daily papers or can be obtained from the River Forecast Center in Portland. The correlation between gauge reading and flow is given in Appendix B. The flow of Lake Creek at Deadwood is approximately one third that of the Siuslaw at Mapleton.

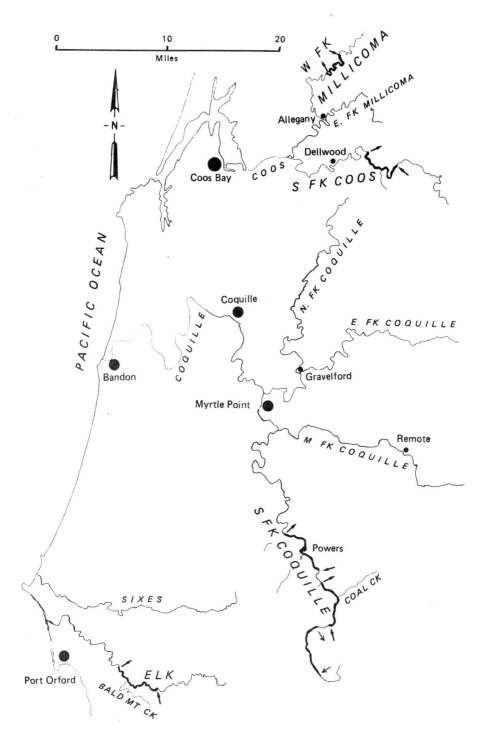

0   10   20
Miles

- N -

W FK
MILLICOMA
E. FK MILLICOMA
Allegany

Dellwood

S FK COOS

COOS

Coos Bay

PACIFIC OCEAN

N. FK COQUILLE

E FK COQUILLE

Coquille

COQUILLE

Gravelford

Bandon

Myrtle Point

M FK COQUILLE

Remote

S FK COQUILLE

Powers

COAL CK

SIXES

ELK

BALD MT CK

Port Orford

Chapter 3. South Coast Rivers

SOUTH COAST RIVERS
Introduction by Richard Dierks

The rivers of the south coastal area share one characteristic: they are unregulated and therefore very sensitive to the weather. Instead of calling the Corps of Engineers for release information, just look outside for rain or try to guess when the Coast Range snows will melt. High maximum flows, like 14,300 cfs for the Elk River and 48,000 cfs for the South Fork Coquille River, result from large amounts of rain combined with a warming trend over a deep snow pack. It's hard to give upper limits to running these rivers. Boaters need to decide for themselves whether it's prudent to be on a river at a given time. Flow figures in these write-ups are merely best estimates. Due to the steep forested terrain, all of the runs with a medium to high gradient have sweeper problems.

A common riverbank vegetation feature is the myrtle tree, indigenous only to southern Oregon and northern California. When crushed or torn its shiny, deep green, oval leaves release a pungent camphor smell.

Roads closely parallel all described runs, except the South Fork Coquille's Powers run and the West Fork Millicoma River, where road and river mileages differ. Mileages given coincide with roadside mileage markers.

Here is a shuttle hint to save time and 62 miles between the South Fork Coquille River and Elk River. From China Flat drive westward (take a good spare tire) on the well maintained gravel road USFS 3353 for 20.8 miles. Merge into road USFS 5325 for another 3.5 miles (perhaps to stay at beautiful Elk Lake Campground), then on to the Elk River put-in at Slate Creek bar. Total distance from China Flat is 34.8 miles.

WEST FORK MILLICOMA RIVER
Above Allegany
Richard Dierks

Class	Flow	Gradient	Miles	Character	Season
3(4)	300-1500	44 PD	6	forest	rainy

Description: The West Fork Millicoma River is a tributary of the Coos River. All along this shallow, clear, ledge-drop river there are numerous small play holes that are especially appealing to beginning hole riders. Much of this river has a canopy of broadleaf foliage, including evergreen myrtle.

From the put-in, it is a 1.6 mile paddle to the first major rapids, Henry's Falls, a 10-ft class 4+ drop. This falls can be seen from 260 ft above on the way to the put-in. Approximately 1 mile downstream from the falls is a concrete low-water river crossing used for logging and fire fighting. This low-water crossing poses no problems. After another 2.2 river miles, look for Girl Scout Triple Drop, a class 4 rapids which is about 0.2 miles long. This rapids should also be scouted on the way to the put-in for sweepers; on the road it is 0.5 mile inside the Elliot State Forest boundary sign. The last significant rapids is the 6-ft falls (class 3), located about 1.1 mile below Girl Scout Triple Drop, which can be run in the chute on the right. The take-out is 0.2 mile farther downstream on river right.

Difficulties: Henry's Falls should be scouted from the left. It can be portaged easily on river right. If there's enough water it can be run far right, but if a boater becomes caught in the center hole, there's a good chance of a swim. The hole is very symmetrical, has little upstream depth and little paddle support. The left side of the falls has been carved out, but is clean, despite its nasty appearance.

The run through Girl Scout Triple Drop begins with a turbulent chute accelerating into a moving pool directly above a vertical 6-ft ledge drop, which diagonally intersects the river. Continue to the left of a hole located just upstream of a very large boulder. Enter the S-turn drop and then eddy out on river left and enjoy the ender hole just upstream of the Girl Scout camp, river right. The upper rapids in this series are spaced in such a way that swims here have been painful and rescues difficult. A boater without a good roll should at least have a couple of people waiting below the first drop but above the falls. The portage is difficult at Girl Scout Triple Drop--it's left through the brush or, a little easier, right through the boulders.

Shuttle: From Coos Bay follow the shuttle directions given for the South Fork Coos River to the green steel bridge. Cross the bridge, drive a short distance and then turn right toward Allegany. At Allegany, you will be 13.8 miles from US 101 and will have just crossed the Millicoma River. Turn up the West Fork Millicoma River and restart the mileage. Cross the river on the only bridge at mile 4.8. This is the place to check the flow level (described in the gauge section). At the Deans Mountain turnoff, mile 5.3, stay right. The take-out is at mile 8.0 where there is a river access road with a locked steel gate. There's not much parking space here (maybe 2 cars); be sure to park off the road. Continue upstream and, to avoid shuttle confusion, note the spur road to the river just above Triple Drop at road mile 8.7. Continue another 2.1 miles to the put-in; the private gate 0.1 mile farther upstream verifies your location.

Gauge: Stand on the downstream side of the aforementioned 4.8 mile bridge and look from river left to river right at the square concrete abutment. There are two spray paint marks there. If only one is visible, then the water is low but runnable. If both lines are visible, then try the South Fork Coos River, instead.

SOUTH FORK COOS RIVER
Johnson Beach to Below Mile 7 Bridge
Richard Dierks

Class	Flow	Gradient	Miles	Character	Season
2(3)	400-3000	23 C	6.1	hilly logged	rainy

Description: This is a nice beginners' run which will challenge the intermediate paddler at higher flows. The river bed is wide, flat and rocky and is located in hilly, deforested land. It becomes muddy with rainfall. This run can only be made on weekends because Weyerhauser Company restricts access upstream of Dellwood due to truck traffic and logging activities during the week. Unfortunately, Weyerhauser has left no wooded buffer strips along the South Fork Coos system. The resulting visual impact is startling and depressing.

From the put-in at Johnson Beach, it is a 1.1 mile paddle to the splash dam remnant. This dam, used in years past to flush logs downstream during low flows, now poses no obstacle. Cox Creek flows in from the left at mile 3.1. The North Fork Coquille Road junction can be seen at mile 3.7. At mile 5.3 the 7 mile bridge passes overhead. Take-out is just downstream on river right at mile 6.1. During higher flows a safer take-out is found in the lower eddy.

Difficulties: There is a long, class 3 boulder garden just before the take-out.

Shuttle: Traveling south from Coos Bay, turn left off US 101 toward Allegany-Coos River; cross the Isthmus Slough bridge and stay left. After 1.1 mile turn right onto Coos River Highway. Cross Ross Slough bridge at 2.1 miles and continue toward Dellwood. Pass under the green steel bridge (mile 3.4) and cross the concrete Daniels Creek bridge (mile 4.4). At mile 8.7 turn right into Weyerhauser Co.'s Dellwood log dump/truck shop. Drive a half mile through the complex and then restart the car mileage in accordance with the mile markers alongside the road. The take-out is found at a turnout near mile marker 6. To get to the put-in, drive 6.1 miles upstream to Johnson Beach, just past milepost 12.
Gauge: None.

SOUTH FORK COQUILLE RIVER
South Fork Bridge to China Flat
Richard Dierks

Class	Flow	Gradient	Miles	Character	Season
3 T	200-	60 PD	5.3	forest	rainy
4 T	1500			wooded	

Description: Nearly continuous class 3 and 4 boulder drops and gardens typify this busy, exciting run. Several campgrounds are in this area; it is very scenic.

Daphne Grove, 1.8 miles from the put-in, marks the approximate halfway point in the rapids. A bridge is passed at mile 2.2, and in another 0.5 mile paddlers should stop on river right to scout Eight Foot Drop. Kelley Creek enters on river right at mile 3.3 and marks the beginning of a long, wide boulder garden resulting from the exfoliation of the vertically tilted sedimentary rock beds on the left. It is less shallow on the left. In this approximately 3.8 mile stretch from the put-in to Johnson Creek the gradient averages about 90 feet per mile. The remaining mile and a half is relatively flat and uneventful, as is the 2.3 mile section from China Flat to Myrtle Grove. Take out just above the bridge at China Flat on river right.

Difficulties: Most of this run is not easily scouted from the road. Be constantly alert for sweepers. During the shuttle, stop about 0.7 miles above Kelley Creek and look for the gravel turn-off, just past the paved one, to scout Eight Foot Drop. The "easiest" route at gauge level 3.0 ft is down into the cushion, far right--no mistakes allowed! At lower levels the reversal is not so strong to the left of where the cushion was. The river left drop is not clean.

Shuttle: To reach the take-out, drive upriver from Powers to the China Flat Recreational Area. (See the South Fork Coquille River, Powers to Baker Creek section, for directions to Powers.) The graveled boat launch road at China Flat is just upstream of the bridge on river right. The put-in is found by driving upstream to the Coquille River Falls Research Natural Area, South Fork bridge, 16 miles above Powers.

Gauge: There is a water level gauge painted on the concrete support under the 16 mile South Fork bridge. Drive over to river left and look back for the markings. All the runs above Powers on the South Fork Coquille River can be gauged from this scale. The authors have been on the river at flows between 1.5 and 3.5 ft, but higher levels would most certainly be runnable, sweepers permitting.

The section from South Fork bridge to China Flat is tight and technical at 3.0 ft; however, it loses its pushiness and class 4 rating at 1.5 ft.

SOUTH FORK COQUILLE RIVER
Myrtle Grove to Milepost 3
Richard Dierks

Class	Flow	Gradient	Miles	Character	Season
4(5) T	200-2000	53 PD	5.3	forest gorge	rainy

Description: This exciting two-part run can be characterized as tight, technical class 4 boulder drops with connecting pools at lower water levels. Also characteristic of this steep canyon section are plentiful signs of beaver, high cascading side creek waterfalls, and deep, clear steelhead waters. The upper 3.1 miles to Coal Creek provides a good class 4, 42 feet per mile gradient warm-up for the higher gradient 0.9 miles below.

From Myrtle Grove downstream 1.9 miles to the quarter-mile long class 4 Roadside Narrows there are many good class 3 and 4 drops. Roadside Narrows can be easily scouted from the road. After the Narrows it is about a mile of class 3 paddling to Coal Creek. Look for the creek entering through two culverts on river right.

The gorge below Coal Creek cannot be scouted from the road, and would be very difficult to exit on foot with gear. The class 5 rapids is located about halfway through this gorge at what would be milepost 5 on the road above. From the end of the gorge it is a 1.3 mile flatwater paddle down to the take-out, a washed out footbridge road on river right. The center-eroded, gray shale gravel fill "road" reveals an exposed cable a short way up the draw. Lower Land Creek joins the river just upstream on river left.

Difficulties: Both sections must be scouted from the road for sweepers, especially for less obvious pieces caught in the tight drops. The nearly mile-long gorge beginning at Coal Creek has an estimated gradient of 111 feet per mile. It is a continuous pool drop, choked with large boulders throughout its tortuous course, and it is complete with sweepers.

Scout as often as necessary to ensure location of the class 5 rapids in time to permit a portage decision. Especially in high water, four contiguous situations combining large holes and house-size boulders will challenge any good boater. Scout and portage the class 5 rapids on the right. The run begins center, then to the right, back to center and return to the right for the finish. Do not go left of the huge boulder at the top. Good boaters have walked, and will continue to walk, this one. The entire section should be avoided when high water and sweepers combine.

Shuttle: To get to the take-out drive upriver from Powers to milepost 3. (See following write-up for directions to Powers.) Park on the left of the road just past this milepost. Walk upriver 0.15 mile until you come to the end of the field. The soggy trailhead to the river is located there. The put-in is found by driving 5.3 miles upstream to Myrtle Grove. However, it may be best to park the shuttle vehicle at Coal Creek because not everyone will choose to continue past Coal Creek.

Gauge: See the previous write-up for a discussion of the gauge for this stretch of river. At 1.5 ft the stretch from Myrtle Grove to Coal Creek exhibits tight, technical drops. At 3.5 ft the river has respectable drops, but eddies will still be found. The river can be run at levels higher and lower than these levels. The canyon downstream of Coal Creek has not been run since the installation of the gauge. It may be too tight in a couple of places at 1.5 ft. At 3.0 ft the class 5 rapid becomes very pushy and technical. It was not run at 3.5 ft because of river-wide sweepers, the locations of which often change during high flows.

Rick Starr

The river above Coal Creek has a longer running season than the lower section because the lower section is wider and more shallow, and thus becomes more rocky and unrunnable earlier in the season.

Relative upstream and downstream levels will vary due to tributary confluences downstream from the gauge and the relation of snowmelt to rainfall. Snows last longer in the upper end of this drainage.

SOUTH FORK COQUILLE RIVER
Two Miles above Powers to Baker Creek

Richard Dierks

Class	Flow	Gradient	Miles	Character	Season
2 + (4)	400-2000	12 C	6.5	wooded, rural agricultural	rainy

Description: The river is wide, and the scenery is open, wooded and pleasant. As the river meanders through Powers, the elevation difference hides the town, but the scenery is occasionally contrasted by washed out bridges and Powers' dual solution to old automobile disposal and riparian erosion.

The run is a pleasant beginner's run with one turbulent 10-ft class 4 drop, which is located in the canyon section of the run and can be scouted and/or portaged on the right.

Difficulties: The class 4 rapids can be seen from the road far above by driving 0.8 road miles upstream from the Baker Creek junction. Run right off the pillow, avoiding the hole in the center. To avoid the possibility of a nasty swim, beginners should give special attention to the class 3 rapids preceding the the class 4 water.

Shuttle: To reach the take-out, turn south off of Oregon 42 at the Powers turnoff, which is at the confluence of the Coquille River's West and South Forks. The confluence is 17.5 highway miles north of Powers, and 13 miles south of Coquille. Drive 15.5 miles toward Powers from Oregon 42, turn right at Baker Creek and proceed 0.3 mile to the take-out, located at the boat ramp on river right just upstream of the bridge. Proceed to the put-in by driving upstream through Powers, following the signs to China Flat, Illahe, and Agness; you will cross the river twice. Two-tenths of a mile past the City of Powers Orchard Park, you will arrive at the put-in, which is at mile marker 2 (from Powers).

Gauge: None. The upper South Fork gauge might be used, but the river is wider here and correlations have not been made. Besides, the gauge is 14 miles upstream.

ELK RIVER
Slate Creek Bar to Elk River Hatchery
Richard Dierks

Class	Flow	Gradient	Miles	Character	Season
3	200-	47 PD	6.5	forest	rainy
4	2000 +			canyon	

Description: The Elk River is a beautiful pool-drop river with deep green water, narrow rock walls and tall timber overhead. Its rapids are not as technical nor as frequent as those of the South Fork Coquille. It is located on the coast between Langlois and Port Orford.

The first mile of the river is an active class 3 warm-up. Included in this section is Nose Bender, 0.2 mile from put-in, which is a technical class 4 at very low water (gauge 4.5 ft). The rock at the bottom of this 6-ft drop can reorient the nose of a boat, and it caused a pin several years ago. Run right, remembering that the previous drop is similar in appearance but not as steep.

Sluice Narrows, class 4, is found 1.0 mile downstream. It is a very turbulent, 15-20 ft sloped drop. Everything flows left toward the wall at the bottom, especially at low water, so stay right. Before running this rapids be sure to check for sweepers, preferably during the shuttle, beneath the roadside hemlock. The 90 Degree Bend drop is located another 0.4 mile downstream and is also class 4. A strong reversal at the bottom of this 6-ft fall necessitates punching it to the left. These rapids mark the end of a 1.5 mile stretch of river which has an average gradient of about 60 feet per mile.

The next 3.6 miles are class 2 and 3. Bald Mountain Creek flows in on river left (note the bridge over the creek) at mile 4.1. At mile 5.0 the pace picks up again with the Lower Gorge. This is a quarter-mile class 4 rapids which has a gradient of about 150 feet per mile. It's clean, fun, and never really technical.

The final class 4 rapid on this run is appropriately named Last Four and is located about 200 yards downstream from the the Lower Gorge. The easiest route is right. Scout for sweepers. From here it is just another mile to the take-out at the Elk River Hatchery, across from Anvil Creek.

Difficulties: Sweepers are the major hazard; they can be difficult to spot from the water. Scout all the major drops from the road during the shuttle. Very high water eliminates most of the river's eddies, creates sapling sweepers, and flattens many of its drops. The cumulative danger is thus increased, especially in the upper section, where it might be considered up to class 5. During very low flows beware of Nose Bender.

Shuttle: Between US 101 mileage markers 297 and 298, turn east at the Elk River turnoff. Drive upriver 7.55 miles to the Elk River Hatchery, which is the take-out. To reach the put-in, drive 6.35 miles upstream to Slate Creek Bar. At both put-in and take-out, park on or near the gravel bars, being careful not to block access. A shuttle can be arranged by Sandy Slater for $5. Be sure and phone ahead: (503) 332-7921.

Gauge: The gauge is located just inside the parallel concrete fish returnways at the most downstream part of the fishery. A low but runnable reading is 4.5 ft; above 7 ft, the river really begins to "pump". The rise in the river level in the upstream canyon is disproportionately greater than the gauge indicates. There is another gauge downstream.

CHETCO RIVER
Upper Summer Bridge to Loeb State Park
Ron Mattson

Class	Flow	Gradient	Miles	Character	Season
1	300-1500	12 PD	11	forest logging	all year

Description: The Chetco River is a famous southwestern Oregon stream noted for fine fishing and crystal clear water. This section is not a big whitewater run, but makes a pleasant easy-going trip. The trip is mostly flatwater with a couple of riffles along the way. As the riverbed is all gravel, riffles and rapids change from year to year. Two miles from the put-in, the South Fork enters on the left. Just below Redwood State Park, where the road becomes visible from the river again, is a large rock on the left with an ideal swimming hole below. This area makes a good lunch spot with a nice gravel bar on the opposite side of the river.

The next section, down to the concrete bridge, contains many fine swimming holes and beaches for lunch stops. The swimming hole under the concrete bridge is probably one of the most popular on the river. A very nice diving rock is on the right. Loeb State Park, a very large park with overnight camping, restrooms, and picnic area, is 2.0 miles farther. Below this take-out there are many houses within sight of the river.

Difficulties: The river is gentle and easy to run, but expect logs, snags, or river channels which change from one year to the next.

Shuttle: To reach the put-in for this trip, drive up the North Bank Road of the Chetco from US 101 (south of Brookings) to the South Fork of the Chetco. This is an alternate put-in that will shorten the trip by 2 miles. Upper Summer Bridge, a plank bridge that can only be used at low summer flows, is located down a road to the left, approximately 1.5 miles beyond the South Fork Bridge. This point is about 18 miles (including 1 mile of unpaved road) from Brookings. The first reasonable take-out is at Redwood State Park. The 5 mile section from the first swimming hole at Redwood State Park to the concrete bridge has numerous access points. None of them are marked. Loeb State Park is a preferred take-out because afternoon winds, which blow off the ocean every day when the weather is good, make the paddling tough.

Gauge: The flow is unregulated. The river can be run spring, summer, or fall.

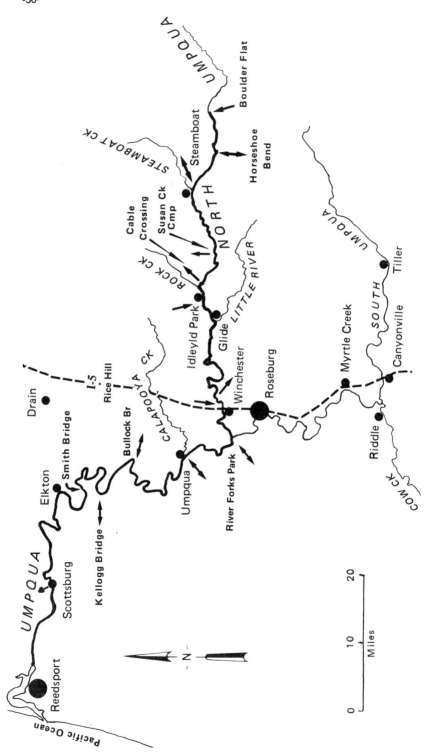

Chapter 4. Southern Oregon Rivers and the Smith River, California

UMPQUA RIVER
Introduction by Kent Wickham

The North Umpqua drains a large region near Diamond Lake in the Cascades. After the river is joined by the South Umpqua near Roseburg and I-5, the Umpqua River flows northwest to the coast at Reedsport. The North Umpqua east of Roseburg provides some truly fine boating along much of its course through a tree-lined canyon. The numerous campgrounds and the road along the river are used by many fishermen, campers, and picnickers. Most whitewater boating is done along the 32 mile stretch between Boulder Flat and Cable Crossing. Normally there is enough water all summer and fall to boat the river.

As well as being a fine boating stream, the North Umpqua is renowned for its incomparable thrills for the angler. As a result the Forest Service has established a few restrictions on boating in order to protect the best fishing areas. A copy of the guidelines can be obtained at the North Umpqua Ranger District Office at Glide. Restrictions affect boating from July through October, when river access is limited to 10 AM to 6 PM except between Island Access and Bogus Creek, which is closed to boating. During September and October, Soda Springs to Wilson Creek is closed for salmon spawning. Please respect these closures. Fisherman are our allies in protecting free flowing rivers.

NORTH UMPQUA RIVER
Boulder Flat to Horseshoe Bend
Kent Wickham

Class	Flow	Gradient	Miles	Character	Season
2	800	39 PD	7	forest	all year
3	2000				

Description: Most of this section can be scouted from the road. The river is characterized by swiftly moving water and fairly continuous activity in moderate-size waves amid numerous rocks and other obstacles. There are no really difficult rapids, though there are several spots where large holes and bigger waves will be encountered. Snags are a hazard at times, and it is not unusual to encounter a tree spanning all or most of the stream. Just beyond the second bridge, a rocky ledge spans 80% of the river, creating a very narrow chute along the right bank. At lower water levels this chute is virtually the only runnable spot. A boater will readily get slammed into the wall on the right by the force of the current here. It is a potential spot for a concentration of lodged debris.

Difficulties: The rocky ledge just below the second bridge should be checked for debris in the right chute. The ledge may need to be portaged.

Shuttle: The put-in at Boulder Flat Campground is approximately 50 miles east of Roseburg on Oregon 138. The take-out is at Horseshoe Bend Camp, also on Oregon 138.

Gauge: Contact the River Forecast Center in Portland for the reading at the Winchester Gauge. The optimum level is 2 to 5 feet. This river is dam-controlled and runnable all year.

NORTH UMPQUA RIVER
Horseshoe Bend to Steamboat
Kent Wickham

Class	Flow	Gradient	Miles	Character	Season
3	800	29 PD	9	forest	all year
4	2000				

Description: This section of the North Umpqua can be described as pool and drop. Between Horseshoe Bend and Apple Creek Campgrounds the river passes through a narrow gorge full of short, steep rapids that vary in difficulty. Most can be scouted from the road. Several of them require meticulous maneuvering between rocks and holes. Pin Ball Rapids is below Apple Creek Campground. The pool-drop pattern of the river continues on to Steamboat. A boater should go slowly and get a look at the rapids that remain.

Difficulties: Pin Ball Rapids is a boulder-choked drop not visible from the road. It is located about 0.3 mile below the bridge below Apple Creek Campground. Scouting is advisable. The rapids occurs on a right bend of the river with a large gravel bar just above it on the left. At water levels that allow for the bar to exist it is possible to pull in at its base and scout from the left bank.

Shuttle: Put in at any of the wide spots along the road from Oregon 138 to Horseshoe Bend Campground. An alternate put-in is the small turnout 0.2 mile upstream from the Dry Creek Store, which is approximately 1.5 miles above Horseshoe Bend. The best take-out is 0.2 mile below Island Camp and 1.5 miles above Steamboat.

Gauge: Contact the River Forecast Center in Portland for the reading at the Winchester Gauge. The optimum level is 2 to 5 feet. This river is dam-controlled and runnable all year.

NORTH UMPQUA RIVER
Steamboat to Cable Crossing
Kent Wickham

Class	Flow	Gradient	Miles	Character	Season
3(4)	1500-3000	21 PD	16	forest	all year

Description: This stretch, although highlighted by several of the Umpqua's best rapids, is generally less technical than the upstream runs. Rapids are separated by long flat stretches.

Steamboat Inn marks the site of an exciting rocky rapids in the left channel, and a sometimes-runnable falls in the right channel. Do not trespass on Inn property when scouting. Six miles below Steamboat is Wright Creek Bridge, which is followed in another 0.2 mile by Bathtub Rapids. At low water Bathtub deserves a scout.

Small fun drops continue for several more miles. A very large cliff rising from water's edge on the left is seen 200 yards above Island (or Staircase) Rapids, the Umpqua's best ride. Several miles below Island Rapids, and marked by the Forest Service boundary sign at the side of the road, is Sleeper Rapids, a long sweeping turn ending in a troublesome hole. A notable rapids encountered at Susan Creek Campground is followed by a notoriously flat 4 miles. At Richard G. Baker State Park, a 5-ft falls known as Little Niagara helps to justify paddling the preceding flat stretch. Cable Crossing is the last convenient take-out above Rock Creek Falls.

The mouth of Steamboat Creek is a holding area for migrating steelhead. From mid-July through October numerous anglers will be encountered here. Confrontations have occurred in the past, and relations between boaters and anglers have been somewhat strained. Please be courteous. During fishing season it is a good idea to plan put-ins after 10 AM and take-outs before 5 PM,in order to leave prime fishing time to the fishermen. If there is an exceptionally high number of fishermen, it is best to avoid the area altogether, and put in 4 miles down at Bogus Creek. With the exception of the rapids right at Steamboat, very few good rapids will be missed.

Difficulties: Rafters might find it necessary to portage Bathtub at low flows due to the narrowness of the chutes. At Island Rapids the river divides into a broad, shallow left channel, which fizzles out to nothing, and roaring right channel that approaches class 4. Island can be scouted from the road with difficulty. Sleeper is a long but rather innocuous rapids that starts out easy but requires a very tricky cut at the end to avoid a very large hole (which reverts to a rock at low flows). It can be scouted from the road.

Below the recommended take-out at Cable Crossing are two very demanding rapids, Rock Creek Falls and The Narrows. These rapids should be considered by experts only.

Shuttle: The best put-in is at the river access just below Island Campground. Bogus Creek Campground is an alternative. The take-out is at Cable Crossing, a poorly marked, but very good access just up from Rock Creek Falls.

This run may be shortened by taking out at the newly built access trail at Susan Creek Picnic Area. The use of Susan Creek Campground as a take-out is discouraged due to the heavy motor home traffic.

Gauge: Contact the River Forecast Center in Portland for the reading at the Winchester Gauge. The optimum level is 2 to 5 feet. This river is dam-controlled and runnable all year.

NORTH UMPQUA RIVER
Idleyld Park to Winchester
Carl Landsness

Class	Flow	Gradient	Miles	Character	Season
2 + (3-) T	1500 and up	11 PD	26	rolling hills	all year

Description: This run is an unheralded gem. In this section, the terrain makes its transition from forested mountain canyon to hilly pastureland. Near sunset, these hills of scattered oak become a breathtaking painted masterpiece of shadow and golden color. By June, the river is comfortably warm, yet mountain clear with plenty of flow, a rare treat for Oregon boaters. What's more, this section contains a fairly continuous offering of class 2 whitewater. All of these factors combine to make this one of the premier whitewater runs of western Oregon for open canoes and a very enjoyable one for novice kayakers.

The first 5 miles to Colliding Rivers resembles the upstream runs complete with emerald green water. Immediately after the put-in is Salmon Hole, a 2 + straightforward drop with some big waves. From here to Colliding Rivers, there are many class 2 and 2 + pool-drop rapids with fairly straight routes through 2-3 ft standing waves. At Colliding Rivers, the river is constricted by several large rock formations; it makes a sharp right turn after colliding head-on with Little River. A narrow class 4 drop makes a shortcut turn to the right. Don't be caught by it. The standard route is generally a class 3- with a rather tight right turn midway. This drop changes with the flow. Scouting is advised.

The river then starts its transition into open hills with a much wider streambed. The rapids take on more of a gravel bar nature with longer rapids (mostly class 2), but also longer flatwater stretches. The waves get smaller, but the drops get very technical, especially at summer flows under 3000 cfs. Play-spots are not as plentiful as on the first 5 miles. About 6 miles below Colliding Rivers, the river makes a bend to the north, announcing Whistler's Park Falls, a class 3- drop with several relatively turbulent routes. Scouting is advised for open boats.

From here, the river makes a horseshoe bend around Whistler's Bend County Park and begins the final 10 miles. About 4 miles down is Dixon Falls, a class 3- drop around the right side of an island. It starts with a slightly technical approach with poor visibility. The drop itself is a turbulent chute with side curlers, but it's a straight shot with a pool finish, so a swim is not too serious. Scouting is advised for open boats. The left channel around the island is a possible alternative, but it is very rocky and technical.

Another 2 to 3 miles downstream is a class 2+ straightforward drop. A curler big enough to swamp an open boat is followed by a whirlpool which can help to flip a water-heavy boat. It can be skirted by those who don't enjoy swimming.

After another 2 to 3 miles, the river makes a big horseshoe bend to the south, with Umpqua Community College visible high on the right bank. When the water slows to a halt due to the Winchester Dam, start looking for a small boat ramp on river left, the take-out.

Difficulties: See description.

Shuttle: Put in just below The Narrows (class 4) at the end of the town of Idleyld Park. It's a scramble down the bank. Another put-in is at a little park named Lone Rock, about 1 mile east of Glide. Most drift boaters put in at Colliding Rivers. Just west of the OR 138 bridge, take the first dirt road to the north and put in over the bank.

Whistler's Bend Park is a convenient access point about 7 miles west of Glide. Take OR 138 and county road 223. Access is also available across the river from the park at Jackson Wayside on county road 200.

The take-out is reached by taking Page Road east out of Winchester along the south side of the river. There is a small boat ramp about 2 to 3 miles upstream.

Gauge: Contact the River Forecast Center in Portland for the flow at the Winchester gauge.

NORTH AND MAIN UMPQUA RIVER
Winchester to Umpqua Landing
Carl Landsness

Class	Flow	Gradient	Miles	Character	Season
2	1000	9 PD	16	valley	all year

Description: In this section the river makes another transition in character as it enters the main Umpqua River valley. The oak covered hills are replaced by bottomland terrain and vegetation not unlike the Willamette River basin. There are surprisingly few houses, considering the proximity of roads. The frequency of rapids decreases, but those that exist have nice standing waves.

The first 7 miles from Winchester to the confluence of the South Umpqua River is Roseburg's "beer and float" run. A warm summer day will find many Roseburg area people leisurely rafting or tubing down to River Forks Park. The first 6 miles to the Garden Valley Road bridge is intermittent class 1 and 2-. The mile following the bridge is locally known as "Sunburn Alley" to commemorate those who fall asleep without their suntan lotion on this notoriously slow and flat stretch.

Afternoon naps are abruptly ended by Burkhardt Rapids, a class 2+ ledge drop which can be a nice jet ferry at higher water levels. Another class 2+ drop with moderate waves quickly follows. A little more whitewater brings you to the confluence of the North Umpqua and the main Umpqua River with a nice beach on the right at River Forks Park.

The first several miles on the main Umpqua River are fairly slow. Some class 2 whitewater appears at a gravel bar and bend to the left about 4 miles below the River Forks. The next couple of miles go through a beautiful canyon with the river constricting dramatically to form two successive class 2+ drops with straightforward standing waves which might swamp an open boat. The last few miles to Umpqua Landing are very flat. The take-out is at a well developed boat ramp under the bridge on the right.

Difficulties: None in particular.

Shuttle: Put in at Armacher Park on the south side of the US 99 bridge in Winchester. The take-out is 8 miles west of Sutherlin near Umpqua, at a county boat ramp under the highway bridge. An alternate access is at River Forks Road Park, about 5 miles northwest of Roseburg off Garden Valley Road on the east side of the river.

Gauge: Contact the River Forecast Center in Portland for the flow at the Winchester gauge.

UMPQUA RIVER
From Confluence of North and South Forks
to Scottsburg (Tidewater)
Dan Valens

Class	Flow	Gradient	Miles	Character	Season
1(2)	1000 and up	4 PD	84	forested farming, roads	all year

Description: From the confluence of the North and South Umpqua near Roseburg, the main Umpqua winds leisurely through the coast range to the Pacific Ocean near Reedsport. Numerous small farms and houses dot its banks, but many stretches show little development, and the development that one does see is fairly unobtrusive. Roads follow most of the river, but significant traffic is noticeable only on stretches below Elkton and along one short stretch near Kellogg. The predominant scenery is the forested hills of the coast range, enjoyable even with its fair share of logging.

The Umpqua's riverbed is quite wide, capable of holding typical winter storm flows in excess of 50,000 cfs and the occasional 100,000 + flood. Yet typical summer flows are in the 1000-3000 cfs range. As one can guess from the low gradient, the Umpqua contains long stretches of slow or flat water interspersed with riffles and small rapids. As the river drops, it becomes restricted in places to narrow channels in the bedrock. Some of these develop into short class 2 to 2+ rapids, depending on the river level.

The Umpqua is runnable year-round by experienced boaters able to deal with the hazards of high volume rivers. Relative newcomers should wait for summer with its lower flows and warm water. This combination provides a good setting for easy-going canoeists.

Note the Bicycle Shuttler's Delight: A trip from Kellogg Bridge to Smith Bridge is about 14 river miles, mostly roadless. But the shuttle is just over two miles, half of which is downhill. Warning: the last rapids above Smith Bridge may be tricky.

Difficulties: Although the rapids are few, they vary with water level and can still be tricky. Be prepared to scout. Inexperienced boaters can still get in trouble if they do not stay alert.

Shuttle: There are many access points along the river: one can pick one's own trip.

Watermarks: Some landmarks are listed below.

Mile

112	Confluence of North and South Forks: Head west on Garden Valley Blvd. from exit 125 on I-5. Follow county route 6 to River Forks Park.
103	Bridge on county route 6 near town of Umpqua. Follow county route 6 from River Forks Park. Or, from exit 136 on I-5 (Sutherlin and Oregon 138), head west to Umpqua on county road 9.
80	Bullock Bridge (county road 57) across the Umpqua. Follow county road 33 along the Umpqua from the town of Umpqua. Or follow Oregon 138 out of Sutherlin until it reaches the river (around milepost 13). Or follow Oregon 138 south from Elkton. One can cross the bridge and go upriver a couple of miles to a boat ramp, or follow Oregon 138 north about a mile to the Yellow Creek Boat Ramp.
71	Kellogg Bridge on Oregon 138, near milepost 6.
57	Smith Bridge on Oregon 138, near milepost 4.
49	Bridge on Mehl Creek Road, county route 67. From the junction of Oregon 38 and Oregon 138 in Elkton, head south about 0.3 mile and turn right to cross the river. There is a boat ramp at Buzzard Bay Park on river left 0.3 mile below the bridge.
27	Oregon 38 bridge at Scottsburg.

Gauge: The level of the Umpqua at Elkton can be obtained from the River Forecast Center in Portland. It is also listed daily in the Eugene Register-Guard. Typical summer flows are in the 3-4 ft range (1100-3000 cfs).

ROGUE RIVER
Above Nugget Falls to Gold Hill Boat Ramp
Garvin Hamilton

Class	Flow	Gradient	Miles	Character	Season
4-	800-3000	20 PD	2	forest houses	all year

Description: This section of the Rogue, which is gaining popularity outside of southern Oregon, provides just enough good play-spots and challenging rapids for an afternoon of boating. The put-in is in the middle of a short flat stretch from which it is possible to paddle upstream to a rapid with some small play waves for warm-up. The first riffle downstream of the put-in is at a broken weir, which has a hole in the right center. There is an excellent ender hole on the downstream edge of the broken weir, but use caution at lower flows since some boats have been folded here.

Nugget Falls immediately follows. This is a class 3+ or 4 drop which can be run down the middle of the left channel. It's a good idea to scout the falls on the first time down. Pull off on the left bank under the trees and take the trail to the rock bar. This is an easy scout, and the trail can also be used to rerun. There is a big surfing wave below the drop.

ROGUE RIVER   *Clayhill Rapids*   *Rick Starr*

Nugget is followed by a fairly long flat stretch which ends at the dam above Powerhouse Rapids (class 4). There are two slots through the dam, both of which are right of center near the downstream bend in the dam. The best route
from here follows the base of the dam downstream, weaves through some grassy clumps, and follows the channel through the main class 4 drop that is nearest the island on the left. For those wishing to avoid the maneuvers described above, there is a route on the far right side of the river where the dam joins the bank. This slot leads to a class 2 + route around the main drop.

Difficulties: Nugget and Powerhouse. Powerhouse can't be scouted from the river, so must be scouted from Upper River Road on the east side of the river. Upper River Road turns off of Oregon 234 east out of Gold Hill just after the road crosses the river. Go upriver about one mile to a pullout on the left. The last drop can be seen from here but the entrance is hidden by some trees. It may be a good idea to run Powerhouse with someone who has been through before since the entrance is tricky.

Shuttle: Take Oregon 234 out of Gold Hill toward Sam's Valley and Crater Lake. It's less than a mile to the take-out, a boat landing on the right. A little more than a mile farther (in a long straight stretch), a gravel road turns off the main road and goes back to the river and the put-in. To make a longer trip, a class 2 + section can be added by driving a few miles farther up Upper River Road where there are a number of spots to put in along the road.

Gauge: Contact the Grants Pass Filtration Plant or the Grants Pass Daily Courier.

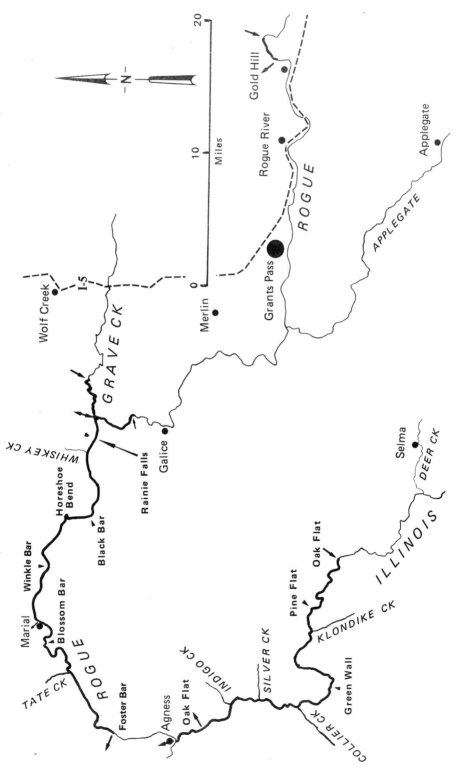

GRAVE CREEK
Six Miles to Confluence with Rogue River
Karen Wilt

Class	Flow	Gradient	Miles	Character	Season
3	500-1000	42 PD	4-6	forest	rainy

Description: This is a small technical stream with the best drops in the section not visible from the road. These are short twisting blind drops. There are very few play-spots; just nice scenery. The run can continue down to the confluence with the Rogue River, and even include Grave Creek Rapids.

Difficulties: A few possible hazards are some swinging footbridges and brush along the bank.

Shuttle: The take-out is at the boat ramp beneath the Grave Creek Bridge across the Rogue River (see shuttle description for the Rogue River). To reach the put-in take the road towards Wolf Creek from the northeast end of the bridge. Follow this for 4-6 miles to the point where it returns to Grave Creek after winding up the hill.

Gauge: There is no gauge on Grave Creek. Flow is flashy and depends on rainfall. The author made the run when the Rogue was running 4000 cfs at the Marial gauge; however, it is unlikely that there is a dependable correlation between the Rogue and Grave Creek.

ROGUE RIVER
Grave Creek to Foster Bar
Bo Shelby

Class	Flow	Gradient	Miles	Character	Season
3 +	2000-6000	13 PD	35	protected popular	all year

Description: The Rogue is one of the best known whitewater runs in the Northwest. It originates in the Cascades near Crater Lake and flows about 180 miles to the Pacific Ocean at Gold Beach. In 1968, 84 miles became part of the Wild and Scenic River System. About 40 miles of the river, flowing through the Siskiyou Mountains northwest of Grants Pass, is classified "Wild," with the river preserved essentially in its natural condition. The banks vary from steep forested slopes to vertical rock walls. The river provides class 3 rapids connected by slower stretches and deep pools.

Recreational use of the wild section has a long and diverse tradition. Private lodges and cabins are located in several places, and many of these are reached only by boat or trail. Jet-boats from Gold Beach originally delivered the US Mail, but later took passengers on popular excursions; these boats will be seen cruising at water-skiing speed along the lower 12 miles of the wild section. Driftboaters have long floated the river for the fine steelhead fishing. Zane Grey's writings were inspired by the solitude and wild setting of his cabin at Winkle Bar.

The scenery, rapids, easy access, and possibility of 2-5 day float trips make this a very popular run. Permits are required from Memorial Day to Labor Day, although not for the flatwater stretches above and below the wild section. At the time of this writing, a drawing for permits is held in mid-February, with leftover or unclaimed launching dates sometimes available on a first-come-first-served basis. Permit information may be obtained from the River Permits and Information, 14335 Galice Road, Merlin, Oregon 97532. Phone (503) 479-3735.

The wild section is a forgiving and enjoyable stretch of water. Dam-controlled flows normally are above 2000 cfs, and the river is runnable throughout the year. Warm summer weather, warm water, rapids ending in pools, and sandy beaches for camping make this a great place for a laid-back trip. One should expect to see lots of other people during the summer season, although the author's first trip was a cold and snowy one in February, when he saw no one else.

The river is described in considerable detail in several published river guides. The Rogue River Map, available from the Forest Service, contains a handy blow-by-blow description, which to this writer seems unnecessarily replete with dire warnings. Follow it for the first few rapids and make up your own mind. Even more detailed accounts are given in the books (Appendix D) by Arighi et al. (1974), Quinn et al. (1978), and Schwind (1974). The account given here will just hit the highlights.

Rainie Falls, 2 miles below the Grave Creek put-in, is the first of the two major rapids on the Rogue. In the next 20 miles tributary streams such as Russian, Howard, Big Windy, and Kelsey Creeks provide pools for swimming, nice camps, and places to scramble up the stream beds. There are numerous play-spots for kayaks, including an ender hole at Black Bar Rapids. Take care not to hurry.

At Marial the river takes a sharp bend to the southwest and enters Mule Creek Canyon. The narrow canyon, with vertical walls, is one of the few continuous stretches of whitewater (about 0.5 mile). Blossom Bar, about 1 mile below Mule Creek Canyon, is the Rogue's second major rapids. Tate Creek, about 7 miles below Blossom Bar, is a stop that should not be missed. About 0.2 mile up the creek is a pool with an exciting rock slide. Hiking above the slide is very beautiful.

Try not to be annoyed by the jet-boats on the lower part of the river. This section also has lots of wildlife; it is common to see great blue heron, salmon, deer, otter, and bear.

Difficulties: Rainie Falls: a short portage trail is located on the left bank, and offers the best place to get a close-up view of the falls which are always fun to look at. The falls have occasionally been run, but seldom right-side-up. Most people run the small fishladder channel on the far right bank, while the more adventurous run the steeper channel through the middle of the rock "island" between the fish ladder and the falls. Any run other than the fish ladder should be scouted.

In Mule Creek Canyon, the major obstacles are turbulence caused by constriction rather than large waves or holes. Everything seems to wash out of here eventually, but several places have been known to hold boats, spin them around, or push them into the walls. Swimmers are difficult to pick up until they get out of the narrow part of the canyon, but even they should remember to appreciate the scenery here.

At Blossom Bar, stop on the right and clamber up the rocks to scout. The run starts on the left side in a channel that ends in a bunch of boulders, so the next move is to the right into a center channel. At low water this ends in boulders, so scout carefully and move fast. Dodge a few more rocks and that's it!

Shuttle: The put-in at Grave Creek is reached by taking the Merlin Exit off I-5 and proceeding west towards Galice. The road follows the river on the north side and then crosses to the south. Stay along the river until the road crosses again to the north; this is the Grave Creek launch site. An optional put-in is about 4 miles upstream at Almeda Bar.

The shuttle to the take-out goes back along this same road just past the town of Galice, then over the mountains and west to Agness on USFS 3400 or 3406. These roads may be closed by snow early in the season, so check with the Forest Service or inquire locally. If the roads are impassable, one must drive to Grants Pass, take US 199 to Crescent City, then US 101 to Gold Beach. After rejoining the Rogue, proceed upstream, cross to the north side of the river, and take the first right turn to Foster Bar landing. Shuttle services can usually be arranged at the Galice Store. **Gauge:** Contact the River Forecast Center in Portland for the Agness reading. The Galice Ranger District gives the Grants Pass reading.

ILLINOIS RIVER
Oak Flat to Agness
Ron Mattson

Class	Flow	Gradient	Miles	Character	Season
4 +	500-3500	24 PD	34	forest	rainy

Description: The Illinois, a crystal clear tributary to the Rogue River, is one of the premier whitewater runs on the West Coast. In 1984 it received protection under the National Wild and Scenic Rivers Act. Flowing out of the Siskiyou Mountains south of Cave Junction, the Illinois runs in a northwesterly direction through the north end of the Kalmiopsis Wilderness Area. The canyons and mountains here are as steep and rugged as any found in Oregon.

Once a trip on this river is undertaken, boaters are on their own. The trail is miles away from the river in places, and very difficult to reach except at Pine Flat, approximately 7 miles from the put-in, and below Collier Creek. The whitewater is tough and demanding, even for the best of boaters.

The Illinois River flows through the northern boundary of the Klamath Mountains, an area that was formed about 200 million years ago. The area is largely devoid of topsoil. Kalmiopsis, a plant in the Heather family, grows here. The Illinois drainage basin is fragile. Natural landslides and erosion are evident along the river. Look at the landscape and enjoy it, but treat it kindly.

The Illinois is truly a wilderness river that tests both the skill and strength of the boater. Help is hard to get. One group spent a miserable evening clinging to the cliffs at Green Wall before being rescued by helicopter. They neglected to check the weather forecast, and a heavy rain transformed an 1800-cfs trip into an 8000-cfs nightmare.

The river is very technical at levels below 800 cfs and very scary at the higher levels. Flows of 1000 to 1500 seem to be the easiest, when most of the technical drops are flushed over enough to make them easier to run. High levels turn the river into boiling holes and rapids.

The first 10 to 12 miles of the run are typified by long, calm pools with very steep boulder-bar drops of up to 10 ft, or long rock gardens that require skillful boat handling. River mile 7 brings the boater to an area called Pine Flat where the canyon opens into large meadows on both sides of the river.

About midway through Pine Flat the river swings to the left, offering what appears to be two channels around a large rock in the middle of the river. On the left side is a gravel bar that can be run only at high water. On the right side is a chute with a raft-stopping hole at the bottom. Scout this one carefully from the right. The hole is tougher than it looks. Rafts and kayaks have been flipped end-for-end in it. There is a sneak route on either side of the hole.

Pine Flat makes an excellent campsite for a first night of a 3-4 day trip. The best camping is on the left, up an easy 40-ft bank. Do not build fires indiscriminately or leave trash. Sand bars and gravel at the edge of the embankment are the best cooking spots. Backpackers are seen frequently on the opposite bank, as this is one of the few places where they have easy access to the river.

From Pine Flat down to South Bend the river continues in pool-drop fashion through beautiful deep green pools and many nice class 2 + to 3 drops. Along this stretch are two more campsites, Klondike Creek and Deadman's Bar. Klondike Creek, named for the mining done along its banks, enters from the left about 2 miles below the last meadow of Pine Flat. The river makes a sharp right turn just past Klondike Creek. Stay far left to catch the eddy below the creek.

Deadman's Bar is a large area about 2 miles farther downstream on the right. It is difficult to spot from the river because it is up a 75-ft rock bank. Several groups can share the grassy area without intruding on each other. Beware of poison oak when scrambling up the rocks, especially in the spring when it's not in leaf.

South Bend should be called Last Chance, because it is the last chance to camp before Prelude and Green Wall, two of the toughest rapids on the river. If it's late in the day, don't miss it unless you're satisfied with cliff and boulder camping. South Bend Bar is located on the inside of a tight right turn in the river. Look for a large creek cascading down the left bank, a fern covered cliff, and an emerald green pool. Don't always count on finding a campsite here because high water can cover the bar or wash most of it away.

The next 4 miles are the toughest of the trip. Immediately below South Bend is a good class 3 + drop, followed in a 0.5 mile by Prelude, the rapid which leads to Green Wall. Prelude doesn't look like much on the approach through a sweeping rock garden, but it leads to a solid 3 + drop which can't be seen from above. An eddy on the left, next to a cliff at the bottom of the rock garden, provides a good spot to scout the remaining portion of Prelude. There are two alternatives, the falls on the left, or the tricky maneuvering on the right.

Immediately after Prelude is Green Wall. Stay to the left and pull in above the innocent-looking rock garden that leads into the main drop. A portage here is a tough 400 yards through a maze of truck-size boulders and a tangle of poison oak. Scout the upper lead-in as carefully as the lower section, because proper entry to the main rapids is the key. The lead-in is quite technical at low water and has a large hole at the bottom. Below the lead-in is a short section of relatively calm water that leads to the first drop of 7 to 8 ft. Take the middle or left channel; the right side is a keeper for all but the largest of rafts. From here down you can breathe more easily and try to stay off the right wall. The higher the water, the more important it is to run the middle section as far left as possible. As the water rises, the hole on the right begins to creep to the left. Stay away from this hole at all cost.

From Green Wall to Collier Creek the river has a half dozen class 4 to 4 + drops that are quite technical and will challenge the best of boaters. It is wise to stop and scout them since it's still a long swim to the take-out. The canyon is steep and rocky through this 3-mile section, and there are no campsites. Unless you are willing to spend a very uncomfortable night, allow at least 4-5 hours to run from Green Wall to Collier Creek.

The end of the major rapids is signaled by Collier Creek on the left. About 100-200 yards below Collier Creek campsites can be found up the bank. Camping is also possible downstream on the right if the water isn't too high. Other campsites are located 2-3 miles downstream and less than an hour from the take-out. Most notable is a site high above the river on the right at Silver Creek. Land on the downstream side of the creek, climb 30 ft to the trail and follow it upstream, across the bridge, and up to the top of the bluff.

ILLINOIS RIVER

Rick Starr

From here to the take-out, the river flows placidly through country that is a feast for your eyes. Sit back and enjoy it. You're one of the lucky ones who have run the Illinois.

Difficulties: Pine Flat, Green Wall, and the 2-mile section below Green Wall are the most difficult rapids on this stretch.

Shuttle: To reach the put-in at Oak Flat, drive west on US 199 from Grants Pass to Selma. A turn to the west in the middle of town will put you on USFS 3504. Drive 17 miles to Oak Flat, which is only a short distance from the junction of the road with the river at a broad gravel bar. To reach the take-out, return to US 199 and continue to the coast, then north on US 101 to Gold Beach. Drive up the road on the south bank of the Rogue River approximately 34 miles to a bridge over the Illinois. Take the first road on the right and continue 4 miles to a broad grassy area that is also called Oak Flat, the take-out. This area may be muddy during wet weather.

An alternate take-out is located 4 miles downstream from Oak Flat, past the confluence of the Illinois with the Rogue, at a public boat landing on the right just downstream from Agness. Shuttle service can usually be hired in the town of Galice.

Gauge: The River Forecast Center in Portland can give combined flow at Kerby of the East and the West Forks of the Illinois.

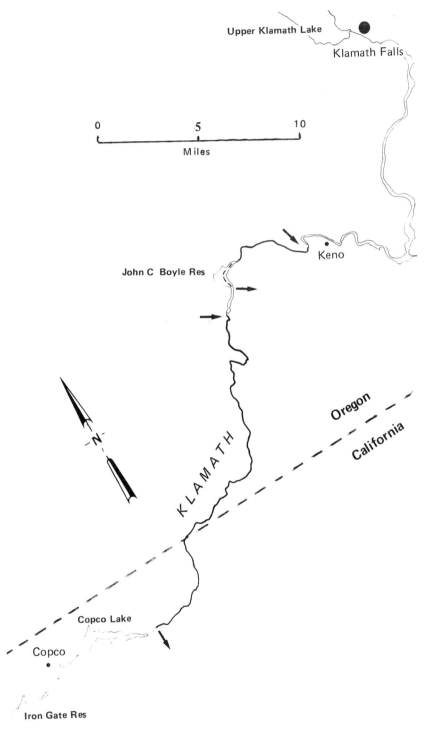

Upper Klamath Lake

Klamath Falls

0   .5   10
Miles

Keno

John C Boyle Res

Oregon

California

K L A M A T H

N

Copco Lake

Copco

Iron Gate Res

KLAMATH RIVER
Keno to John C. Boyle Reservoir
Karen Wilt

Class	Flow	Gradient	Miles	Character	Season
3 +	2000	50 PD	6-7	forest agriculture	rainy

Description: This seldom-run section of the Klamath is difficult to scout from the banks. The river leaves the road at the put-in and is hardly accessible until the take-out. A few logging roads go to the edge of the river's south side, and a dirt road from Keno is used by fishermen on the north bank. None of these roads is easy to find.

The river flows below the dam for about 2 miles of short, busy rapids. Then an easier section culminates in a rapids with a sharp drop at the bottom. The next notable rapids has waves that pile up on a wall at the bottom and could become more of a face-wash in higher water. Next is a section of rocky, pebbly, wide river. The water gathers together again for one last rapids, a good play-spot, before the lake. This last drop may require scouting, depending on the water level and the skills of the party.

The best points of this run are the large number of rapids in a few miles, relatively few flat spots, and accessibility to Ashland and Klamath Falls paddlers. Most of the rapids are wide open and can be run by eddy-hopping behind boulders. Unfortunately, the water is very dirty from pasture run-off. This is not the river for making many practice rolls.

Difficulties: The last rapids before the reservoir may require scouting.

Shuttle: To put in below the dam at Keno, drive through Keno on Oregon 66, cross the river, make an angled left turn before an overpass, and take the very next left to parallel the logging right-of-way. Continue to a stop sign where a road crosses the right-of-way, bear left (instead of crossing the right-of-way), and drive to a point below the dam where it is convenient to put in. Some of the best play-spots are in the rapids immediately below the dam. The take-out is on John C. Boyle Reservoir, where Oregon 66 crosses the Klamath at a roadside rest area.

Gauge: Gauge information is unknown.

KLAMATH RIVER
John C. Boyle Power Plant to Copco Lake
Lance Stein and Dan Valens

Class	Flow	Gradient	Miles	Character	Season
4	1500	51 PD	15	no roads	all year

Description: This dam-release run provides paddlers with some of the most exciting brownwater in the Northwest. Brownwater? The Klamath drains the warm, shallow Upper Klamath Lake, which supports an abundant growth of algae during the summer. The results are beautiful brownwater rapids and suds-filled slackwater. Don't let that deter you from wetting your blades in this challenging river. After all, that nasty looking stuff is organic. The releases provide some of the best class 4 summertime paddling in Oregon.

The run starts just below the John C. Boyle Power Plant, where the release from the turbines augments the minimum flow of 300 cfs. One unit (1200 cfs) provides this pool-drop river with plenty of action for the expert paddler and the intermediate with a bombproof roll. An occasional release of two units adds to the excitement.

The action begins immediately with 1.5 miles of class 2 to class 3 warm-up rapids. The brown water adds another aspect to reading the river, as waves and holes that look safe conceal rocks just below the surface. After the warm-up stretch, the river flattens out for the next 4 miles, presenting an opportunity to enjoy the abundant wildlife: bald eagles, red tailed hawks, cormorants and herons.

The river gets more exciting in the next 3 to 4 miles, as the gradient increases to over 100 feet per mile. Most rapids drop out of sight; the only way to look them over is to scout from the bank. Eddy-hopping is often difficult and is not recommended for first-time runners. Do not count on memorizing a route. With a hundred and fifty yards of class 4 water between you and the pool below, the river can create unplanned detours. Names of rapids like the Caldron, Satan's Gate, and Hell's Corner let the imagination run wild as to what lies around the next bend.

The length of the trip depends upon which of the six designated access points is chosen for the take-out. Access 6, the farthest upriver, provides a 10.5-mile trip. Access 1 adds about 4.5 miles of class 2 water. The take-outs are provided by the power company and farmers along the river. Respect their property rights and use only the designated access points.

There are no camping areas at the take-out or around Copco Lake. Topsy Campground is just off Oregon 66, between Keno and the powerplant turn-off. There is no potable water at Topsy or along the river.

Difficulties: The approach of the real excitement, which begins around mile 5, is identified by a long pool and a large camping area on the right. For those who have had enough, a jeep road leads back to the put-in. Just past this point, the river narrows and enters the Caldron, the first of a dozen major rapids.

The length of the rapids, proliferation of holes and rocks, and the brown water all add to the difficulty of paddling through these exciting high gradient drops. The water is moving fast enough to flush boats out of most holes, but the rocks are still hard.

Several rapids below the Caldron lies Satan's Gate, a steep drop that disappears around a corner to the right. A very short pool separates it from Hell's Corner. Less pushy than the Cauldron, Hell's Corner is considerably longer, and advanced knowledge of what lies ahead is helpful. Scout from the left.

Shuttle: The road to the put-in heads south from Oregon 66, between mileposts 42 and 43. It is marked with a sign to John C. Boyle Power Plant. Follow the road about 5 miles to the power plant; continue another 0.5 miles to a steep switchback road that leads to the river's edge and the put-in. There are two shuttle routes to the take-out; both require returning to Oregon 66.

The shorter route takes an hour and a half, but should be considered only in good weather. Drive west on Oregon 66; between mileposts 25 and 24, look for a row of mail boxes, a dirt road and a defunct sign post, all on the left. Turn left onto this road. At mile 2.5 take the right fork. Just beyond a group of houses and a farm at mile 8.5, take a right fork again. A mile and a half of very steep class 4 road starts near mile 10.7. At the junction with a better road near the bottom of the hill, take a left. From this point take every major left fork until you reach the bridge across the head of the lake at mile 18.5. Cross the bridge and take another left. Access 1 is 0.5 mile upriver from the bridge; access 6 is another 4.5 miles. Total mileage from the put-in to access 6 is 47.5 miles. The access points are clearly marked from the road and river.

The other shuttle is recommended in winter. Drive west on Oregon 66 to I-5, then south on I-5 to Hornbrook. From Hornbrook, drive east 16 miles, following signs to Copco Lake. This is the south side of the lake; do not cross the bridge at the head of the lake. Proceed 0.5 mile to access 1. **Gauge:** Call Pacific Power and Light (800) 452-9912 for a recording of expected releases from the Boyle Power Plant . Releases occur fairly regularly, but the system is usually closed for cleaning for a short period every summer.

ILLINOIS RIVER   *The Green Wall*   *T.R. Torgerson*

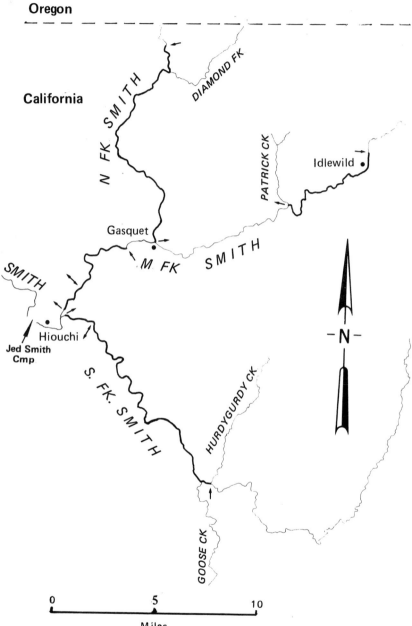

Oregon

California

DIAMOND FK

N FK SMITH

PATRICK CK

Idlewild •

Gasquet •

M FK   SMITH

SMITH

Jed Smith
Cmp

Hiouchi •

S. FK. SMITH

HURDYGURDY CK

—N—

GOOSE CK

0   5   10

Miles

SMITH RIVER (CALIFORNIA)
Introduction by Bo and Kathy Shelby

This edition of the Soggy Sneakers Guide to Oregon Rivers includes several border rivers just outside of Oregon. The North, Middle, and South Forks of the Smith River in Northern California are in this group. If there were ever a movement to appropriate the best whitewater rivers just out- side Oregon, these gems should be first on the list. In addition to terrific whitewater rivers and spectacular scenery, this area offers the coast and beautiful redwood forests. At Jedediah Smith State Park you can camp right on the river among 15-ft diameter trees. Like the Rogue and Illinois Rivers, the Smith is a substantial drive from the population centers in the Willamette Valley. The solution is to plan a trip for a full two or three days.

With torrential coastal rains and the porous serpentine soil, river levels on the Smith can go up and down like a yo-yo. Although the gorges on the Middle and South Forks are runnable with as little as 1000 cfs on the gauge at Jed Smith State Park, it is not uncommon for a good winter storm to bring the water up to 40,000 cfs overnight. When it stops raining, the river often drops to 20,000 on the first day and 10-12,000 on the second, giving it a "half life" of a day. Water levels dramatically affect both the character and difficulty of all the runs on the Smith. High water means big hydraulics and extreme turbulence, even in some innocent-looking places. Good paddlers have taken bad swims here; be careful!

The gauge for the Smith River system is located at Jedediah Smith State Park. This reading gives the flow for all three forks combined. In- dividual flows can be estimated by multiplying the Jed Smith gauge read- ing by the following percentages: North Fork = 33%; Middle Fork (above North Fork confluence) = 17%; Middle Fork (below North Fork but above South Fork confluence) = 55%; South Fork = 45%. Flow information can be obtained from the California Department of Water Resources in Eureka; phone (707) 443-9305 for a recording with levels for all of the Northern Coastal streams.

NORTH FORK SMITH RIVER
Thirteen Miles above Gasquet to Gasquet
Bo and Kathy Shelby

Class	Flow	Gradient	Miles	Character	Season
3	800-	45 PD	13	wilderness	rainy
5	12000			clear water	snowmelt

Description: This is a run of rare isolation and beauty. Even at high levels the water is crystal clear, like a river of bubbling champagne. Although the authors have run this stretch in as little as 1.5 hours at high water, it is best to start early and plan a long day. Hiking out after dark would really take all the fun out!

There are many distinct drops as well as a couple of small gorges on this run, but the entire trip is less severe than the Middle and South Fork Gorges, ranking between them and the stretches above them in terms of difficulty. Big (but generally friendly) hydraulics develop at high water.

Difficulties: This is a long run with a long shuttle, so give yourself plenty of time. The isolation makes walking out or getting help difficult, so plan to be self-sufficient.

Shuttle: The take-out is in Gasquet at the confluence of the North Fork with the Middle Fork. To drive there, take Gasquet Flat Road from the east end of town and drive about 0.2 mile to the bridge over the Middle Fork. Just over the bridge walk left down a dirt road about 200 yards to the North Fork. From the river the confluence and large rock outcropping on river left will be obvious. An alternate take-out is the put-in for the Gasquet to Oregon Hole Gorge section.

To reach the put-in, take US 101 north to the town of Smith River. From there take Rowdy Creek Road east. At the first fork, bear left up the hill on County Road 308. After about 5 miles County Road 308 ends where it joins County Road 305; continue east on County Road 305. This shuttle route climbs several thousand feet and then winds back down, but don't lose heart; County Road 305 crosses the North Fork about 25 miles from US 101. Put in at this bridge.

The area around the bridge where County Road 305 crosses the North Fork is private land. Stay on public land by walking down the steep bank on river left just upstream of the bridge. The shuttle from Gasquet takes about 1.5 hours one way. The drive is long over a small, steep, but well maintained dirt road to a remote put-in.

Gauge: The flow is approximately 33% of the flow at the Jed Smith gauge; see the introduction for the Smith River.

MIDDLE FORK SMITH RIVER
Six Miles above Patrick Creek to Patrick Creek
Bo and Kathy Shelby

Class	Flow	Gradient	Miles	Character	Season
4 (5)	500-2000	65 PD	5-6	canyon forest	rainy snowmelt

Description: This little-run section has a spectacular but very tight gorge. The authors ran it when the Jed Smith gauge read about 8000 cfs, a good level. The most difficult parts of the gorge can be scouted by walking along US 199 for a mile or so above Patrick Creek. The remainder of the run is not visible from the road. Other drops need careful consideration from the river.

The following section, Patrick Creek to Gasquet (class 3-4), is described by Schwind (1974).

Difficulties: The gorge itself, most of which is visible from the road, is the major difficulty. Scout for trees and logs.

Shuttle: Take out where Patrick Creek enters the Smith. Put in approximately 5.7 miles upstream; just look around for a place to scramble down the bank.

Gauge: The flow is approximately 17% of the flow at the Jed Smith gauge; see the introduction for the Smith River.

MIDDLE FORK SMITH RIVER
Gasquet to Above Oregon Hole Gorge
Bo and Kathy Shelby

Class	Flow	Gradient	Miles	Character	Season
2+	1000-	20 PD	6	clear water	rainy
3+	22000				snowmelt

Description: This delightful section provides a good warm-up for the more demanding runs on the Smith. There are several good rapids and play-spots.
Difficulties: No particular difficulties.
Shuttle: At the downstream end of the town of Gasquet, put in at the first place where the river is right next to US 199. There is a laundromat, trailer park and a wide spot in the road. The obvious put-in is on private property, but no one seems to mind so far. The take-out is approximately 5 miles downstream. During the shuttle, look for a highway warning sign that says "Slippery When Wet", where a small dirt road angles down to the river (river is not visible from the road here). Walk down and scout the take-out; it isn't obvious from the river.
Gauge: The flow is approximately 55% of the flow at the Jed Smith gauge; see introduction for Smith River.

MIDDLE FORK SMITH RIVER
Oregon Hole Gorge
Bo and Kathy Shelby

Class	Flow	Gradient	Miles	Character	Season
4	500-	50 C	1.5	gorge	rainy
5	22000			clear water	snowmelt

Description: The only thing wrong with this gorge is that it is over too soon! The character of the run changes dramatically with the water level. At low water the drops are steep but distinct, requiring some tricky moves around big boulders. At high water the gorge becomes an awesome, turbulent flush in which eddies are hard to find. Oregon Hole Gorge is also known as Middle Fork Gorge.
Difficulties: Most of the Gorge is visible from US 199, but the road is several hundred vertical feet above the river, luring the unsuspecting paddler into an inappropriate complacency. Be sure to take the time and effort to scramble down to river level and scout carefully; the water is bigger and faster than it appears from above. The last major rapid in the gorge is just barely visible downstream; it can be scouted from river left.
Shuttle: Put in either at Gasquet or just above the gorge (both access points are described in the "Gasquet to Oregon Hole Gorge" section). Take out at the bridge where the South Fork Road crosses the river (paddle under the bridge and land on river right at a small gravel beach). A steep trail leads up to a parking area where the South Fork Road takes off from US 199.
Gauge: The flow is approximately 55% of the flow at the Jed Smith gauge; see the introduction for the Smith River.

SOUTH FORK SMITH RIVER
Upper Bridge to South Fork Gorge
Bo and Kathy Shelby

Class	Flow	Gradient	Miles	Character	Season
3(4)	1000-20000	35 PD	10	forest canyon	rainy snowmelt

Description: This section is less demanding, comparable to the Gasquet to Oregon Hole Gorge section on the Middle Fork. Most of the drops are gradual and straightforward, with the exception of the sharp drop visible from the road several miles up from the gorge (past the point where the road climbs away from the river and then returns).

Difficulties: The sharp drop mentioned above develops a nasty hole at some water levels; it can usually be avoided by running river left.

Shuttle: Take the South Fork Road off of US 199 about 1 mile northeast of Hiouchi Hamlet. Cross the Middle Fork and the South Fork, then turn left and go up the South Fork. The take-out is about 1 mile above the South Fork Bridge (2 miles from US 199). There is a large pull-out (75 yards long and 40 yards wide), with trails leading down to the river. The river is not visible from the road at this point. Scout the take-out if you don't want to run the gorge; it isn't obvious from the river. To reach the put-in proceed upstream, crossing the river twice on bridges high above the river. The put-in is at a small bridge about 10 miles up. The river is generally visible from the road. It is possible to shorten the run by putting in farther down.

Gauge: The flow is approximately 45% of the flow at the Jed Smith gauge; see the introduction for the Smith River.

SOUTH FORK SMITH RIVER
South Fork Gorge
Bo and Kathy Shelby

Class	Flow	Gradient	Miles	Character	Season
4	500-	60 PD	1.5	gorge	rainy
5	9000			clear water	snowmelt

Description: This gorge is a bit longer than the Oregon Hole Gorge, but it still isn't nearly long enough! Although the South Fork Road follows the river, the water is generally out of sight. With persistence and scrambling it is possible to scout most of this stretch from the road; we suggest you do this before committing yourself to the run. This is one of the most beautiful gorges anywhere, complete with all the classic gorge characteristics: steep blind drops, tough landings for scouting, and powerful turbulent water. This run is particularly difficult and potentially dangerous at high water levels.

Difficulties: The run has several distinct drops, which vary markedly with the water level. Be prepared to do your own scouting and make your own decisions.

Shuttle: Put in anywhere on the Upper Bridge to South Fork Gorge run, or at the take-out for that run. Take out at the South Fork Bridge by paddling under the bridge and landing at the small beach on river right. A trail goes sharply up the bank to the end of the bridge.

Gauge: The flow is approximately 45% of the flow at the Jed Smith gauge; see the introduction for the Smith River.

Chapter 5. Upper Willamette and McKenzie Drainages

ROW RIVER
Dorena Dam to Scaling Station Bridge
Larry Mooney

Class	Flow	Gradient	Miles	Character	Season
	300	35 PD	4	rural	dam controlled
2(3)	and up				

Description: This section includes four major drops (4 to 6 feet each) and several minor drops, all of which make this a quick, exciting run.

The first quarter of the run winds through some narrow channels where riverside brush can be a hazard. About 0.5 mile below the first bridge is a major drop. Watch for rocks in the middle of the river. Scouting this rapids is advisable since considerable maneuvering is required to negotiate this drop, which occurs over a distance of 50 to 75 feet. At high levels (greater than 700 cfs) a right channel can be used.

Within 100 yards of the first drop is a second major drop which should be scouted. This is usually run on the left, although at high water an exciting channel exists on the right.

Within the next mile is a third drop, again heralded by the presence of rocks in the middle of the river. This one is not of the same proportions as the first two but requires careful maneuvering. On the third drop, start on the right bank and guide through the slot on the left. Coming off the 3-ft drop at the bottom, do not be afraid to move the bow into the right-hand rocks.

The last major drop is another 0.8 mile downstream, right next to the road (to the delight of the passersby). Since this rapid was scouted on the way up, boaters should have no difficulty hitting the narrow slot.

The remainder of the trip is not so exciting, but is still fun because of the many ledges which are found traversing the width of the river and the sneaky rocks that inhabit the streambed.

Difficulties: The first two class 3 rapids, at the 0.5 mile mark, should be scouted. The third major drop, 1 mile farther, and the fourth major drop 0.8 mile after that should be scouted on the first trip down the river.

Shuttle: Travel south from Eugene on I-5 and take the first Cottage Grove exit. At the stop sign turn left towards Dorena Reservoir (past the Village Green Motel). A convenient take-out is at the first bridge just past the log scaling station. Continue on this road for 3 miles to a "Y" in the road. Take the right branch and travel an additional mile to the USFS Dorena Tree Improvement Center. Turn left and follow the road to the river. This is the upper section of Schmidt Park, a nice place to picnic before the river run. The gate to the park may be locked in the winter, which necessitates a 0.2 mile walk with boating gear.

Gauge: The flow of the Row can change by a factor of two within hours, so contacting Lookout Point Dam is recommended. The dam can provide the present flow as well as any changes which may occur that day. A flow of 300 cfs is probably the minimum flow that should be attempted. Summer flows can be as low as 100 cfs. Late fall, winter, or early spring are the most likely times to enjoy this run.

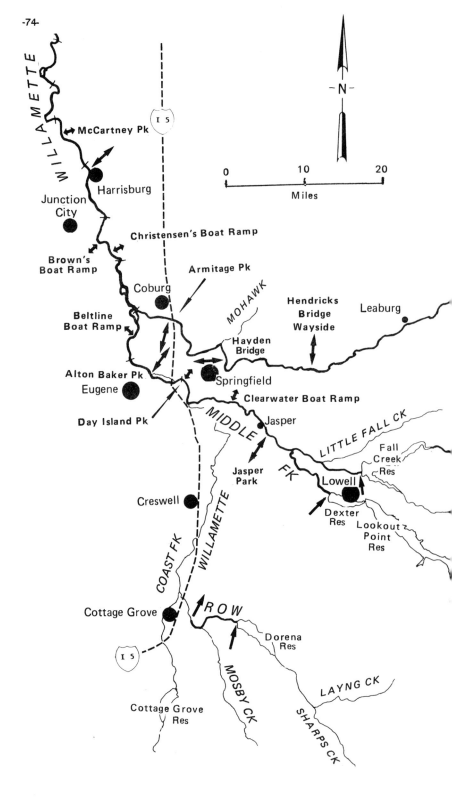

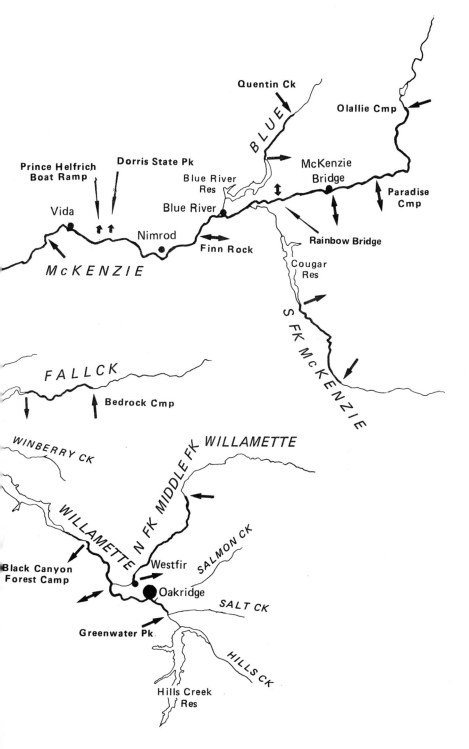

MIDDLE FORK OF THE WILLAMETTE RIVER
Oakridge to Lookout Point Reservoir
Rob Blickensderfer and Rich Brainerd

Class	Flow	Gradient	Miles	Character	Season
2 +	1000-3000	18 PD	10	forested hills	all year

Description: This is a beautiful run for a sunny day in October, in the period after Hills Creek Dam increases its discharge at the end of summer, and before the winter rains bring up the unregulated rivers along this stretch. The banks are lined with trees so that houses and roads do not often intrude into the river landscape. The current is fast, creating frequent class 1 and 2 rapids of all shapes and sizes. It is a challenging run for the novice, exciting for most open canoers, and nice and splashy for more experienced boaters. You will probably see a number of drift boaters and shore-bound fly fishermen; be courteous, giving them a wide berth where possible.

Immediately below the Greenwater Park put-in is a long class 2 + rapids, which has lots of waves and cross currents, but requires little technical maneuvering. At 3.5 miles the river crosses under Oregon 58. There is a small Forest Service park, Ferrin Park, on river right just below the bridge. At 4.8 miles there is a second bridge, on the road that leads to Westfir. There is a good eddy and road access on river left, just below the bridge. Immediately below this is Hell's Gate Rapids, a rocky and technical class 2 at low water and class 3 at high flows. The remaining 5 miles to the take-out are similar to the first half, except that the highway is more visible and audible. Depending on the water level in Lookout Point Reservoir, the last 0.2 mile of the trip may be flatwater.

Difficulties: For novice boaters, there is no warm-up before the long, splashy class 2 + rapids near the put-in. Hell's Gate Rapids, just below the second bridge, is the most technically difficult of this section. It is easily scouted from the bridge on the road to Westfir.

Shuttle: From the Willamette Valley, take Oregon 58 east from I-5, just south of Eugene, and proceed upstream about 28 miles to the take-out at Black Canyon Forest Service Campground, at the head of Lookout Point Reservoir. There is a boat ramp at the downstream end of the park. This boat ramp remains open later into the fall than the rest of the park.

To reach the put-in, continue east on Oregon 58 another 4 or 5 miles to Westfir Junction. Take a left, cross the bridge, turn right towards Oakridge, and rejoin Oregon 58 in 1.3 miles, at the east end of the Oregon 58 bridge over the Middle Fork. The put-in is at Greenwater Park, at the upstream edge of Oakridge.

There is an alternate put-in 2 miles farther upstream near the base of Hills Creek Dam; this put-in appears to be popular with the drift boaters. This section has not been run by the authors, but is reputed to be class 2 - 2 + .

Gauge: The flow in the dry season comes principally from Hills Creek Dam. In dry years there may not be enough water released in July and August for a good run. If Hell's Gate Rapids, which can be viewed from the bridge, looks runnable the whole run should have enough water. Contact Lookout Point Dam for more precise flow information.

N. FK. MID. FK. WILLAMETTE   *The Gorge*   *Kathy Shelby*

MIDDLE FORK OF THE WILLAMETTE RIVER
Dexter Dam to Jasper Park
Rob Blickensderfer

Class	Flow	Gradient	Miles	Character	Season
1+	2000	14 C	8	rural	all year

Description: The Willamette River makes its transition from the wild water of the upper reaches to the slower water found below Eugene on this and the next section described. The trip begins with fairly fast turbulent water from the run-out of Dexter Dam and continues at a brisk pace. The rapids are fairly small and straightforward, although at low water several exposed rock shelves require careful maneuvering.

About midway down is an area where trees have been deposited by high water and the river subdivides into several channels (as of 1978). The exact configurations of the channels and log jams can vary each year. This is also typical of the conditions of the lower McKenzie and lower Santiam Rivers were the faster water slows as it enters the valley floor. The Middle Fork is a little less steep on the second half of the trip. Take out on the left at Jasper Park, where picnic tables can be seen from the river, or 0.2 mile downstream at Jasper Bridge.

Difficulties: There is a potentially dangerous section about midway on the run where the river splits into several channels and where there are log jams. At some flows a portage may be required. The casual boater without solid class 2 experience should not attempt this section of the Willamette.

Shuttle: Dexter Reservoir is along Oregon 58 about 18 miles southeast of Eugene. It is easiest to drive first to the take-out at Jasper Park. The park is 0.2 mile upstream from the Jasper Bridge on the south side of the river. An alternate take-out is at the bridge. To get to the put-in follow the road along the north side of the river through Fall Creek to Lowell and thence to the base of Dexter Dam. The put-in is a bit of a scramble down riprap.

Gauge: Contact the River Forecast Center in Portland and ask for the reading at the Jasper Gauge. The flow is regulated so that the minimum is runnable.

NORTH FORK OF THE MIDDLE FORK OF THE WILLAMETTE RIVER
The Gorge to Westfir
Gene Ice

Class	Flow	Gradient	Miles	Character	Season
4(5)	2000	29 PD	9	forest	rainy

Description: The North Fork is one of the premier whitewater runs of the Willamette drainage. It offers exciting whitewater, superb scenery, and easy access. The North Fork flows into the Middle Fork of the Willamette just below Westfir, near Oakridge. Except for Ledges, all major rapids can be scouted on the drive to the put-in. The difficult Gorge section should be carefully scouted before boating.

The run below The Gorge is a good class 3 with three noteworthy rapids. These are Shotgun, Bull's-eye, and Ledges. Shotgun is a twisting left turn with a small 3-ft drop that can be seen from the road. Bull's-eye can be recognized by a large rock that blocks the main channel on the left. The boater can go either right or left of the rock, but some paddlers have been known to go right over the top, giving it the name Bull's-eye!

Ledges is difficult to scout from either the river or the road. It consists of a narrow channel on the far left that becomes apparent only at the top of the drop. Ledges can be recognized by a wall of rocks on the left just at the start of the drop. This rapids, which is located very near the end of the run, is often called Little Ledges by fiendish paddlers trying to worry anxious first-timers on the river. A section above the normal run can also be paddled, but is not recommended because it contains mostly flatwater and one very technical section of whitewater that is often blocked with logs.

Difficulties: The Gorge, a half-mile section of class 4, is located between the two bridges on the main road. At high water the hydraulics in this section are very powerful. The Gorge has three main obstacles: a drop on the right, a very large curling wave that crosses the entire river about halfway through the Gorge, and a tight class 5 boulder garden at the end. Kayakers normally run the boulder garden through slots barely wide enough for their boats, so rafters should scout this section very carefully. Shotgun, Bull's-eye, and Ledges are the class 3 rapids mentioned in the description.

Shuttle: To reach the river, take Oregon 58 east from I-5 just south of Eugene, and proceed to Westfir, about 32 miles to the southeast. At the covered bridge in Westfir, continue on through the log storage yard on the road that follows the south bank of the river. A paved road appears just past the park. A convenient take-out is at the weigh station located about 0.5 mile upstream of Westfir; from the river it is just around the corner from the Ledges.

The normal put-in for experts is just above the second bridge; this gives boaters a short warm-up for the Gorge. Those who do not wish to run the Gorge can put in at the bridge just below it.

Gauge: To our knowledge the flow of the North Fork cannot be readily obtained. However, past observation indicates that it is runnable whenever the South Santiam above Foster Reservoir is runnable. Contact Foster Dam for the Cascadia reading. Flows of 900 cfs and greater are runnable.

FALL CREEK
Bedrock Campground to Fall Creek Reservoir
Doug Tooley

Class	Flow	Gradient	Miles	Character	Season
3(4)	800-3000	42 PD	7.5	forest	rainy

Description: Upper Fall Creek is one of the most exciting and beautiful runs in the Eugene area. With the exception of two very difficult rapids the run can be made by intermediate paddlers. Within 0.5 mile of the put-in is the first class 3 drop. The river starts out with a river-wide ledge, then narrows considerably. The water in this slot is turbulent and will flip an unwary boater. This drop is usually run best on the left. Below this rapids, the river has a series of ledges and pools. Several class 2 and 3 rapids are interspersed in this green Eden. The beauty of the stream's banks contrasts with the water which is usually muddy at high flows.

Beyond the second bridge, begin preparing for Fish Ramp Rapids, which can be a very difficult and potentially dangerous rapids with a strong guard hole at the top. Scout this rapids during the shuttle. It can be reached by a short unmarked road leading down to a BLM boat ramp. This road is the only one leading to the river above the open rural lower section of the run; immediately above this turn-off for this road the main road follows the river for a short distance.

Between the last bridge and the take-out lurks another class 4 rapids with a 6-7 ft slide ending in a diagonal hole! Scout this drop before attempting to run it.

Difficulties: The worst drawbacks on this run are the unpredictable flow, cold water, and the difficult put-in and take-out. Scout Fish Ramp Rapids and the rapids between the last bridge and the take-out. Intermediate boaters may wish to portage around Fish Ramp Rapids. At flows above 2000 to 2500 cfs this river is strictly for experts.

Shuttle: The put-in for this run is at Bedrock Campground, 7.5 miles upstream from Fall Creek Reservoir on USFS 18. The trail just above the campground bridge leads to the river and sometimes looks more like a mudslide than a path. Be careful! A boater can take out either at Fish Ramp Rapids or at Fall Creek Reservoir

Gauge: Contact Lookout Point Dam for the flow.

FALL CREEK
Fall Creek Dam to Jasper Park
Doug Tooley

Class	Flow	Gradient	Miles	Character	Season
2(3)	1000	10 PD	10	rural	dam controlled

Description: With the exception of the Willamette River and the McKenzie River at Hayden Bridge, this run on Fall Creek is the closest whitewater to the Eugene-Springfield area. It contains some excellent play-spots and would be a good river for beginners to try their hand at surfing. As this section of Fall Creek is not prone to high peak flows, fallen trees remain in the river. There are usually a couple present anytime, so keep your eyes open.

The first 0.5 mile of the run is a nice series of short class 2 rapids; this is actually the most interesting portion of the entire run. Throughout this section many good play-spots are to be found, with good eddies on both sides of the river. The run ends with a class 3 rapids located just downstream from the Pengra covered bridge. The class 3 rapids can be scouted easily from the bridge. Decked boaters should have no problems with this rapids. Open canoeists run a risk of swamping in the 3-4 ft standing waves. Boaters who do not wish to run this drop can take out on river left, at the base of the bridge. One take-out for those who elect to run this rapids is just around the corner where Jasper Road bends near the river. It is also possible to paddle down to the confluence with the Middle Fork of the Willamette River and then continue to Jasper Park for a 4-mile longer trip.

Difficulties: Some boaters may opt to scout the class 3 rapids just below the Pengra covered bridge; see above.

Shuttle: The put-in is reached by driving out Jasper Road off US 126 to the Fall Creek Dam access road. The take-out is 4 miles below the Pengra covered bridge at Jasper Park on the Middle Fork of the Willamette River.

Gauge: Flow on Fall Creek is regulated. Call Lookout Point Reservoir for discharge information.

McKENZIE RIVER AND TRIBUTARIES
Introduction by Gene Ice

Of all the whitewater rivers in Oregon, few are more popular than the beautiful McKenzie. The river begins in the Cascades and flows in changing moods to the Willamette Valley. The upper McKenzie River Basin is historically and geologically fascinating. The basin was the site of frequent volcanic activity and the river has cut through numerous layers of tuff (consolidated volcanic ash) and basalt flows. A geologically recent basalt flow is responsible for the formation of Clear Lake, which is the origin of the McKenzie River.

H.T. Stearns (Geology and Water Resources of the McKenzie Valley, United States Geological Survey Water Supply Paper, 1929) describes how this lake must have formed. "Clear Lake occupies a part of the ancestral valley of the McKenzie River. This valley cannot be traced in the area north of the lake as that area is covered by lava flows. Observations indicate that the ancient McKenzie River carved out a wide and deep canyon with many tributaries on the slope of the Cascade Range, but the numerous lava flows have completely buried all traces of the former stream pattern. The lava is chiefly permeable basalt, and it is through the cavities and interstices in this lava that the groundwater flows. Hence many of the former streams continued to flow in practically the same channels, but far beneath the surface. As the part of the valley now occupied by Clear Lake was not filled with lava, it became the exit for the subterranean McKenzie River, and the lava dam at the outlet caused the formation of a lake instead of the usually relatively small spring pool.

"At the time the lava entered the valley a forest bordered McKenzie River at this place, for a submerged, but still upright forest is visible in the shallow northern part of the lake. The tree trunks, many of them two to three feet in diameter and 40 feet high, were particularly noticeable. They have remained erect because the water is not agitated by violent storms or strong currents."

Carbon 14 measurements of the submerged trees place the date of the lava flow at 3,000 years ago.

Over the lava flows which poured from the Belknap Crater, early pioneers blazed the McKenzie River Trail. McKenzie Pass provided a more direct route to the fertile Willamette Valley than other passes through the Cascades, but the rough terrain and high elevations must have taken a terrible toll. Remnants of this trail can be seen at the observatory on the old McKenzie Highway. These old ruts in the crumbly basalt make us appreciate even the worst of modern roads. The setting and terrain are so rough and desolate that American astronauts used this as a training area for subsequent lunar exploration.

The stark foreboding of the volcanic formations is in contrast to the dense forest stands which thrive in the soils. The French Pete Drainage, which leads into the South Fork of the McKenzie, is a favorite hiking area for Eugene-Springfield residents. This area was recently established as a Wilderness Area. The H.J. Andrews Experimental Forest is located near the town of Blue River. This area is used by the U.S. Forest Service to research the impacts of logging activities on water quality and to monitor undisturbed basins. Filbert orchards, Christmas tree plantations, and other farmlands crowd the lower McKenzie Valley between the forests of the upper McKenzie and the confluence with the Willamette River below the city of Springfield. Whether one's interests lie in hiking, boating the main river, or paddling one of the exciting tributaries, the McKenzie truly has something for everyone.

McKENZIE RIVER
Olallie Campground to Paradise Campground
Gene Ice

Class	Flow	Gradient	Miles	Character	Season
3	700 and up	60 C	9	forest	all year

Description: Within its tree-lined banks, the McKenzie rushes with almost nonstop rapids between Olallie and Paradise Campgrounds. This run is an excellent cruise, but has few play-spots. The first few miles are a fun, bouncy ride. At the first bridge, there is a wave on the left which can be surfed at some water levels.

A few miles downstream lies Fishladder Rapids, class 3, the most difficult rapids on this run. Below Fishladder, the river continues to offer miles of interesting rapids. Just across from Belknap Hot Springs is an interesting eddy, to which Belknap provides some welcome hot water which can warm cold hands during winter runs. Watch for the plumes of steam on the right.

Paradise Campground, with flush toilets, is a fitting name for the isolated boating stop. Take out on the left.

Difficulties: Fishladder Rapids should be scouted from the road by those unfamiliar with it. It starts at a left turn in the river located near milepost 16 and about 5 miles above Paradise Campground. Look for a series of power lines which cross the river, and a clearcut on the west bank. To scout, pull off onto a dirt road at milepost 16 and walk the 100 yards to the river. From the river the rapids is marked by the power lines crossing just above the rapids.

Shuttle: Drive east from Springfield on Oregon 126 to the take-out at Paradise Campground, located about 4 miles east of McKenzie Bridge. The put-in is at Olallie Campground, about 9 miles upstream on Oregon 126. Paradise is partially closed during the winter. Boaters should take a close look at the take-out before setting out. The highway bridge across the river at McKenzie Bridge and the covered Rainbow Bridge on McKenzie River Drive offer alternate take-outs for longer trips.

Gauge: The reading of the gauge at McKenzie Bridge can be obtained from the River Forecast Center in Portland, but the minimum flow is runnable.

McKENZIE RIVER
Paradise Campground to Finn Rock
Gene Ice

Class	Flow	Gradient	Miles	Character	Season
2 +	700 and up	31 C	15	wooded cabins	all year

Description: Below Paradise Campground the McKenzie loses some of its continuous nature and takes on a pool-drop character. A long boulder garden beginning at the town of McKenzie Bridge and ending above the covered Rainbow Bridge is one of the most significant rapids on this stretch. About a 0.2 mile below the Rainbow Bridge, where the river nears the main highway, is an S-curve which ends in a rocky stretch with a strong diagonal wave on the right.

Below this the river eases into a nice class 2 paddle for experienced open canoeists with a good backferry! Play-spots are few, but are high-lighted by an excellent ender hole just across from the Redsides log scaling station, about half-way down. Even C-2's can do incredible enders on the wave on the right. At most water levels the boats survive without serious damage. Local paddlers sometimes spend a whole day here seeking the perfect ender. Below Redsides the river becomes flatter and includes some shallow stretches.

Difficulties: The class 2 + stretch below McKenzie Bridge is the most difficult on this section.

Shuttle: Take Oregon 126 east from Springfield to the rest area at Finn Rock. Kayakers can take-out here, but rafters will find the gentle, gravelly bank opposite the rest area easier. Cross the river on the concrete bridge just downstream and turn left. Restrooms are available at the Finn Rock rest area.

The put-in is at Paradise Campground about 5 miles upstream from McKenzie Bridge. Alternate put-ins are at the bridge at McKenzie Bridge (watch for traffic) and at Rainbow Bridge, which is located off the main highway on McKenzie River Drive.

Gauge: Contact the River Forecast Center in Portland for the flow at McKenzie Bridge or Vida. The minimum flow is runnable.

McKENZIE RIVER
Finn Rock to Leaburg Dam
Gene Ice

Class	Flow	Gradient	Miles	Character	Season
2(3)	900 and up	21 C	15	wooded cabins	all year

Description: When people speak of "The McKenzie" they usually mean the run from Finn Rock to Prince Helfrich Boat Landing. This run might well be the most popular one-day trip in Oregon. It offers rapids negotiable by paddlers of many skill levels, good scenery, and outstanding play-spots. This "lower" run consists of long quiet stretches interspersed with exciting rapids and play-spots. Few rapids are powerful; however, cold water is a danger to the unprepared.

One of the best play-spots is at Clover Point, just above and within sight of the bridge at Nimrod. On the river it is marked by a large flat rock outcrop on the right bank following a series of cottages. In low water a hole on the right is excellent for pinwheels, while in high water the waves here are the largest on the run.

McKENZIE RIVER   *Brown's Hole*   *Cheryl Mattson*

About 0.8 mile downstream is Eagle Rock: a huge rock wall which rises abruptly from the left bank of the river. Just upstream from Eagle Rock is a fun rapids with outstanding eddies. This is an excellent spot to work on ferrying and on using eddies to climb up the side of a rapids. Approach this rapids on the left for the best ride. About 0.5 mile below Eagle Rock is a long rapids with numerous surfable waves. The best are on the left near the top of the rapids.

Of several well known holes on the river, the most famous is Brown's Hole, one of the highlights of the run. Located about 2 miles below Rennie Boat Landing, Brown's Hole is found about 50 yards upstream of a sharp right jog in the river at the end of a long straight section. A rock wall on the left bank about 30 yards upstream of the right jog marks the specific location of Brown's Hole, which lies hidden from upstream. Those looking for a thrill can try to punch through the hole, about 15 feet from the left wall. If this is not enough, boaters can try to meet the real challenge of going in and trying to paddle out. This is more easily accomplished on the left, but boats rarely emerge right side up.

About 3 miles downstream the river passes Ben and Kay Dorris State Park. Ahead is Marten Rapids, an excellent hunting ground for scuba divers stalking watches, glasses, wallets, and other items "contributed" by unwary drift boaters, kayakers, and rafters.

Most people take out 0.5 mile downstream at Prince Helfrich Boat Landing, but boaters may continue on to Leaburg Dam if they do not mind some flatwater.

Difficulties: Brown's Hole, mentioned in the description, can be nasty for unprepared boaters. It also can be totally avoided by going on the right.

Marten Rapids can be a fun ride, but many people end up swimming through it. To run Marten, look for a large boulder in the center of the river at the top of the rapids; there is a good channel about 10 feet to the right of the rock at most river levels. Beware of a large hole on the right towards the bottom of the rapids. This is a notorious ender spot, but should be approached only by competent paddlers. It can be much more violent than Brown's Hole, and contains some dangerous rocks.

Special attention should also be given to the water temperature, which even in the heat of the summer is quite cool. A long swim through Marten Rapids with little on but a swimsuit (quite a common occurrence) can be quite dangerous, especially without a life jacket.

Shuttle: Put in at the small rest area at Finn Rock on Oregon 126. Rafters may prefer to cross the bridge just downstream and use the dirt boat ramp on the left. Some boaters with limited time choose to put in just above Brown's Hole. The most common take-out is at Prince Helfrich Boat Landing, located at the end of Thomson Lane, on the south side of the highway about 1 mile below Ben and Kay Dorris State Park. From the river the take-out is marked by a suspension footbridge across the river.

For those who wish to continue and who do not object to some flatwater, take out at the boat landing at Leaburg Dam, just below Finn Creek on the right. The landing is off Oregon 126.

Gauge: The minimum flow is runnable. The Vida gauge is most appropriate if flow information is desired.

McKENZIE RIVER
Leaburg Dam to Hendricks Bridge Wayside
Gene Ice

Class	Flow	Gradient	Miles	Character	Season
2	900+	14 C	11	agriculture	all year

Description: This run is fairly quiet compared to the upper runs, but is very enjoyable for open canoes. The river meanders in deep pools around large islands and runs swiftly through sharp turns with tricky currents. The scenery here is more typical of Oregon's agricultural countryside than the dense forests found upstream.

Although some of the turns require careful attention, there are no major rapids until the very end. All of the channels around the islands appear to be open, but close inspection for the best route is required, especially at low water. About half-way through the trip the river runs under the only bridge, then past a golf course and some farm land.

Difficulties: The most significant rapid is about 0.5 mile above the take-out, identified by the high ridge on the left that slopes down to river level. The river drops to the right, forms some high waves, and then runs swiftly out through some large rocks. Some of the turns are tight with brush at low water and require controlled back-paddling by open canoeists.

Shuttle: Take Oregon 126 to Leaburg Dam, cross the dam, and use the drift boat slide just below the dam. The take-out is at Hendricks Bridge Wayside, at Mile 11.5 on Oregon 126.

Gauge: The flow is controlled by the Leaburg Dam; for further information contact the River Forecast Center in Portland.

McKENZIE RIVER
Hendricks Bridge Wayside to Hayden Bridge
Gene Ice

Class	Flow	Gradient	Miles	Character	Season
2	900 and up	11 C	9	agriculture paper mill	all year

Description: Although this run is practically at the doorstep of Springfield, it has much to offer and is an ideal run for beginning boaters and for boaters without much time. During the summertime the banks are lined with juicy blackberries and the cold water provides refreshing relief from the summer heat. Several surprisingly good rapids, including Hayden Bridge Rapids, are in store for paddlers.

The first few miles are quite calm and provide a good warm-up. In low water some rapids near the top can be scratchy, but things get better. About half-way down there is a tricky right turn, with strong eddies on both sides. This is a good place to practice ferrying.

Watch the trees and sky; on several trips eagles have been sighted. Don't look skyward too long, however. There is a rapids with large standing waves to contend with. This is a fine place for surfing, but the waves can be easily avoided on the left.

The best rapids is at the end of the run at Hayden Bridge. This is actually a whole series of rapids near the Weyerhaeuser Paper Mill, whose smoke stacks can be seen from the river. Eugene paddlers often come here to practice surfing. There are excellent eddies which allow a skillful paddler to work to the top of the rapids.

Difficulties: Hayden Bridge Rapids is difficult. The best channels are to the left. The rapids climax in a sharp left turn. Open canoes should run to the inside of the turn to avoid swamping, but should watch out for the eddy. Don't underestimate the water. Statistics say this is one of the most dangerous rapids in Oregon! Certainly the power of the water is not the problem; it is the coldness of the water. Wear a life jacket!

Shuttle: Take I-105 to Mohawk Road. Hayden Bridge is about 0.5 mile north on Mohawk Road. The take-out is a boat landing on the left bank next to a water intake station. To get to the put-in, return to I-105, travel east to the junction with Oregon 126 and drive to Hendricks Bridge Wayside, at which is a paved parking lot and boat ramp.

Gauge: Contact the River Forecast Center in Portland for the flow at Vida. The minimum flow is runnable due to dam control.

McKENZIE RIVER
Hayden Bridge to Armitage Park
Gene Ice

Class	Flow	Gradient	Miles	Character	Season
1	900 and up	7 C	8	agriculture houses	all year

Description: The Hayden Bridge to Armitage Park run is another excellent canoe paddle close to Eugene-Springfield. This paddle has very few rapids, but is a pleasant float. The most difficult rapids is just above Armitage Park, but can be avoided if desired. One of the most enjoyable parts of this float is gliding by the Coburg hills. After finishing the run, Armitage Park makes a fine spot for a picnic.

Those who want a longer run may continue about 2.5 miles to the confluence with the Willamette. See the section on the Willamette River for a description of this run.

Difficulties: None to speak of.

Shuttle: See the previous section for directions to the put-in at Hayden Bridge. The take-out at Armitage Park is located on Coburg Road. It may be reached from the north by taking Coburg exit from I-5, and turning south on Coburg Road in the middle of town. From the south, exit from I-5 onto Belt Line Road. Follow Belt Line west to the first exit, which is Coburg Road, and go north.

The shuttle may be run via I-105 or via the following back roads: cross Hayden Bridge and take an immediate left on Mohawk Road. After about 1 mile turn left on Hill Road and continue for about 0.5 mile. Turn left again on McKenzie View Drive, which intersects Coburg Road just across the river from Armitage Park.

Gauge: The minimum flow is runnable. For further information contact the River Forecast Center in Portland for the flow at Vida.

SOUTH FORK OF THE McKENZIE RIVER
Near French Pete to Cougar Reservoir
Gene Ice

Class	Flow	Gradient	Miles	Character	Season
3	1500	81 C	8.5	forest	rainy
4(5)	3500-4500				

Description: For most McKenzie boaters, the South Fork is just another tributary which enters the main river unnoticed somewhere between Rainbow and Blue River. Above Cougar Reservoir, however, lies the free-flowing South Fork of the McKenzie, one of the most interesting rivers of the Upper Willamette system. At flows above 2000 cfs the South Fork is a superb experts-only run. At flows below 2000 cfs the long rapids are no longer continuous, and the South Fork can be attempted by paddlers with dependable rolls.

The South Fork drainage is adjacent to the North Fork of the Willamette, but tends to have an unusually spiky flow pattern. It is usually runnable only during or shortly after a hard rain. The spring snowmelt is undependable, and is not as high as runoff during heavy rains. Furthermore, one of the best rapids is exposed only during the fall and early winter when Cougar Reservoir is lowered.

Some rapids can be scouted on the drive to the put-in, but the South Fork is so continuous that it is impractical to memorize routes. The first part of the run is fairly shallow and rocky. Soon, however, side creeks begin to add volume and the gradient begins to pick up. Watch for logs! Below the confluence of French Pete Creek lies a long major rapids with holes and large waves. After French Pete Rapids the river quiets down for about 1 mile, passing below the bridge at the top of the reservoir.

Below the bridge the river cuts deep into mud walls of the lowered lake. The second major rapids soon follows. This rapids has two 90-degree right turns which can be run to the inside. There are few eddies to catch for this 0.8 mile stretch. The rapids finally comes to an end in the lowered reservoir. The walk to the take-out is a bit muddy, but well worth the trouble. A welcome treat is a soak at the Cougar Reservoir Hot Springs on the way home.

Difficulties: The whole run. See Description.

Shuttle: To reach the put-in, take Oregon 126 east from Springfield past Blue River and take the Cougar Reservoir exit on the right. Proceed to the top of Cougar Dam. It is worthwhile to stop at the top of the dam to note the tremendous drop. We can only guess (with a shiver) at the rapids buried beneath the reservoir.

From the dam, drive along the west bank. Along the way are numerous creeks and waterfalls. Toward the end of the lake it is possible to spot a boat ramp on the other side of the reservoir; this is the take-out. Proceed to the bridge crossing the South Fork. The take-out is to the left; the put-in is to the right, towards French Pete. Put in about 8.5 miles upstream of the boat landing.

Gauge: Contact Cougar Dam and ask for the flow information on Cougar Reservoir.

BLUE RIVER
Quentin Creek to Blue River Reservoir
Ron Mattson

Class	Flow	Gradient	Miles	Character	Season
4(5)T	220	91 PD	3-5	forest	rainy
	900			logging	

Description: Blue River is a technically demanding, high gradient tributary of the McKenzie River and is located only 39 miles east of Eugene. Approximately 0.5 mile below the Quentin Creek put-in is a triple drop called Food for Thought. This drop has been run successfully, but may require a portage. The remainder of the river requires extensive scouting both from the road and the river.

Technical drops of 3 to 10 feet are numerous, as are extensive boulder gardens that require precise boat handling. Due to logging activity in the area, boaters should be wary of log debris and sweepers. From Tidbits Creek, located 1 mile from the take-out, the river broadens and flattens, building up for one last boulder garden just before the take-out.

Difficulties: This run is composed of a nearly continuous series of difficult chutes and drops. Worthy of special note is the class 5 Food for Thought, which is just below the put-in.

Shuttle: Turn north from Oregon 126 onto USFS 15, 2 miles east of the town of Blue River. The take-out is located at a boat ramp at the upper end of Blue River Reservoir, about 4 miles from the 126 turn-off. The put-in is about 5 miles farther, at the confluence of Quentin Creek and Blue River. Put-ins for shorter runs are possible if low water warrants.

Gauge: Water level information is available through the Lookout Point Dam. Ask for the flow above Lookout Creek.

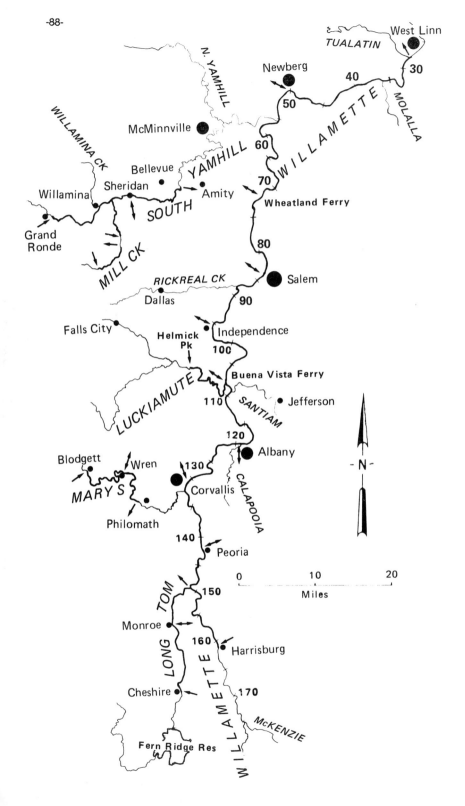

Chapter 6. Willamette River and Western Tributaries

WILLAMETTE RIVER

Introduction by Gene Ice and Ellen Oliver

The Willamette River runs like a giant artery north through the heart of western Oregon. It drains an immense valley which holds the major population centers of Oregon: Eugene, Corvallis, Salem, and Portland. Many small communities which lie along the banks think of the Willamette as their own. In fact, more than half of all Oregonians live in cities touched by the Willamette. Perhaps because it is so much a part of Oregon life, this river enjoys a special place among Oregon rivers. Much of the river is protected by a Greenway Program which seeks to preserve the river corridor for public enjoyment. Other sections are bordered by parks.

Even though the river traverses the heartlands and major population areas of Oregon, boaters will see surprisingly little of the impact of civilization, especially on the upper and middle sections. The sharp-eyed drifter will observe a variety of plants and wildlife, and the fishermen may catch dinner. Edible foods include red huckleberries, wild strawberries, blackberries, cherries, and apples. Do not pick produce from a farmer's field! Fish include trout, steelhead, salmon, sturgeon, sucker, carp, bass, and bluegill. Other wild animals and many species of birds, especially the Great Blue Heron, will be seen.

During the summer months, upper sections of the river can be like a carnival with the frenzy of innertubers and paddlers. In contrast, during the winter the river is isolated; a place of solitude. It is perhaps the contrasts of the Willamette that are most striking. Parts of the river are lined with homes, factories, and parks. Other sections cut through Oregon farmland or forests. From the clear, wild, and free North Fork, to the stately regulated Main Fork, the Willamette holds paddling opportunities for boaters of all skill levels and interests. For the curious, there are relics of abandoned bridges, dams, and old canals. This is a river to explore!

The mid- and lower Willamette are well suited for extended camping trips of several days. Beginners should take a few short trips on the river before attempting overnight trips.

Some islands and camping spots have people, dogs, sheep and cattle living nearby. Leave your dog at home if you want to see wildlife and coexist peacefully with other neighbors.

The mid- and lower Willamette appear slow and calm, but many unsuspecting canoeists, both novice and expert, have misjudged the capacity for danger. Cable lines from a dredge can suddenly rise out of the river without warning. A lazily drifting canoe can hit a submerged log and swamp. High winds can blow upriver on a sunny afternoon and push boaters upstream. An inviting side channel can become blocked with debris after a mile or more. Willamette Falls, an unrunnable 30-ft drop at Oregon City, must be portaged. Water flowing fast through trees when the river is near flood stage can capsize a boat and leave boaters stranded in trees far from shore.

Because the Willamette Valley has a thorough network of roads, most shuttle routes can be discerned from an Oregon road map. If you must leave your vehicle unattended overnight, contact the local sheriff's office and explain how long the car will be left. The officers will usually check the car for you on their rounds. There is sufficient water to run this river all year. The river is dam controlled.

An additional reference on the Willamette is the "Willamette River Recreation Guide" published by Oregon State Parks and Recreation Branch and available at State Highway Division offices in towns along the river. Information concerning the Greenway Program can also be obtained from the Oregon State Parks and Recreation Branch in Salem.

Regulations on the Willamette require personal flotation devices for all passengers. Boats on the Willamette River are subject to laws and regulations enforced by the U.S. Coast Guard, Oregon State Police, and county sheriffs.

WILLAMETTE RIVER
Jasper Park to Alton Baker Park
Gene Ice

Class	Flow	Gradient	Miles	Character	Season
2(3)	2000	16 C	14	houses industry	all year

Description: The Jasper to Alton Baker Park run is a popular summer run for Eugene residents and the site of the annual Willamette River Race. Although racing boats try to finish this stretch in under 1.5 hours, the run is more often enjoyed at a leisurely float pace. Do not expect a wilderness run here; rather enjoy a gathering of happy folks, especially during the summer when hot weather drives rafts, canoes, and crafts of all pedigree onto the water.

Despite its popularity with novice paddlers, the river needs to be respected. During the summer the water is warm, but rocks are plentiful. During the spring, winter, and fall the water can be brutally cold.

The run begins on the Middle Fork of the Willamette. The biggest rapids on this run come below the Clearwater Boat Landing where the river splits around an island, resulting in whitewater on both sides. About 4 miles below, look for the confluence with the Coast Fork, below which the river enters Springfield. Just downstream from a train bridge are the Main Street Bridge and Day Island Park on the right. Day Island Park is a possible take-out. Beaver can often be seen near the island guarding the park. The section of river below the park is generally good for seeing signs of beaver.

Below Day Island the river offers Pizza Rapids, named for a local pizza establishment of the left bank. A flat section extends below this rapids to I-5 Rapids. A sign posted on the river bank warns boaters that the coming stretch is the most dangerous on the river. DO NOT EXPECT TO SEE THIS SIGN FROM THE RIVER. The weir at the head of I-5 Rapids is about 100 yards upstream of the I-5 bridge. At this point, boaters have a choice of two routes for the remaining 2 miles to Alton Baker Park.

Those wishing easy paddling to Alton Baker Park should take out at the boat landing on the right above I-5 Rapids and paddle the rest of the way on the Eugene Canoe Path. A portage of only 200 feet is needed to reach the Canoe Path, a pleasant canal that flows to Alton Baker Park.

Those continuing on the river should scout I-5 Rapids, which consist of a low rock wall and a broken weir with various slots followed by a reasonably long rapids with a large wave at the bottom. The far right slot is the only route. Under no circumstances should any of the other slots be run, as debris and reversal action can make them unrunnable under some conditions.

Boaters should be forewarned that the waves and holes become quite large at high water. Rafts are particularly prone to being trapped in the hydraulics behind the weirs. Below I-5 Rapids the river passes under two of Eugene's four bike and foot bridges. At the second one, about 2 miles below I-5 Rapids, there is a large standing wave in the main channel on the left. Boaters flock to this spot in the summer to try to do enders and prolonged surfs. Open boats may avoid the wave by sneaking to the right. A mile downstream the Ferry Street Bridge signals Alton Baker Park and the end of the run.

Difficulties: The weir ahead of I-5 Rapids is dangerous at all water levels. Do not attempt to run any slot except the right. I-5 Rapids will swamp open boats at high water.

Shuttle: Jasper Park is on the south side of the Middle Fork of the Willamette about 0.2 mile above the Jasper Bridge. There is good parking at Jasper Park, but it is about a 50-yard carry to the water. An alternate put-in under the Jasper Bridge has less desirable parking but a shorter carry to the water. Another put-in or take-out is about 5 miles downstream at Clearwater Boat Landing, on the road between Jasper and Springfield.

The take-out above I-5 Rapids is off Centennial Boulevard east of the I-5 underpass. Alton Baker Park is on the north side of the river near the junction of Centennial Boulevard and Coburg Road (Ferry Street Bridge).

Gauge: The flow is regulated such that the minimum is runnable. Jasper Gauge gives the flow for the Middle Fork; Eugene Gauge gives the flow for the Willamette. These flows can be obtained from the River Forecast Center in Portland.

WILLAMETTE RIVER
Alton Baker Park to Harrisburg
Gene Ice

Class	Flow	Gradient	Miles	Character	Season
1(2)	6000	5 C	14	suburban rural	all year

Description: The Alton Baker Park to Harrisburg float seems less popular than the trip from Jasper Park, perhaps because the water is a bit slower and the trip a bit longer. This section is somewhat more enjoyable, however; passing through rural Oregon makes for interesting exploration of the river banks. For an alternate route to Harrisburg, beginning on the lower McKenzie, see the next section.

After the put-in at Alton Baker Park (Ferry Street Bridge), the river immediately passes Skinners Butte Park and the Eugene Rose Gardens on the left. The first rapids is across from the Rose Gardens, just above the Jefferson Street Bridge. Below the rapids the water is calm, and it is possible to paddle to the left for a better look at the roses.

Below Jefferson Street the river passes the Valley River Shopping Center and then passes under a bike and foot bridge. This section, although basically flat water, is interesting because of the numerous small islands which divide the river into channels. Between Valley River Shopping Center and the Beltline Bridge lies Marist Rapids, the most difficult rapids on this run. Marist Rapids is fairly straightforward with large waves in the center. It can be scouted and/or portaged on the left, but watch out for the slippery rocks!

The next major landmark is the Beltline Bridge, a possible take-out. Below Beltline, the signs of Eugene give way to rural Oregon. A few miles downstream on the right, the McKenzie adds some cool water to the Willamette; however, it is easy to miss this confluence. Two possible take-outs are located about midway between Eugene and Harrisburg (see Shuttle). The second half of the river broadens and has fewer curves. The railroad bridge signals the approach to Harrisburg. After passing the highway bridge, the boat ramp will be found on the right.

Difficulties: Marist Rapids, between Valley River Shopping Center and Beltline Bridge, should be scouted on the left by open boaters or those unfamiliar with the rapids. Below Eugene, a section with downed trees frequently develops. These "strainers" can be extremely hazardous.

Shuttle: Alton Baker Park, the put-in, is located on the north bank near the Coburg Road and Centennial Boulevard junction. A possible take-out is located about halfway to Harrisburg at Christensen County Boat Landing. To find this take-out, follow Coburg Road north to Crossroads Lane. Another take-out is nearby on the other side of the river at Brown's Boat Landing. The boat ramp at Harrisburg is toward the north side of town.

Gauge: The minimum flow is runnable.

WILLAMETTE RIVER
Armitage Park to Albany
Ellen Oliver

Class	Flow	Gradient	Miles	Character	Season
1 +	2000-20,000	4 C	58	rural	all year

Description: Armitage Park is actually on the McKenzie River, 2.5 miles from the confluence with the Willamette. The boat landings at Harrisburg and Peoria allow shorter trips. The typical river speed of 4 mph requires constant attention. There are no large rapids but many swift, shallow spots that could mean scraping bottom. Logs lying just under the surface are always a hazard. If the water ahead shows a downstream V, follow it.

Boaters will find many good camping spots on the upper stretch of this river. Agates and petrified wood can be found on the banks. Some of the islands have state parks for boaters only. Fishing is usually good.

Difficulties: None in particular.

Shuttle: The shuttle can be arranged by scanning the following watermarks.

Gauge: The River Forecast Center in Portland has flow information for the Willamette at several locations.

Watermarks:

Miles from mouth

'178 Armitage Park on Coburg Road, under I-5 between Eugene and Coburg.

'175 Confluence of McKenzie and Willamette Rivers. As you leave the McKenzie, edge into the Willamette carefully. The meeting of the two rivers causes cross currents that can swing a canoe crosswise.

'161 Harrisburg. A good boat ramp towards the end of town on the right. Stores are within walking distance.

'156.5 McCartney Park. A good boat ramp on the right. Water is swifter here, so plan ahead before landing. There are many excellent camping spots between here and Peoria.

'142 Peoria. Just before Peoria is a fast water stretch with homes above the river on the right. Large boulders can be seen under the water. A large whirlpool is near the right bank. This whirlpool is dangerous when the water is high. Keep left.

'141.5 Peoria Boat Landing is on the right. It is hard to see so keep close to the shore on the right if you plan to land. Many boaters leave the river here after a weekend on the river.

'141 Islands. If your canoe is loaded (or you are short on time) keep to the right of the islands just below the Peoria Boat Landing. The camping spots are numerous and at about mile 136.5 the

'134   river swings around a large island. Keep left and land at the end for a nice spring-fed pool, good for swimming.

'134   Willamette Park. Not a good take-out because of high steep banks.

'133   Lower Willamette Park Boat landing.

'132   Marys River Landing (Pioneer Boat Basin), Corvallis. This boat landing is not visible from the Willamette River because it is on the Marys River, a hundred yards upstream from the confluence with the Willamette. The mouth of the Marys River is on the left where the Willamette makes a curve to the right as the bridge in Corvallis comes into view. In the summer when the water is low, this is not a good landing because mud sometimes blocks the entrance.

'131   Boat landing on the left just below the two bridges in Corvallis and across from the OSU boat dock. It is accessible to cars and many canoeists unload here. This is a busy spot for waterskiers and motorboats on hot days.

'127   More excellent camping spots on the way to Albany. At river mile 127 there is Half Moon Bend; at river mile 125, Riverside Landing. These are accessible only by boat.

'122   Hyak Park is on the left. It is a good place to take out and end a trip from Eugene. The large water intake on the left side of the river marks the boat landing.

'120   Bryant Park in Albany. Large boat landing on the right side of the river at the mouth of the Calapooia River and above three bridges over the Willamette. This is a very busy place. By car, follow Third Avenue west from downtown Albany.

'119   Bowman Park in Albany. On the right side of river, downstream of the third bridge.

WILLAMETTE RIVER
Albany to Portland (West Linn)
Ellen Oliver

Class	Flow	Gradient	Miles	Character	Season
1C	2000 20,000	1.3 C	95	rural	all year

Description: The river continues to become larger and slower, with an average speed of 2 to 3 mph. Homes and houseboats are present. Highways can be seen. Islands are larger. The power boat traffic definitely increases below Independence. Below Newberg camping places become difficult, but not impossible to find.

Difficulties: Willamette Falls at mile 26.5. See Watermarks.

Shuttle: Consult the following watermarks and a local map to pick your shuttle.

Gauge: Contact the River Forecast Center in Portland for the flow at several places on the river.

Watermarks:

Miles from mouth

'120   Bryant Park at mouth of the Calapooia River. Albany is left behind as the boater slips under the bridge and passes Bowman Park on the right. Bowman Park is an alternate put-in.

'113.5   Island in middle of river could be good camping in summer, keep right.

'109   Luckiamute Landing on left. Primitive camping and toilet.

'108   Here the Luckiamute comes in on the left and the Santiam

River comes in on the right. The water here boils with back current and whirlpools.

'106.2 Buena Vista Ferry, still in use. A small park on the left side before ferry cable crossing.

'106 Wells Island Park. Go to the right of the island, which is about 1 mile long. The best camping area, with toilets, is identified with a sign. The river runs pretty fast here so plan landings ahead of time. Paddling upstream against the current is almost impossible.

'95.5 Independence. Town is accessible to boaters. A good place to get fresh water and food.

'92 Large island on the right; keep left. Camping is allowed in Greenway strip.

'85 Salem. River becomes smoother and wider. Two bridges are passed.

'83 Two miles out of Salem the river divides. The main channel is to the left. If the water is high the boater can make it through the right channel.

'78.5 Large island on the left. Check here for camping spots because they will be harder to find below here. Power boats and water skiers are present in summer.

'72 Wheatland Ferry. Time your crossing to give the ferry wide berth. There is a nice beach for stopping to watch the ferry. Possible take-out on the left side.

'65 Lambert Slough comes in here. There is a large island on the left.

'52 Large Island. Keep right.

'50.5 Newberg. Paddling begins in earnest as the river slows and camping spots become hard to find. Homes and houseboats are on the river. Water activists are numerous in the summer.

'38.8 Boones Ferry Park on the left just below bridge. Gas and supplies available at store on right side of river.

'33 Herb Park. This is a lovely park and a good lunch stop on a busy river. Just below Herb Park stay to the left. When you come around the large bend keep left and enjoy the scenery!

'31.5 Peach Cove Landing. Primitive camping; boats only.

'30 Rock Island Landing. Keep left of island.

'28.5 Willamette Park, city of West Linn, on the left where the Tualatin River comes in. Good take-out but busy in the summer. The river is very wide in this area with lots of boats, tugboats, barges, mills, and log rafts. There are no signs indicating the large falls ahead.

'26.5 Willamette Falls: DANGER! The slow flowing pool drops abruptly 30 feet.

'26.5 West Linn Locks. Keep against left bank. Wait for larger boats to move ahead and ask them to alert the lock-keeper of your presence. It is wise to contact the lock-keeper BEFORE you start your trip down river. He may recommend a certain time and day as being better for small craft.

'25 Clackamette Park on the right at the mouth of the Clackamas River. Possible take-out.

'24 Meldrum Bar Park on the right. Possible take-out.

LONG TOM RIVER
High Pass Road to Willamette River
Allen Throop

Class	Flow	Gradient	Miles	Character	Season
1 + (P)	50 +	5 PD	17	accessible pleasant channelized	all year

Description: The Long Tom is an alternative to the Willamette for those who desire to float down a quiet stream away from the crowds. Elementary paddling skills can be practiced while maneuvering around rocks in slow-moving water. It is also an excellent river for novice poling practice. For the farmer's benefit, much of the river channel has been lined with riprap. The water level is regulated for irrigation. A narrow riparian vegetation strip separates the Long Tom from most of the agricultural activity in the area.

The river can be run at all levels except flood stage. It is best in late spring or in the fall. Many sections are rocky below 50 cfs; be prepared to hop out and wade in places. Caution is advised near each of the 3 dams. For a shorter trip, the river can be reached at 5 of the 6 bridges along the way; Stow Pit Road is the exception.

Difficulties: The only major problems are the 3 dams. The first dam is just upstream, but within sight, of the second bridge (Ferguson Road), 2.5 miles below the put-in. The next dam is another 2.5 miles farther downstream. The final dam is at the Monroe mill, after another 3 miles downstream. All of the dams are over 10 ft high and have very powerful reversals. Portage all three to the right. At the Monroe dam, take out about 100 ft past the US 99W bridge. Because of thick blackberries, there is no path closer to the dam.

Shuttle: The put-in is at the bridge on High Pass Road, which connects Junction City with the Monroe-Cheshire Road, 3.2 miles south of Monroe. To reach the take-out, turn east from US 99W, 11 miles south of Corvallis, onto Eureka Road. Follow Eureka Road for 2 miles, crossing one bridge. Turn right onto another gravel road and go south to the take-out bridge. This bridge is within sight of a channel of the Willamette River. The take-out is a very steep pull up the right bank just past the bridge. (Note the upstream flow of water on the Long Tom here!)

An alternate and much easier take-out can be reached by turning east off US 99W onto Old River Road, about 0.5 mile south of Eureka Road. Follow Old River Road to the take-out, which is on river left about 100 yards downstream of the Old River Road bridge. This is the third bridge below Monroe.

Gauge: The flow at the Monroe gauge is regulated by the Corps of Engineers at the Fern Ridge Dam. A minimum flow of 50 cfs is maintained except from July 1 to September 30 when the flow drops to 30 cfs. In October the flow is greatly increased while Fern Ridge Reservoir is drawn down to catch the winter rains.

MARYS RIVER
Blodgett to Wren
Bill Ostrand

Class	Flow	Gradient	Miles	Character	Season
1 +	500	10 C	9	wooded	rainy
				railroad	

Description: The Marys River flows from the Coast Range east to its confluence with the Willamette in Corvallis. It is a mild-mannered and isolated stream ideal for canoeists and kayakers interested in scenery and mild whitewater. The rapids on this section are slightly easier and farther apart than on the Wren to Philomath section.

Difficulties: The brushy banks can be a problem for novice boaters on this narrow stream. The brush can also become a serious hazard to the swimming boater. If you are in the water just remember to swim to shore at an open area. The Marys is also likely to contain a few downed trees.

Shuttle: The put-in is at the US 20 bridge in Blodgett. Alternate put-ins may be found with the aid of a Benton County map. Take-out at the US 20 bridge in Wren or at the covered bridge on the Marys River Road upstream from Wren.

Gauge: Presently no gauge is available for the Marys. It is usually runnable several days after a storm. Corvallis residents can make a subjective evaluation of the flow by checking out the rapids on the Marys in Corvallis' Avery Park. If water is flowing on any part of the walk along the rapids the upper sections will be runnable.

MARYS RIVER
Wren to Philomath
Richard Hand

Class	Flow	Gradient	Miles	Character	Season
1 +	500	10 C	8-12	wooded	rainy
(2)				rural	

Description: The first part of this stretch is class 1. The pace picks up approximately 7 miles below the upper put-in where the river enters a section with hills on both sides. The current here forms more eddies and play-spots than on the upper stretch.

Difficulties: Brush and downed trees can be a hazard on this river. Approximately 0.5 mile below the covered bridge is a short series of shelves that must be portaged at low to moderate flows. Portage on the left to avoid confrontation with residents. When this shelf is runnable it is a solid class 2 drop.

Shuttle: The put-in is at the covered bridge between Wren and Blodgett. From US 20 west of Philomath take the Wren exit and go to the railroad tracks. Take a left and follow the Marys River Road to the covered bridge. Another put-in is at the US 20 bridge in Wren. Putting in at the Oregon 223 bridge in Wren will shorten the trip, include most of the rapids, and give boaters a 7 to 8 mile run with a 4 mile shuttle. Take out west of Philomath at the Oregon 34 bridge or the US 20 bridge near the lumber mill.

Gauge: None. See preceding section on the Marys.

LUCKIAMUTE RIVER
Helmick State Park to Buena Vista
Carl Landsness

Class	Flow	Gradient	Miles	Character	Season
1	500+	1 C	15	wooded	rainy

Description: The Luckiamute wanders slowly out of King's Valley northwest of Corvallis on its way to the Willamette near the Buena Vista ferry crossing. The current is very slow except after significant rainfall, so this trip can take the better part of a day. While the banks are generally high and brushy, there are very few snags that present problems. However, this can change from year to year, so be alert. For additional information, see Jones (1982).

Difficulties: There are two small class 1+ ledges and a few narrow spots that require the boater to wake up.

Shuttle: This is a great trip on which to "run" the shuttle because the distance is only 6 miles. From the take-out at the Buena Vista ferry, drive (or run) west 2 miles to the Independence Highway and turn north. After about 1 mile, turn west and follow signs to Oregon 99W. Take Oregon 99W north to Helmick State Park, the put-in.

Gauge: There is no gauge for this river. It is generally runnable all winter and spring.

MILL CREEK
Upper Bridge to Mill Creek Park
Rob Blickensderfer and Steve Holland

Class	Flow	Gradient	Miles	Character	Season
3(4) T	400-1000	50 C	5.5	forest hills	rainy

Description: There are at least four Mill Creeks in Oregon--this one flows from the Coast Range toward the northeast and into the South Fork of the Yamhill River. The stream is quite narrow and gives one a more intimate feeling with the water than any other river the authors know. From the put-in at the upper bridge, the water is fairly gentle for about a mile. Then comes the class 4 Triple Drop, which should be scouted on the drive to the put-in.

Just below Triple Drop the river slows on a 90-degree curve to the left, then begins a 0.2 mile accelerating drop through a gorge with a dynamic class 4 ending. Once a boater enters this fast water in the gorge, there is almost no turning back or getting out. Below here, some stretches of the river are relatively quiet. After a 0.5 mile, an island is passed, and then another island.

The next watermark is a bridge, downstream of which the road is on river left. Straight downstream from this bridge is a fast, steep drop. After another mile is the second bridge and the road is back on the right. Just below this second bridge is The Claw, class 3. At low water The Claw has a large exposed rock area in the middle and the route must be picked. At high water, the rocks are covered. In either case, the bottom hole tends to reach up and claw at the sterns of boats.

The third and last bridge is a mile farther downstream and warns you that you are near the take-out. The water picks up speed below this last bridge and leads to the final drop, The Twist, a 3-4 ft blind drop that is quite fast with a turbulent run-out. Take out immediately on the left, at Mill Creek Park.

Difficulties: Triple Drop is aptly named. It can be seen from the curve in the road at a pull-out about a mile below the put-in. This class 4 rapids has been run at estimated flows of 500 to 700 cfs; at lower flows it appears too steep and rocky.

The gorge below here is similar in difficulty but potentially much more dangerous. The gorge is a mandatory scout, since a log block here could become fatal. There are only a few small eddies for stopping, and the rock walls are too steep to allow one to climb out of the boat. To scout, first look upstream from the road for the whitewater at the lower end of the gorge. Check for logs. Then go up the road about 300 ft and climb down to the creek. There is a place where one can get down to creek level. By walking downstream as far as possible, one can just barely see if the upper part of the gorge is obstructed. The two major drops in the gorge are bigger than they look from here.

The Claw, class 3, is easier than the gorge. It can be seen from the road just a short distance below the second bridge. It is technical at low water when the large rock area in the middle becomes exposed, and easier at high water. The Twist, the last drop, is straightforward and can be observed from the take-out at Mill Creek Park, just opposite the parking lot. Caution: do not continue below Mill Creek Park. Within 0.2 mile is a steep, twisting, narrow class 6 gorge.

Shuttle: Oregon 22 crosses Mill Creek about 22 miles west of Salem. Just west of the bridge, a crossroad runs along Mill Creek. Drive upstream 2.3 miles to reach Mill Creek Park (a county park), the take-out. Continue upstream another 5.6 miles to a concrete bridge, the put-in.

Gauge: Not known. Unregulated flow. Best at high water after heavy or sustained rains.

MILL CREEK
Buell Park to Sheridan
Rob Blickensderfer

Class	Flow	Gradient	Miles	Character	Season
2- T	1000	21 C	7	forest	rainy
1		5 C	3	agricultural	

Description: This section of Mill Creek is quite enjoyable at high water when there are numerous class 1 to 2 surfing waves. At low water, below 600 cfs, it might be a bottom scraper. After 7 miles, Mill Creek empties into the South Fork of the Yamhill River, but because there is no access there, the boater must travel 3 miles on down the Yamhill to the take-out in Sheridan. The 3 miles of the South Fork of the Yamhill, with its gradient of 5 feet per mile, are uneventful; but when Mill Creek has adequate water, the Yamhill will be rolling along to make it a 15 or 20 minute trip.

Difficulties: Trees can block the entire river, but the alert boater will find it possible to land in time.

Shuttle: Oregon 22 crosses Mill Creek about 22 miles west of Salem. Just west of the bridge an intersecting road runs along Mill Creek. Drive downstream 0.3 mile to Buell Park (a county park), the put-in. To reach the take-out in Sheridan, go back to the community of Buell, on Oregon 22. Take the county road to the north which more or less follows Mill Creek and crosses it before intersecting Oregon 18. Turn right (northeast) and go about 3 miles to the road that goes to Sheridan. The boat ramp is in downtown Sheridan, one block upstream of the highway bridge on river right.

Gauge: None. Unregulated flow. Runnable after long or hard rains.

SOUTH FORK OF THE YAMHILL RIVER
Grand Ronde to Sheridan
Rob Blickensderfer

Class	Flow	Gradient	Miles	Character	Season
2(3) T	700-3000	10 PD	14	wooded flatland	rainy

Description: Draining the coastal mountain side of the Willamette Valley, the river wanders through the foothills and then meanders through the valley. The boater has several options of put-ins and take-outs.

This section will keep the open canoeist busy and entertain the beginning kayaker with many good surfing waves. Put in at the upstream right side of the bridge on Oregon 18. Only 0.2 mile downstream is a 3-ft ledge, class 2, followed by a mile of riffles. At about mile 2 is an old log bridge followed by a highway bridge. About 0.5 mile farther is a small ledge drop. After another 0.5 mile is a second highway bridge. For the next 2 miles a secondary road runs along river left.

Five miles below the put-in is a modern concrete bridge and a mile farther is an old suspension footbridge. A half mile farther is a 1.5-ft ledge followed in 100 yards by a 2-ft ledge; then, 0.5 mile farther is another 2-ft ledge with a channel on the right. After another 0.5 mile the river passes under a very high concrete bridge, Oregon 18, then an older concrete bridge, Oregon 22, that provides a reasonable access.

Just below here (mile 7.5) is another ledge rapids, class 2, with a maze of willows in fast water. After 0.5 mile is a steel bridge (which might be removed in the future; it is closed) near the town of Willamina. At mile 9, in the town of Willamina, Willamina Creek enters from the left. A mile downstream is The Ledge, class 3. A sawmill on the left bank is the landmark. Fast water leads to The Ledge. To scout, land on the left. The chute about a third of the way across the river from the right bank has been run at high water.

The river gradually slows as it approaches the town of Sheridan. A mile below The Ledge (at mile 11), Mill Creek enters from the right. A mile below Mill Creek is a maze of willows in medium fast water. Two miles farther is the railroad bridge near Sheridan and the highway bridge in downtown Sheridan (mile 14). The boat ramp is on the right, one block upstream of the highway bridge.

Difficulties: The Ledge, at mile 10, is difficult to scout because the river banks are so steep that it is difficult to get out of one's boat. A fast riffle leading to The Ledge makes it difficult to get close enough in a boat to pick a safe route. Parts of The Ledge have potentially dangerous reversals. To scout, land on the left bank above the sawmill. The far left chute, and the chute about one third of the way across the river from the right bank, are feasible. Probably the second greatest difficulties are the willows, especially the group at mile 7.5. The other ledges can be run by experienced boaters without scouting.

Shuttle: Several accesses to the river are available and the choice depends upon the section to be run. The upper put-in is on Oregon 18 about 26 miles west of McMinnville (34 miles west of Salem) where a bridge crosses the river just east of the community of Grand Ronde. There is a parking lane and a good path to the river on the west side of the river, between the highway and the railroad trestle. Other accesses are available along the road that follows the river from river mile 3 to 5, south of Oregon 18 and 22.

The next good access is at the Oregon 22 bridge on the downstream left bank. The bank is fairly steep, but there is a good parking area above. Another access can probably be found in the town of Willamina. In Sheridan, a boat ramp is located on the east side of the river, one block upstream from the highway bridge.

Gauge: River Forecast Center, Portland. Unregulated flow.

SOUTH FORK OF THE YAMHILL RIVER
Sheridan to Near Amity
Rob Blickensderfer

Class	Flow	Gradient	Miles	Character	Season
1	700-3000	4 C	12	rural flatland	rainy

Description: Below Sheridan the river meanders through the valley. The scenery is quite pleasant considering that the route passes considerable civilization. The fastest water on this lower stretch is just below the highway bridge (Oregon 18), a mile below Sheridan, where the river flows through some willows. These willows can be seen from the bridge.

After another 3 miles, a secondary road to Ballston crosses on a wooden bridge. No take-out is possible here because of the very thick brush. After 8 miles of meandering, the sight of the steel bridge, on the road between Amity and Bellevue, will be welcomed. Take out on the right side, downstream of the bridge.

Difficulties: The willows a mile below the bridge at Sheridan require attention.

Shuttle: In Sheridan a boat ramp is located on the east side of the river, one block upstream from the highway bridge. The take-out is at the east end of the bridge on the paved road between Amity and Bellevue.

Gauge: River Forecast Center, Portland. Unregulated flow.

Chapter 7. Eastern Tributaries in the Mid-Willamette Valley

CALAPOOIA RIVER
Bridge 13.3 miles upstream of Holley to near Holley
T.R. Torgersen

Class	Flow	Gradient	Miles	Character	Season
3	740-2500	48 PD	8-10	forest logging houses	rainy

Description: The Calapooia is named after the Indians who once inhabited the Willamette Valley. It is a fine small river whose uppermost runs are within an hour's drive of many southern Willamette Valley communities. The river tumbles through forested land in the foothills of the Cascades. Winter storms augment the Calapooia's flow and normally make boating possible from about mid-November through the first week in March.

The beginning of the run is swift, and the combination of gradient and rocks immediately below precipitate the boater directly into class 2 to 3 rapids. Spend a few minutes warming up by playing the easier holes near the put-in. Within several hundred yards, the river demands some decisive maneuvering, particularly at a heavily rock-strewn section that sweeps to the left past a point occupied by a log and debris jam (1981). At low flows only a narrow boatable channel skirts the jam to the right center of the river. At higher flows this rapids is passable throughout most of its width. The rocky stretch is about 0.2 mile long and requires considerable rock dodging at low flow. Opportunities exist for some thrilling surfing at higher flows. A dump on this section could involve a rather long swim. At mile 1.5 the river veers right with a rocky class 3 drop. The drop can be taken on either side of a small stony bar and large boulder at high flows, or on the right at low flows.

Big Creek enters on the right at mile 2, and a single cable marks mile 3.2. A double cable with a hose crosses at mile 4.4, marking a nice play spot. Below this, the channel narrows and a ledge develops a tricky curl that can dump a too complacent boater. Below is the Narrows with a rocky little drop; run on the left at most flows, or to the right of the rocky bar at higher flows. One mile downstream look for a small brushy gravel bar and a prominent culvert protruding from the road fill on the right. This marks a short class 2 drop and interesting play spot. Approach the drop on the left of center and watch out for the nasty rock near the bottom of the fast flush! Dollar Drop, named for the former town of Dollar, is at mile 6.5. Pull out on the right to scout the 4-ft drop over a ledge.

Difficulties: Dollar Drop at mile 6.5 should be scouted. A bridge crosses the river about 0.2 mile upstream. While the drop is not technically demanding, a potentially hazardous reversal is along much of the base. A reasonably good run-out and a good eddy are below the drop on the right.

Shuttle: The Calapooia is reached from I-5 by taking the Brownsville exit and turning east on Oregon 228. McKercher County Park is about 6 miles beyond the Brownsville turnoff, and from a gravel turnoff at milepost 12 one can view a falls in the park. This is a popular local swimming hole in summer. The run described here begins 20 miles farther upstream. At the village of Holley, 4 miles from McKercher Park, turn right. The put-in is 13.3 miles from Holley where the road forks to the right and crosses the river on a bridge blocked by a gate. A gravel bar on the right bank above

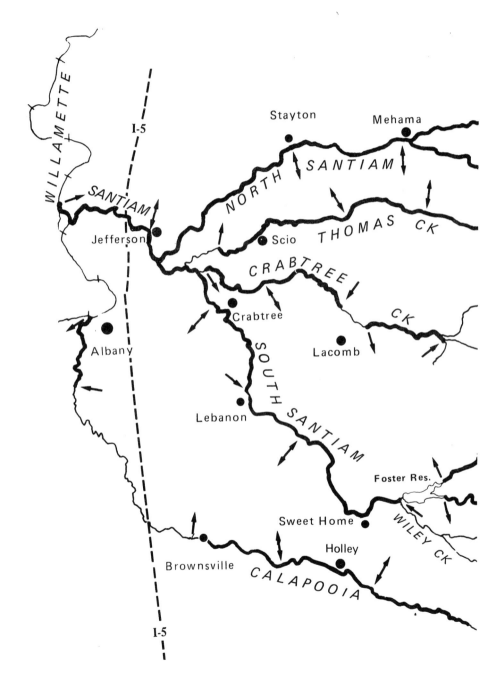

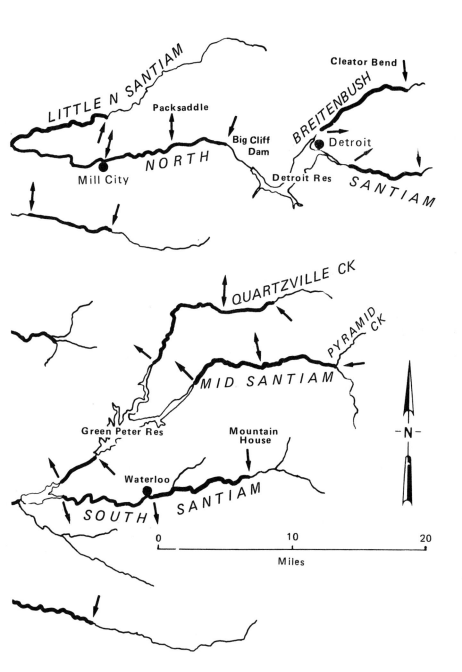

the bridge provides a good put-in. Two take-outs permit runs of 7.9 or 9.8 miles. The take-out for the longer run is under the bridge about 4 miles from Holley on the Upper Calapooia River Road. Land on the right immediately before or under the bridge. This is a poor take-out with a difficult carry up a steep embankment.

A much easier take-out is about 5.6 miles from Holley. There is an undeveloped parking area right at river level. The spot is immediately above a drop with a large rock ledge on the right.

Gauge: Just downstream of the bridge at Holley there is a gauge-house and stick on the right. To view the gauge stop at the house just across the bridge, on the north side of the road, and ask permission to cross the property. A reading of 3.1 feet on the gauge represents a minimum runnable flow (740 cfs). Flow fluctuates widely and rapidly in response to rainy periods.

CALAPOOIA RIVER
Concrete Bridge 4 miles above Holley to McKercher Park
T.R. Torgersen

Class	Flow	Gradient	Miles	Character	Season
2	400-1200	18 PD	10	rural	rainy

Description: On this section the gradient slackens considerably compared to the upper run. The relatively easy rapids and numerous riffles make it a good choice for open canoes. There are two rather rocky drops within the first 0.5 mile and another at Crawfordsville.

Difficulties: Because this section is boatable during the winter, take suitable precautions for cold water. Widely fluctuating storm-influenced flows also make sweepers and debris jams potential hazards. A very rocky rapids 0.2 mile below the double bridges at Crawfordsville may warrant scouting; land on the left.

Shuttle: The put-in is at a concrete bridge about 4 miles from Holley on the Upper Calapooia River Road. There is a good parking place here. The carry is a little steep. Launch under the bridge. The take-out is at McKercher Park, 5.8 miles east of Brownsville. A good landing can be made at the upstream end of the park. Be certain not to overrun the take-out, as there is a class 3 drop a few hundred yards downstream.

The river swings close to the road at several points along the run and there are alternate put-ins. The bridge at McClun Road, about 2.5 miles above Holley, is one of these.

Gauge: See remarks on the upper run. At 2.0 feet on the gauge this run had enough water for open canoes. Some spots required walking and lining. Minimum flow for this run is 400 to 450 cfs, or 2.5 feet at the Holley gauge.

CALAPOOIA RIVER
McKercher Park to Brownsville
T.R. Torgersen

Class	Flow	Gradient	Miles	Character	Season
1 P	400	11 C	7	agriculture	rainy

Description: The gradient of this run is much less than that of the two upper runs. This river assumes a gentle, meandering course with occasional riffles, and flows through pastoral country. This is an ideal stretch for a gentle canoe run.

The section from Brownsville to US 99E Bridge south of Tangent contains a log jam several miles long. This log jam has blocked the river for many years. Do not run this section unless you prefer carrying your canoe to paddling it.

Difficulties: There is a weir about 3.75 miles from the put-in. The weir should be portaged.

Shuttle: McKercher Park is a quaint county park about 6 miles east of Brownsville on Oregon 228. The put-in is immediately below the falls at a small sandy beach. A good unloading point is the turn-out at milepost 12, just after a bridge, but before the park entrance; a short path leads down to the beach. The park offers picnic tables and restrooms. The take-out is at the city park downstream from the bridge at Brownsville. The landing is on the right.

Gauge: The location of the gauge at Holley is described in the narrative for the upper run. Water levels above 2.0 feet correspond to flows above 400 cfs and indicate acceptable levels. The telemetered gauge on the Calapooia at Albany can serve as an estimation for the river above Brownsville. Flows of about 600 cfs on this gauge indicate acceptable flows from McKercher to Brownsville.

CALAPOOIA RIVER
Oregon 34 to Albany
Allen Throop and Rob Blickensderfer

Class	Flow	Gradient	Miles	Character	Season
C	300	3 C	9	agriculture	rainy
1 +	1000				

Description: The river follows a very serene and sinuous course on this stretch. The shores are heavily vegetated, so despite the proximity to human activity, the river has few obvious encroachments by man. There are some nice sandy beaches at low water.

Difficulties: Because of the heavy brush bordering the river, reasonable care should be taken to avoid being swept into strainers. Small debris jams that require portaging are normal at low water.

Shuttle: The put-in is under the bridge where Oregon 34 crosses the river several miles east of Corvallis. A small access road is on the south side of the highway, on the river's east side. Alternate put-ins are possible where Lake Creek Road crosses the river, about 2 miles west of Tangent, and where US 99E crosses the river, about a mile south of Tangent. These upper sections have more brush and downed trees, but provide a unique jungle-like experience.

Several take-outs are available: where Riverside Drive crosses about 6 miles from the put-in; near the mouth, at Bryant Park; or at the confluence of the Calapooia and the Willamette behind the Senior Citizen's Center on Water and Washington Avenues in Albany.

Gauge: There is a telemetered gauge above the confluence with the Willamette. Flow information can be obtained from the River Forecast Center in Portland.

SOUTH SANTIAM RIVER
Mountain House to Foster Reservoir
Chet Koblinsky

Class	Flow	Gradient	Miles	Character	Season
4(6)	800-	45 PD	5-14	forest	rainy
P	3000			canyon	snowmelt

Description: The upper South Santiam is magnificent. This run can be made only after substantial rainfall or snow melt. The rapids are pool-drop and all of the more difficult rapids can be portaged. The Upper South Santiam can be divided into five short sections.

Section 1 is from Mountain House to Trout Creek Park. This class 2 portion is somewhat of a rock scraper at lower water, but is much easier than what lies ahead.

Section 2, Trout Creek Park to the US 20 Bridge, is mostly flatwater with some nice warm-up class 2 rapids. The highlight is Longbow Falls, an abrupt 3-ft drop with a fast entry. The run-out from the falls is somewhat turbulent, but free of rocks.

Section 3 extends from the US 20 bridge to the Monster. This is the most exciting stretch of whitewater on the river. Most of these rapids are peppered with large rocks and require quick judgment and skillful maneuvering or a good roll and a strong boat. As in most high Cascade rivers, logs can be a problem. The Monster, at the end of this section, is class 6 and should be portaged. This conversation piece makes a nice lunch spot. Crawdad Rapids, a small twisty drop only 20 yards below the Monster, looks easy but munches a lot of boaters.

Section 4 of the trip begins about 1 mile downstream from the Monster, at what has become known as Tomco Falls, adjacent to Tomco Mill. This true waterfall has a 5-15 ft double drop. The height of the falls is usually about 8 feet; however, the estimate varies as the boater scouts it, goes over it, and looks back up at it. As the flow increases, the drop decreases. The run-out is turbulent, but free of rocks and other rapids. The easiest portage is on the left.

Below the falls is a long gorge. This may be the most scenic stretch on the river. Here, the river runs for a mile between 30-50 ft tall rock walls. Notwithstanding the proximity of the road, the boater feels incredibly isolated. The rapids in the gorge are less violent than those upstream. One rapids, the Plug, is worth noting. Shortly after Tomco Falls, a series of large haystacks are followed by a small drop with a tricky hole that throws boats against the left wall. Eddies exist on both sides above the hole. Catch the right eddy and sneak the hole on the right. Shortly after this hole the river narrows to less than 10 feet in width. This gap can be blocked by a log, hence the name "The Plug." The gorge section ends at Cascadia Park. A gravel bar on the right, upstream from the bridge is the take-out. Stairs and a railed path lead to the parking lot. This lovely park is complete with restrooms, picnic areas, and a soda spring.

Section 5, beyond Cascadia Park, is well worth the effort. After a few miles of relatively easy water is Tree Farm Rapids (class 4 to 4 +). This maze of rocks and turbulence can be scouted from Tree Farm Park during the shuttle. Just beyond the rapids is a good set of play waves. A nice sandy beach take-out is found on the left, 0.5 mile below Tree Farm Park. A short hike behind some river homes will get the boater to the highway. The run could continue another several miles to Foster Reservoir.

Difficulties: Several rapids should be scouted before running: Longbow Falls, Monster, Crawdad, Tomco, the Plug, and Tree Farm. The first three can be scouted from the road. The Monster (class 6) is seen from a right turn (driving downriver) of the road about 1 mile upstream of Tomco Lumber Mill. Portage Monster. Portages can be made on either side and require some effort. The Plug is scouted from just upstream of Canyon Creek; Tomco from just beyond a deserted white house in a cow pasture 0.5 mile above Canyon Creek; Tree Farm from the river bank inside Tree Farm Park.

Shuttle: US 20 follows the river. The Mountain House Cafe is located at Upper Soda, about 24 miles east of Sweet Home. The uppermost put-in is along the road above Mountain House where the river is visible. Above this put-in the river makes a tumultuous 40-ft drop. The Trout Creek Park put-in is about 3 miles downstream from Mountain House. There are several possible take-outs where vehicles can be parked along the road.

Gauge: Contact Foster Dam for flow information at Cascadia.

SOUTH SANTIAM RIVER
Foster Dam to Waterloo
John VanSickle

Class	Flow	Gradient	Miles	Character	Season
1	900-	11 C	14	rural	all year
2	1500 +				

Description: This stretch is excellent for novice kayakers and whitewater canoeists, or anyone who wants a trip with small, evenly spaced rapids to keep things interesting. At low summer flows, the rapids are class 1 +. At high flows, canoeists find the run an exciting class 2. At flood level, kayakers will find some of the best surfing waves in Oregon on the short stretch between Foster and Sweet Home.

The put-in is an excellent boat ramp in the park just below Foster Dam on river left. The most difficult rapids is the S-turn, about 2 miles down from the put-in, as the river bends left, then right over a short drop. About 1 mile farther down, just past the water intake for Sweet Home, is a fine surfing wave as the river drops into a large pool. A boat ramp on the downstream side of this pool, on river left, can be reached from Sweet Home.

The other major rapids, Highway 20 Rapids, occurs 2 miles downstream from Sweet Home as the river bounds to the right off the highway embankment. Strong eddies and large standing waves make this rapids an excellent spot for practicing surfing and ferrying. Below here a few more small shelves occur before the river levels out to become fairly flat for the rest of the trip. Take out on the left at Waterloo Park and above Waterloo Falls.

Difficulties: Open canoes should be alert for S-Turn Rapids, about 2 miles below Foster Dam, and Highway 20 Rapids, about 2 miles below the Sweet Home bridge. Waterloo Falls, class 4, can be seen from Waterloo Park. It can be run by open boats at certain water levels.

Shuttle: From US 20 in the town of Foster, turn north at the sign to Foster Dam and follow your sense of gravity to the boat ramp in the pleasant park at the foot of the dam. The take-out is at Waterloo Park, about 6 miles east of Lebanon, and about a mile north of US 20. An alternate access in Sweet Home can be reached by turning north off US 20 onto McDowell Creek Road at the west end of Sweet Home; before crossing the bridge, turn right on the access road to the waste treatment plant and continue to the boat ramp.

Gauge: Contact Foster Dam for information. A minimum flow of 900 cfs is maintained during the summer.

SOUTH SANTIAM RIVER
Waterloo to Crabtree
Rob Blickensderfer

Class	Flow	Gradient	Miles	Character	Season
1 P	500-3000	7.5 C	16	rural	all year

Description: Below Waterloo the South Santiam is typical of the rivers in the Willamette Valley: tree-lined dirt banks, gravel bars, riffles, and sweepers. The river flow is rather slow, but the scenery is better than one would expect so near population centers.

From the put-in below the falls at Waterloo the river flows nicely for about 2 miles. The water slows and gravel pit workings are seen as a dam is approached. Portage on the right and continue 2 miles through the city limits of Lebanon. An alternate put-in is the Lebanon City Park on the left. Continue another 9 miles to the covered bridge near Crabtree. Take out on the left below the bridge. Take care of this access! Private land owners are trying to close it and there has been one court battle already.

Difficulties: The dam, about 10 feet high, between Waterloo and Lebanon must be portaged. Be alert for sweepers along the bank.

Shuttle: Waterloo can be reached by turning north off US 20, 6 miles east of Lebanon. It is about 1 mile to the put-in at Waterloo County Park. An alternate put-in with a boat ramp is at the City Park in Lebanon. From US 20 in downtown "old" Lebanon take the street north that goes to the bridge over the South Santiam. The park is near the bridge on the south side.

The take-out is near the Oregon 226 bridge, about 1 mile off US 20. The highway junction is 7 miles east of Albany and 6 miles from Lebanon. The road to the boat ramp is about 0.5 mile west of the bridge and goes to a large gravel area downstream of the bridge. This was the highway to the former steel bridge. The land belongs to the state. However, the land upstream and downstream is privately owned and the owners are justifiably highly sensitive about abuse of their land.

Gauge: Contact the River Forecast Center in Portland. The flow is controlled at Foster Dam. A minimum flow of 900 cfs is maintained during the summer.

SOUTH SANTIAM RIVER
Crabtree to Jefferson
Rob Blickensderfer

Class	Flow	Gradient	Miles	Character	Season
1	500-3000	6 C	10	agriculture wooded	all year

Description: The South Santiam continues its gradual descent for 8 miles below Crabtree to the confluence with the North Santiam. There are numerous class 1 riffles that can become bottom-scrapers during low water. The scenery is pleasant with almost no houses to be seen. The confluence with the North Santiam is 2 miles above Jefferson. Take out below the bridges (the highway and railroad bridges are close together) on the right at the boat ramp.

Difficulties: Be alert for sweepers and brush along the bank.

Shuttle: The put-in is downstream of the Oregon 226 bridge on the river left. See preceding section for more detail. Cars will encounter a vast area of loose river rock, but drift boats can be launched. The take-out is a boat ramp one block below the bridge in "downtown" Jefferson. Jefferson is 2 miles east of I-5. Take the exit about 6 miles north of Albany. County roads connect from Crabtree.

Gauge: Contact the River Forecast Center in Portland. Flow is controlled at Foster Dam. A minimum flow of 900 cfs is maintained during the summer.

MIDDLE SANTIAM RIVER
Wilderness Run
Bill Ostrand

Class	Flow	Gradient	Miles	Character	Season
3(4) T	700 +	77 PD	8	forest	rainy
				wilderness	snowmelt

Description: This is the most pristine river run in Oregon's Cascades and the only Cascade wilderness run. The trip begins in a broad basin with scenic views of neighboring mountain peaks. Initially, rapids are class 1, giving boaters a chance to take in the scenery. The tempo picks up at mile 3 with class 2 and 3 drops appearing frequently. There is a class 4 rapids, about two thirds of the way through the trip, which is likely to have its main channel blocked with logs. After the class 4 rapids, the water is more consistently class 3.

The end of the wilderness is marked by a huge clearcut that gives you a real appreciation of the unscarred vistas and huge trees you have just left behind. The last mile through the clearcut contains some of the liveliest water on the run.

Difficulties: Because of snow and mudslides, getting to the river is difficult. Storms big enough to raise the river to a runnable level usually dump snow at Cool Camp, thereby closing roads. The Forest Service Ranger Station in Sweet Home will usually know whether the pass is open.

There are many logs in the river on this section and a few require portaging. The class 4 drop, because of its constricted nature, is likely to contain logs.

Shuttle: To reach the put-in, drive to Upper Soda on US 20, about 22 miles east of Sweet Home. Turn left on USFS 2041 (USFS 1263 on old Forest Service maps). Drive over the pass at Cool Camp (3000 ft elevation) on USFS 2041 and down to the river. The final mile to the river was cut off by a soil slump in 1979. Park above the slump and carry down the slump to the put-in.

The take-out is located 7 miles upstream from Green Peter Reservoir. To locate it, drive across the Green Peter Dam and continue along the reservoir for 15 miles to the river. The road continues along the river. The take-out is at the fourth bridge across the river up from the lake.

Gauge: The river is unregulated. Contact Foster Dam for the the South Santiam's Cascadia reading. The Middle Santiam flows about 100 to 200 cfs less than the South Santiam.

MIDDLE SANTIAM RIVER
Seven Miles above Green Peter Reservoir to Reservoir
Bill Ostrand

Class	Flow	Gradient	Miles	Character	Season
4	900-2000	50 PD	7	logging	rainy snowmelt

Description: The Middle Santiam is the major water source for Green Peter Reservoir. This is a difficult and challenging run for advanced boaters only. The character of the river changes according to flow levels. At 900 cfs the rapids were continuous, featuring technically demanding boulder dodging with steep twisting drops lurking beyond blind turns. At 2000 cfs downstream visibility increases and scouting is necessary at only two points.

This is not to say that the run becomes easier at higher flows. Boulders become holes; the speed of the river seems to double; eddies disappear; twisting drops become screaming chutes of water dumping into waves or boat-eating holes. Scouting while driving along the river is very deceptive. Unlike normal pool-drop rivers, the continuous gradient of the Middle Santiam is difficult to perceive from the road.

The river gives several warm-up rapids for the first 0.8 mile, then action starts with a class 4 that continues for 0.6 mile. More class 3 to 4 water follows. The 3-mile point is marked by a wooden bridge and the Ice Follies (a class 3 rapids named for Gene and George Ice, who took a brisk swim here on the first descent).

At 4 miles, the river leaves sight of the road and enters a steep-banked gorge. This section should be scouted either on the way to the put-in or from the river. The first time that the gorge was run, a huge fir tree was jammed in the second drop.

The river relaxes after the short gorge, giving the boater a chance to relax and work some adrenalin out of the blood stream. Just above the third bridge (5.3 miles into the run) the pace briefly picks up to a class 3. About 0.3 mile farther is a gauge and a good take-out for a shorter run.

The remaining 1.4 miles of river to the reservoir is mostly class 2. There is another short gorge (where the road swings away from the river) which has a class 3 lead-in rapids to a short steep ledge drop. A good take-out is at the bridge where the river flows into the reservoir.

Difficulties: The whole run. See Description.

Shuttle: To get to the run, cross the Green Peter Dam and continue along the reservoir to the river, 15 miles from the dam. The put-in is at the fourth bridge across the river (7 miles upstream from the lake). Possible take-outs are at any of three bridges, the gauge 1.4 miles above the lake, or at the bridge at the head of the reservoir.

Gauge: Contact Foster Dam for the South Santiam's Cascadia reading. The Middle Santiam runs about 100 to 200 cfs less than the South.

MIDDLE SANTIAM RIVER
Green Peter Dam to Foster Reservoir
Ron Mattson

Class	Flow	Gradient	Miles	Character	Season
4	2000-4000	36 PD	2.5	canyon abrupt releases	dam controlled

Description: This run, although short, offers some of the best whitewater available in the mid-Willamette area during the summer. Green Peter Dam has two generating turbines, each of which require 2000 cfs. The flow from the dam is determined by electricity demand. When one turbine (also called one "unit") is operating, the flow is up to 2000 cfs; if both generators are kicked in, the flow can be up to 4000 cfs. The water released comes from the bottom of the reservoir and is very cold even on a very hot day, so do not forget your wet suit.

Difficulties: The last three rapids, called Swiss Cheese, Scrawley's Wall and Concussion, are the most difficult on the run. Swiss Cheese consists of several ledge-drops which produce nice playing waves at a flow of 1 unit. At 2 units the ledges produce many large holes. The right is the usual route.

A short pool gives time for a party to regroup before Scrawley's Wall, the second drop, which should be run on the right. The river forms many standing waves and can push the boater very close to the left wall.

Another short pool provides a second regrouping spot before Concussion, the grand finale. Concussion is formidable and has lived up to its name at both water levels. At 2 units the water is swift and turbulent. The boater chooses between trying to miss the huge holes and turbulence on the right or the huge holes and turbulence towards the center. At 1 unit the central chute is recommended, but the right can be run with momentum. The rapids end abruptly as Foster Reservoir backs up the river for the remaining distance to the take-out. Concussion can be scouted by parking at road mile 3.3 from US 20 and hiking down the steep bank to the river.

Shuttle: The put-in is located across the river below Green Peter Dam. Cross the dam and take the first dirt road to the right and drive to the bottom of the hill. The river is reached after a short class 5 hike of 150 feet down through the briars. The take-out is 2.6 miles from US 20 on the road to Quartzville. A wide turn-out on the right near a gate in the fence that parallels the road gives access to the river.

Gauge: The schedule for water release can be obtained one or two days in advance from Foster Dam.

QUARTZVILLE CREEK
Above Gregg Creek to Galena Creek
Ron Mattson

Class	Flow	Gradient	Miles	Character	Season
4+	700-2000	120 PD	6	forest mining	rainy snowmelt
5					

Description: At the put-in the river is fairly broad and shallow, but 0.2 mile farther around a right turn the fun starts with a 6-ft drop that can result in a tailstand. About 100 yards downriver is a very technical lead-in to a 7-ft waterfall. These kinds of drops are very typical of Quartzville, which winds down through a steep narrow canyon. The run is definitely not for beginners.

Quartzville was first run after extensive scouting from the road, which revealed one double drop (class 5) that consisted of two waterfalls separated by 25 feet of semi-flat water. The two falls, named the Double Dip, give one something to think about while paddling the first 4 miles above it.

Difficulties: The entire run requires scouting steep drops and looking for debris. This run is for experts only.

Shuttle: From Green Peter Dam drive towards Quartzville on USFS 11. The put-in is at a grassy wide spot on the left side of the road approximately 32.5 miles above the dam. The take-out is by the log bridge where Galena Creek enters Quartzville Creek about 26.4 miles upstream from the dam.

Gauge: Flow information can be obtained from Foster Dam. This creek is unregulated. At a gauge reading of 6.02 the run is class 4; at 7.3 the run is class 5.

QUARTZVILLE CREEK
Galena Creek to Green Peter Reservoir
Ron Mattson and Lance Stein

Class	Flow	Gradient	Miles	Character	Season
4	800-3000	65 PD	10	forest	rainy snowmelt

Description: This lower run on Quartzville Creek is a good prelude to the upper run described in the preceding write-up. The lower section does not have quite the gradient and is not as intense as the upper section, but its pool-drop character still presents a challenge.

At 800 cfs, very long stretches of relatively calm water are culminated in 6-8 ft vertical or very technical drops; the whole run is quite rocky and marginal for boating. At 1500 cfs the run is at its easiest and play-spots abound. Above 2500 cfs large waves and holes punctuate almost every rapids, but routes are fairly easy to find. The possibility of great runs at very high flows looks promising.

Difficulties: Two drops that are definitely worth scouting on the way to the put-in are at mile 24.4 and 24.8, just upstream from Yellow Bottom Recreation Site. Both have nearly vertical ledge drops. Downstream, and within sight of the drop at 24.8 is another treacherous drop which should be scouted. A house-sized boulder marks the spot. At low flows keep right and punch the hole between the boulder and the side of the cliff. At higher flows, a sneak chute on the extreme left is recommended.

Most of the other more difficult rapids can be scouted from the road on the drive up, except those below Dogwood Recreation Site. Several class 4 rapids spice up this last pitch into the reservoir.

Shuttle: Driving east on US 20 out of Sweet Home, take a left on the road to Quartzville at the upper end of Foster Reservoir. Proceed to Green Peter Dam where the mileages start.

Several put-ins are possible. The uppermost is at a log bridge just upstream from the turn-off to the old Quartzville townsite. Another is at Yellow Bottom Recreation Site. This put-in is just below the two ledge-drops at Miles 24.4 and 24.8. Take out at the first convenient pull-out after the river empties into the reservoir. For a shorter run, Dogwood Recreation Site is a convenient take-out, but some of the best rapids are between here and the reservoir.

Gauge: Flow can be obtained from Foster Dam.

CRABTREE CREEK
Snow Peak Camp to Larwood Park
Lance Stein

Class	Flow	Gradient	Miles	Character	Season
3 T	700	91 C	6.7	forest	rainy
4	2000				

Description: Crabtree Creek is located between the South Santiam River and Thomas Creek. It is easy to reach, enjoyable to run, and interesting as the river makes the transition from mountain to valley. The upper 2 miles are tight and rocky at low flows. The river sieves its way through large cobble-bar rapids in the middle section of the run, and the lower section has several large bedrock ledges that spice up the end of the run. Due to the continuous gradient, none of the rapids are exceptionally steep, but seeing the bottom of each drop is often quite difficult until someone decides to go for it.

A heavy rain is needed to bring this river up to a runnable level. At bank full flows, rocks and eddies disappear on the upper section, replaced by large holes and great waves, brush patches and trees. Cobble islands create blind channels which could dead end in alder stands or possibly contain sweepers. Play-spots are found everywhere on the lower part.

Difficulties: About 1 mile from the put-in is an interesting class 3 rapids. At high flows the speed of the water and brushy banks create eddy-hopping problems. Sweepers could be a problem in this narrow stream bed.

Shuttle: To reach Crabtree Creek take Oregon 226 east off of US 20. A few miles past the Crabtree exit look for Fish Hatchery Road. Turn east and continue about 7 miles to an intersection near Larwood Park. Bear right (south) on Meridian Road towards Lacomb. After 0.2 mile bear left on E. Lacomb Road, proceed another mile, and then make a left onto Island Inn Drive. Head upstream following the river for about 2 miles. The take-out is located where the river is right next to the road. A good landmark is the house with an interesting tower.

To reach the put-in continue upstream for a mile or so to the first intersection. Turn right then immediately turn left onto Snow Peak Road. Cross the river and continue up the road to Willamette Industries Snow Peak Camp. (This is private property.) Just past the camp, turn right and head downhill about 0.5 mile to the North Fork Bridge, cross it, continue up and over the ridge and back down to the South Fork Bridge, the put-in.

Gauge: No known gauge.

CRABTREE CREEK
Roaring River to Oregon 226
Carl Landsness

Class	Flow	Gradient	Miles	Character	Season
2-	600	21 C	8	rural wooded	rainy

Description: This section contrasts dramatically with the upper section as Crabtree Creek suddenly empties into lightly wooded farmland. The first 6-mile section is a steady collection of class 1 + and 2- water with a few play-spots. The last few miles to Oregon 226 are still swift but with only occasional class 1 + riffles. An alternate put-in a few miles upstream at the take-out for the previous section provides a class 3- rapids.

Difficulties: None in particular.

Shuttle: Put in at a small park where a covered bridge crosses the river 3 miles north of Lacomb, at the confluence of Roaring River with Crabtree Creek. Take out where Oregon 226 crosses the river between Crabtree and Scio.

Gauge: This river is not regulated or measured. It is generally runnable whenever the upper Santiam drainage rivers are runnable after rain or snowmelt.

CRABTREE CREEK
Oregon 226 to South Santiam River
Carl Landsness

Class	Flow	Gradient	Miles	Character	Season
1 (2)	400 +	7 C	8	rural wooded	rainy

Description: The current slows dramatically on this section and the river loses some of its open feeling as the bank vegetation becomes thicker. Several herons and beavers call this section home, making for an occasional surprise in an otherwise silent drift. At the 4 mile mark, under a railroad bridge, there is a class 2 ledge drop which has a clear path down the center.

Difficulties: Novices may wish to scout the one drop mentioned above. A few miles below the put-in, a barbed wire fence extends most of the way across the river. It can normally be skirted on the left.

Shuttle: Put in at the Oregon 226 bridge between Crabtree and Scio. To reach the take-out, go 1 mile west from Crabtree, then 2.5 miles north to the bridge across the creek near the S. Santiam River. Alternatively, one can continue down the S. Santiam River to Jefferson.

Gauge: This creek has no reporting gauge. This section is generally runnable throughout the winter and spring.

THOMAS CREEK
Below Thomas Creek Falls to Log Bridge
Curt Peterson

Class	Flow	Gradient	Miles	Character	Season
3(4) T	800	68 PD	7	forest logging	rainy

Description: The Thomas Creek drainage is situated between the North Santiam River and Crabtree Creek. It is fed by winter rain run-off. The upper section of Thomas Creek descends in pool-drop fashion through a steep-sided river valley that has limited access by road. A scenic 40-ft falls can be found one mile upstream of the put-in. One-half mile below the Hall Creek put-in is a nasty chute that plunges into a wall. Scout, and possibly portage, on the left.

The next 2 miles of river provide easy class 2 and 3 rapids. The river then enters a narrow, forested canyon and descends to the take-out in pool-drop, class 3 rapids. Three ledge drops were portaged on the exploratory run. Thomas Creek flows through clearcuts and thickly forested areas, so all drops should be scouted for logs. One particularly susceptible section occurs at mile 2.5 where, on the exploratory run, a debris dam blocked a portion of the river.

Difficulties: Three ledge drops located at 0.5, 3.0 and 4.5 miles below the put-in should be scouted and possibly portaged--most easily on the left. The first drop is a nasty chute that plunges directly into a wall from a perched pool trapped by several very large boulders. The second drop occurs at a constriction as the river bends right away from a 20-ft vertical wall on river left. The last of the major drops is a ledge that extends across the full width of the river, with a reversal along the foot of the ledge. This last rapids can be seen on the drive to the put-in; it has not been run.

Shuttle: To reach the put-in and take-out for this run, locate the intersection of Oregon 226 and Thomas Creek Road, 9.2 miles northeast of Scio. Proceed 4.6 miles up Thomas Creek Road to a log bridge, the take-out. To reach the put-in, continue east along the north side of the river. Turn left (north) at an intersection 2.3 miles above the take-out and 100 yards downstream of another bridge. This could be an alternate take-out for a shorter run. From this intersection the road ascends the north side of the river valley and temporarily leaves the river. Stay right at all intersections until reaching the ridge top intersection, 5.2 miles from the take-out, and stay left at this intersection. Make an immediate right at the next intersection, 5.4 miles above the take-out. Descend to the river, pass the first two intersections, and turn right on one of the short access roads 6 to 7 miles above the take-out, or continue on until the road ends just below Hall Creek, which joins Thomas Creek from the south.

Gauge: A high run-off is crucial to running this small, scenic stream. The water level is easily determined from the old Jordan power dam, located where a bridge crosses Thomas Creek 8.2 miles northeast of Scio along Oregon 226. Water flowing over the top of the unbroken section of the dam indicates a water level sufficient to run the upper section of Thomas Creek.

THOMAS CREEK
Log Bridge to Hannah Bridge
Mark Hower

Class	Flow	Gradient	Miles	Character	Season
2 + T	500	40 PD	7	forest	rainy
(P)				logging	

Description: From the log bridge at the put-in, the river moves right along. There are some rather steep rocky drops, but no blind drops as in the upper section. The rapids seen from Oregon 226 between Hannah bridge and Jordan bridge are typical of the difficulty of this section. The mean river gradient is actually closer to 30 feet per mile for most of the river run; however, there are two areas where the drop is much steeper. Between miles 3 and 4 above Jordan, the river drops 100 ft, but with uniformity. And at the Jordan Dam, which should be portaged, the drop is about 15 ft.

Difficulties: The old Jordan Power Dam and its chute should be portaged. Along several of the banks at low water, the main current sweeps under the brush. This section would undoubtedly become class 3 at higher flows.

Shuttle: For put-in, see the upper Thomas take-out. Hannah bridge, described in the next section, is the take-out.

Gauge: Unknown. Judge it for yourself at the rapids along Oregon 226, between Hannah and Jordan bridges.

THOMAS CREEK
Hannah Bridge to Gilkey Bridge
Rob Blickensderfer and Mark Hower

Class	Flow	Gradient	Miles	Character	Season
1 + T	400	15 C	10	wooded	rainy
	1500			agricultural	
				houses	

Description: This run passes beneath a covered bridge and ends at a covered bridge. The narrowness of the stream bed as it drops near rocky banks or trees makes the run technically challenging for open canoes. Although it passes quite a few houses and goes through the town of Scio, the general feeling is one of isolation and intimacy with a wooded stream.

Access at the Hannah bridge put-in is on either side of the river. The first 3 miles to the concrete bridge on Oregon 226 are the steepest. This part resembles the section just upstream, from Jordan bridge to Hannah bridge. There are no named rapids, but numerous short drops. Below the concrete bridge on Oregon 226 (an alternate put-in), the stream flattens somewhat, although some careful maneuvering is still required at low water, and some waves develop at high water.

About midway between the concrete bridge and the town of Scio the stream appears to run under a large red barn. This is Shimanek covered bridge, 130 ft long, on Richardson's Gap Road. The approach to Scio is heralded by a drop over a small ledge followed by a sharp right turn. This spot is easily seen from the road. Below Scio the stream becomes broader and slower for the last 3 miles to the take-out at Gilkey covered bridge, on river right.

Difficulties: The stream is very simple for experienced kayakers but could prove too tricky for novice kayakers. It is relatively technical but not very dynamic for experienced open canoeists. The first 3 miles are much more difficult than the small ledge drop that can be seen from the road in Scio. For comparison, this section is more technically difficult than the main Alsea River.

Shuttle: The put-in is at Hannah bridge just off Oregon 226 on Camp Morrison Drive, 6.5 miles east of Scio. An alternate put-in is the concrete bridge on Oregon 226, 3.5 miles east of Scio. The take-out is at Gilkey covered bridge. From Scio take Oregon 226, 0.5 mile south of the downtown bridge over Thomas Creek. Take Gilkey Road west, follow the zigzags for 3.2 miles, cross a railroad track, stop at the T-intersection, turn right and you will see Gilkey covered bridge. The take-out is between the covered bridge and the railroad bridge on river right. The take-out can also be reached by county roads from Crabtree or Jefferson. An alternate take-out is about 4 miles below Gilkey Bridge, where the river comes close to the road from Crabtree.

Gauge: None. Unregulated.

NORTH SANTIAM RIVER
Whispering Falls Campground to Detroit Reservoir
Laurie Pavey

Class	Flow	Gradient	Miles	Character	Season
3	1300	67 C	6	forest	rainy
3 +	1700 +				snowmelt

Description: The North Santiam River has its headwaters in the Mount Jefferson Wilderness. This upper stretch of the river is usually runnable when the snow begins to melt (usually in late March or early April) and continues its season until late spring. It may also be runnable after several days of hard rain during the fall or winter. It is not uncommon to tramp through snowfields at the put-in area. The water is always very cold.

On the river, boaters will find a continuous gradient that offers constant action all the way through the run. Play-spots are abundant. At 1700 cfs the river is not very technical; however, the drops demand good boat control and a strong brace and roll. Eddies are small. At 1300 cfs the drops become more technical but eddies are more numerous. On a clear day spectacular views of Mount Jefferson reward boaters who turn around and look upstream.

The first 3 miles of the river are class 2 + to 3 at 1700 cfs and class 2 + at 1300 cfs. After the first bridge, which is about halfway through the run, the river becomes class 3 + at 1700 cfs (class 3 at 1300 cfs) with some significant drops and pushy water. All the rapids can be scouted from the river by eddy-hopping. The road is always nearby on river right, but it never seems obtrusive. Some of the best rapids occur as one passes several lumber mills, but the paddling and playing along this stretch is so much fun that one barely even notices them.

When the reservoir is low, the final rapids, a steep class 5, is uncovered. Be sure and scout these rapids at the take-out. It is possible to take out above them; they were not run by the author.

Difficulties: Cold water and the final class 5 rapids.

Shuttle: To reach the take-out drive up Oregon 22 to the headwaters of Detroit Lake. Look for a log scaling station on the right. Turn right off the highway here and drive downstream on a dirt road for about 200 yards to the road's end. The put-in is found by returning to the highway and driving upstream 6 miles to Whispering Falls Campground. At this writing (Spring, 1985) there were several sweepers and logs crossing the river above Whispering Falls, which demand portages.

Gauge: Contact Detroit Dam and ask for the flow of the North Santiam River coming into the reservoir. The author has run this stretch only at 1300 and 1700 cfs. The lower limit for boating is judged to be 1300 cfs. Somewhat higher flows than 1700 cfs would probably also be runnable, but may increase the difficulty.

NORTH SANTIAM RIVER
Big Cliff Dam to Packsaddle Park
George Ice

Class	Flow	Gradient	Miles	Character	Season
3(5) P	2000-3200	26 PD	5	forest	all year

Description: The North Santiam River is regulated by Detroit and Big Cliff Dams above Gates. However, these are not the first attempts to harness the North Santiam. In the early 1890's two brothers, Edward and Frank O'Neil, and an associate, C.W. Callagahan, planned to build a mill to make paper from straw. The site of the mill was originally set at the small town of Niagara, where a natural formation constricted the flow of the North Santiam to a channel only 4.5 feet wide at certain flows. Niagara was a stop on the Corvallis and Eastern Railroad, which snaked from Yaquina Bay to the Willamette Valley and up the canyons of the North Santiam past Detroit.

The O'Neils and Callagahan began construction of a rubble-masonry dam to provide power for the mill. However, the construction proved difficult. The narrow channel was scoured by extremely rapid flows and the undercut rock formation was difficult to plug. After spending $37,000 they decided to relocate the mill in the town of Lebanon. In 1909, Byllesby and Co. leased the site and spent $65,000 to redevelop and expand the Niagara Project. Again the river won and by 1912 attempts to tame the North Santiam at Niagara ended.

At the turn of the century, the community of Niagara consisted of a tavern, a hotel, a store, and several homes. It also claimed the nation's smallest post office (6X8 feet). With the lost dreams of the railroad, paper mill, and dam, the town of Niagara faded into history. Today there is nothing left of the town. The masonry dam remains at Niagara State Park. A half century after the last attempt to build the dam at Niagara, the North Santiam was finally tamed with the construction of Detroit Dam.

The numerous class 2, and several class 3 and 4 rapids make the Niagara run a fun and exciting stretch of whitewater. The two named rapids in this stretch are the Narrows and Niagara. The Narrows, about 0.8 mile downstream from the put-in is preceded by a class 3 rapids which turns to the left. At the bottom of this entry rapids is a large eddy on the right. The current continues on the left side and funnels into the Narrows, a 100-yard-long constriction with a large drop. The upper section has a large wave across it, followed by a diagonal hole, very turbulent water and a good pool at the bottom. The exposed rocks are covered at higher water. At low discharges, experts report that this rapids should be portaged. Scout this one before running.

Niagara is a twisting class 5 drop at Niagara State Park. The entrance, at which the river squeezes to a width of merely 4.5 feet, is followed by a swirling pool that leads into a turbulent snake of water and a drop into a huge, potentially dangerous eddy. The first time this rapids was attempted by a group of WKCC boaters there was a log caught in the eddy below the slot. Boaters had to time their approach as the log circled, so that the slot would be clear. The swirling pool leads into a turbulent snake of water that finishes with a drop and extremely dangerous eddy. Niagara is a sharp S-turn with violent waves and dangerous undercurrents. Boaters should be prepared for a difficult rescue if a kayaker is out of his boat. A description of the first WKCC run follows:

NORTH SANTIAM   *The Swirlies*   *Lance Stein*

"On June 1, 1975, Gene and George Ice, Bob Porter, Jim Henderson, and Jim Brumelsey ran through Niagara Park at 3200 cfs. In running the S-turn and drop both George Ice and Bob Porter rolled and Jim Brumelsey was forced out of his boat. Below the last drop Jim was caught in a large and violent eddy from which he was unable to escape. The eddy repeatedly circulated Jim into the hole at the bottom of the rapids and into the sucking eddyline. Even with the lifejacket, Jim was underwater much of the time in the highly aerated froth. Jim was rescued when Jim Henderson threw him a lifeline that Bob Porter brought along on the trip. Without the line Jim Brumelsey may not have escaped the hole."

While the Narrows may become more runnable at larger flows, Niagara becomes more difficult, and the eddy and drop at the bottom keep building. There are several other memorable rapids and features in this stretch. Just above Niagara is a major rapid which can have some very large holes. Below Niagara, ender holes can be found at some discharges. About 2 miles below Niagara is Packsaddle Dam. The dam is a 12-ft slide which is used to divert salmon and steelhead for capture to supply eggs for fish hatcheries. The reversal at the bottom is dangerous, and reinforcing irons are embedded at the bottom. THIS IS A PORTAGE. DO NOT RISK IT! Portage on the right. Just a couple hundred feet below the dam is Packsaddle County Park on the right.

Difficulties: The Narrows and Niagara are technically demanding rapids. See details above. Portage around Packsaddle Dam.

Shuttle: The take-out at Packsaddle County Park is about 3 miles east of Gates on Oregon 22. Proceed to the put-in at Big Cliff Dam about 5 miles east on 22. Stop at Niagara Park to scout Niagara. About 1 mile east of Niagara there is an abandoned gas station on the left. The Narrows is found by scouting down the bank opposite this.

Gauge: Contact the River Forecast Center in Portland or Detroit Dam for flow information.

NORTH SANTIAM RIVER
Packsaddle Park to Mill City
George Ice

Class	Flow	Gradient	Miles	Character	Season
2 + (3)	750-2500	27 PD	7	forest houses	all year
3	2500-4500 and up				R44500-

Description: Packsaddle Park to Mill City is one of the more popular boating trips in Oregon. Riffles immediately below the put-in can be used to warm up. Turning the corner, the riffles lead into a small rapids. On the lower right side is a nice mild surfing wave. Following a pool is a class 2 rapids which has plenty of small holes. This rapids leads into a narrow chute which has narrow eddies on both sides and can be very turbulent at certain flows.

The next rapids finishes with an excellent play-spot, sometimes referred to as the Swirlies. On the left is a large rock formation preceded by a nice eddy and followed by another on the lower left. On the right is an enormous eddy. The waves and eddies at this spot make excellent surfing. The expert boater will surf across from the right eddy to the upper left eddy. Pop-ups and enders can sometimes be done by stalling out on the wave at the top of the rock formation. The flow below this spot is extremely turbulent with small whirlpools and collapsing swirls. This rapids is an excellent and difficult practice site for the ol' river roll.

The next play-spot is two enters rapids downstream where the river narrows and turns to the right. Waves above and below a rock on the far right of the channel can be surfed.

After passing under the bridge at Gates, a series of mild rapids begins. At low discharges, the riffle 0.2 mile below the Gates bridge is rocky. The best spot to run this rapids is usually on the left. This riffle can be identified by the tall sheer banks on the outside of the turn.

Spencer's Hole is one of the famous rapids on this river. At Spencer's the river is constricted by rocks on both sides (except at very high flows). On the river, however, a boater first runs into Fake Spencer's, a rapids which looks (from above) similar to Spencer's Hole. An eighth of a mile below Fake Spencer's is the true Spencer's Hole which can be easily scouted (and portaged, if desired). At low flows it has an exposed rock in the middle of the drop; at higher flows a hole develops behind the rock. The preferred route on the right side of the drop is guarded by a hole which can be punched. At very high flows a wave can develop which breaks from the right and acts as a pancake flipper. One covey of 12 kayakers had 10 flipped here. There is a pool below this drop. Occasionally kayakers take out here. A short, steep trail leads to a road which goes to Gates.

About 0.2 mile below Spencer's Hole is Carnivore, hidden on the left side of an island. Jim Oliver named this small, twisting, frothy beast when it was hungry and "ate" him.

There are several mild rapids and play-spots between Carnivore and Mill City. A nice rapids which improves dramatically at higher water with bigger waves is located just where the river nears Mill City. Mill City Falls is usually scouted before the trip begins by walking out on the car bridge. If this was forgotten, one can sneak up on the left side to look over the drop. The middle-left of the drop usually has a clear chute, and there is a favorite slot on the far right.

Difficulties: Spencer's Hole and Mill City Falls should be approached with caution. See Description.
Shuttle: The put-in is at Packsaddle County Park about 3 miles east of Gates on Oregon 22. There are several options for taking out. The easiest is just above Mill City Falls. It is reached by driving through the paved parking lot at the north end of the bridge at Mill City and continuing along a short dirt road to a turnaround. This is a hundred feet from the big eddy above the falls. Taking out at the base of the falls is possible but involves a difficult scramble. Drift boats that have run the falls can continue on to Fishermen's Bend Park, about 1.5 miles west of Mill City and find a spot to park and take out. About 0.2 mile below Mill City kayaks may take out at a wide place in the road.
Gauge: The flow may be obtained from Detroit Dam or the River Forecast Center in Portland. The run, usually considered one of the backyard runs of Corvallis and Portland, can change drastically with high winter flow. At 10,000 cfs, the maximum winter discharge desired by Big Cliff Dam, the current and rapids on the river require expert paddling. Summer levels of about 1,000 cfs are less demanding. A flow of about 3,000 cfs is optimal for playing.

NORTH SANTIAM RIVER
Mill City to Mehama
George Ice

Class	Flow	Gradient	Miles	Character	Season
2	1000-3000	23 PD	7.5	wooded houses	all year
3	3000-10000				

Description: A short pleasant intermediate trip is found below Mill City. The rapids are less demanding than those upstream, but should still be respected. Several broken dories, canoes, and kayaks have been observed along this stretch. The rapids tend to become rocky at flows below 1500 cfs.

Several rapids have standing waves which can be surfed even at 1100 cfs. A favorite play-spot is at North Santiam Park, which is 2 miles below Fishermen's Bend. A small ledge on the right provides boaters with a good place to practice surfing, S-turns and rolls.

About 0.5 mile above the take-out the Little North Santiam River enters from the right. As the Lyons-Mehama Bridge comes into sight, the river splits. The left channel has a nice wave for one last fling at surfing. The right channel is also runnable, with the current plowing into a low wall to produce a nice quick turn.
Difficulties: The Mill City Falls should be approached with caution. See the description in the Packsaddle to Mill City Section.
Shuttle: There are several optional put-ins for this stretch, including Mill City and Fishermen's Bend State Park. See Shuttle for the take-outs of the Packsaddle to Mill City run. Fishermen's Bend provides restrooms and a spot for launching dories. Unfortunately, this put-in is only open in late spring and summer. The take-out is under the bridge on Oregon 262, between Lyons and Mehama. This is about 0.5 mile south of the junction of Oregon 22 and 262. The take-out is reached from the southwest corner of the bridge.
Gauge: The flow can be obtained from Detroit Dam or the River Forecast Center in Portland.

NORTH SANTIAM RIVER
Mehama to Stayton
George Ice

Class	Flow	Gradient	Miles	Character	Season
2- P	1000-2000	20 C	9	agriculture	all year

Description: The coniferous forests found along the upper reaches of the North Santiam gradually shift to foothill and farmland vegetation along this section. After about 0.2 mile of smooth water below the put-in, the river begins a series of mild rapids. Rocks can be avoided even at 1000 cfs. Following these rapids is a nice play-spot on the left known as Beginner's Hole. Houses high on the right bank identify the spot. In low water boaters can surf across this current and into eddies on either side. Nose stands can be accomplished at some water levels. Watch out for snags in the river below this play-spot.

A particularly troublesome chute for beginners occurs just before a group of three power lines comes into view. The chute flows directly into the bank, moving from the left to the right. Boaters attempting to avoid the bank and brush are often flipped in the strong, swirling eddy on the inside of the turn. Watch out!

Another 0.2 mile below this power line is the largest drop on this stretch. At 1100 cfs, the drop should be run on the far left. At higher discharges, the drop can be run on either the far left or middle left. Below this drop is the traditional lunch stop on the right bank. In the summer and fall wild blackberries can be added to the lunch menu.

Below the lunch stop are a number of class 1 rapids and riffles. Following a mild rapids, farmland fringed by birdboxes can be seen on the left bank. The river is split below the birdboxes by a small dam and fishladder. The trip continues in the left channel below the dam, so a portage is required. At 1100 cfs boaters can paddle to the far right of the dam and carry over it. At higher flows boaters should take out on the levee at the right of the dam. Salmon and steelhead can sometimes be seen jumping in the fishladder or up the dam.

The rapids below the dam is rocky and swift. At low flows a boat can easily become bridged and damaged. The route is straight down the middle. Beyond this, the river becomes much more rocky and shallow. A few of the rapids have current moving into brush. Several other rapids are shallow enough that even expert navigators may not avoid scraping rocks.

Difficulties: Portage around the fish dam. See above.

Shuttle: The put-in is a boat landing located beneath the bridge that connects Mehama to Lyons, just off Oregon 22 on Oregon 262. During the summer this popular boat landing can be very congested with fishermen, boaters, and drifters. The shuttle is along Oregon 22. The take-out is under the bridge which crosses the North Santiam in Stayton.

Gauge: Contact Detroit Dam or the River Forecast Center to obtain flow information.

NORTH SANTIAM RIVER
Stayton to Jefferson
John Westall

Class	Flow	Gradient	Miles	Character	Season
1 +	1200	17 C	19	rural	all year

Description: Below Stayton, the North Santiam flattens out and winds its way through farmland and stands of alders and cottonwoods. The scenery is very pleasant: wide gravelbars lined with trees, with almost no buildings in sight. At low water the banks could be characterized as class 1 continuous lunch spots. There is no real whitewater on this run, but a number of sharp turns, a few snags, and some turbulent water require boaters to pay attention. The relatively flat water and high frequency of eddies along the shore makes this stretch excellent for beginning canoers and kayakers who can control their crafts.

The current is continuous through this run except for a long pool beginning about 2 miles above Jefferson. About 7 miles below the put-in the river splits and winds through many channels around a number of islands. The main channel is completely open (Spring, 1985), but this stretch has a well earned reputation for becoming blocked by sweepers. There is an alternate access to the river at Green's Bridge, 14 miles below the put-in and 5 miles above the take-out. About half-way between Green's Bridge and the take-out, the South Santiam flows in from the left.

Difficulties: None in particular, but be alert for downed trees.

Shuttle: All three accesses to the river on this run are well developed boat ramps. To reach the take-out, take Exit 138 off I-5 and follow Oregon 99E 2.5 miles east to Jefferson. The take-out is about 100 yards downstream of the Oregon 99E bridge, on river right. To reach the put-in, take the road from Jefferson to Scio, which turns south off of Oregon 99E about 200 yards east of the bridge mentioned above. About 2.5 miles east of Jefferson this road crosses Green's Bridge, under which, on river left, is an alternate access to the river. Continue on this road to Scio and then take the road north from Scio to Stayton. The put-in is on the south side of the river below the bridge just south of Stayton.

Gauge: Contact the River Forecast Center in Portland for the North Santiam flow at Mehama. The run begins to get a little bumpy at flows below 1500 cfs.

SANTIAM RIVER
Jefferson to Buena Vista
Carl Landsness

Class	Flow	Gradient	Miles	Character	Season
1	1000 +	6 C	11	pastoral hills	all year

Description: This stretch sees surprisingly little use relative to its more popular neighbors, the Willamette, and the upper forks of the Santiam. Gravel bars and the absence of houses provide scenery and solitude within a heavily farmed region. The wide and open nature of the river offers pleasant views of the surrounding hills.

Difficulties: At low flows, be alert for snags.

Shuttle: Put in at a public boat ramp in Jefferson at the base of Ferry Street. An alternate put-in is Green's Bridge public boat landing, approximately 5 miles upstream and 3 miles east of Jefferson on the road to Scio. (See previous description.) The take-out is at the Buena Vista ferry on the Willamette River, about 2 miles past the Santiam confluence. The ferry closes at 5 pm, so judge accordingly if you plan to use it. It also closes occasionally in the winter when the water gets high.

Gauge: This section is runnable all year. Flows for the Santiam at Jefferson may be obtained from the River Forecast Center in Portland.

BREITENBUSH RIVER
Cleator Bend Campground to Detroit Lake
Rich Brainerd

Class	Flow	Gradient	Miles	Character	Season
4 T	800- 2000	80 PD	9	forest canyon	rainy snowmelt

Description: The Breitenbush starts from the crest of the Cascades north of Mount Jefferson and is one of the major tributaries to the North Santiam River. This run is typical of Cascade rivers with high gradient, crystal clear water and steep forested banks. The run requires technical maneuvering and a reliable roll. The Breitenbush has a short season, during the spring snowmelt or after a heavy fall rain. For most of the winter the road and ground are covered with snow. This stretch can be divided into two sections; Cleator Campground to the road bridge and the road bridge to the lake.

The upper section has tight and technical rapids, with many class 3 drops. There are short pools between the rapids and many side eddies. Chutes are narrow, twisting, swift and deep. More than half of the significant drops cannot be seen from the road, but all can be scouted from the river, except Barbell. There are several blind corners which should be scouted for logs by at least one member of the party.

Near the bridge the geology changes; the river becomes broader with frequent stretches of flat bedrock on the bottom. The river volume and velocity increase significantly with the entrance of Humbug Creek, 1 mile above the bridge. There is one class 4 drop and numerous class 3 gems on this lower section. The gauge is 2.3 miles below the bridge and marks the end of the difficult rapids. When the reservoir is full, the lake reaches to just above the small unnamed Forest Service campground, 0.5 mile below the gauge. When the reservoir is low the rapids continue past the town of Detroit.

Difficulties: This run is rated as a class 4 because the drops are so closely spaced and require technical precision to run, although the individual drops are 2's and 3's. It might be said that the whole is greater than the sum of its parts. The pools are short and the route is often not apparent until the boater is almost at the brink of a drop, and sometimes not even visible then; thus the necessity of the scout. This river requires a class 4 level of concentration and quick reactions. A quick reliable roll is mandatory.

The author has run the first 0.9 miles below Cleator Campground only once, because two portages are required around large logs. For other runs he has opted to avoid the portages by putting in just below The Slot, down a steep trail from a very small roadside rock quarry. Logs are always a threat, especially in the narrower upper section, so scout all blind drops!

In the lower section, below the main road bridge, there are two drops that demand attention. Barbell Rapids should be scouted (not without difficulty) on the drive upriver, 2.4 miles above Detroit, since it is even more difficult to scout from the river. It is a complex, pushy, class 4 boulder garden, dominated by a huge barbell-shaped rock that lies parallel to the current, in the middle of the river.

Half a mile below Barbell is Woo-Man-Chew, a 5-ft waterfall into a deep pool. Scout on the left by landing at the low concrete structure. This drop can be seen at a distance by looking downstream from the road.

Shuttle: From the town of Detroit on Oregon 22 at the east end of Detroit Lake, take USFS 46 east along the Breitenbush. The take-out is at the marina in Detroit, or preferably at a Forest Service campground 0.5 miles upstream.

Many put-ins are possible: the main road bridge 3.3 miles above Detroit; a dirt logging road that goes to the river 5.4 miles above Detroit; or a small quarry 8.1 miles above Detroit, where one can park on the left and put in down a steep bank just below The Slot Rapids. If there is sufficient water and no logs, the easiest put-in is at Cleator Campground, 9 miles above Detroit.

Gauge: Contact the Detroit Dam for the flow on the Breitenbush. The gauge is read at 6 am daily. Optimal flow is estimated at 1000 to 1200 cfs.

LITTLE NORTH SANTIAM RIVER
Elkhorn Valley Campground to North Santiam River
Mick Evans

Class	Flow	Gradient	Miles	Character	Season
2(3)T	750-	39 PD	10	forest	rainy
(P)	2500			canyon	snowmelt

Description: The Little North Santiam is a secluded fast flowing river whose headwaters originate in one of the last true wilderness areas of Oregon. Although many cabins lie along the lower part of this run, the road appears only occasionally and due to the lack of public access and other boaters there is a real feeling of isolation on this river.

Before putting in at Elkhorn Valley Campground, walk down and scout the class 3 drop visible from the campground road. This drop may be run on the right at most flows. Three miles downstream is a concrete bridge which is another possible put-in.

There are some minor rapids until 1 mile downstream of the bridge where the river narrows and drops to the right. Just below the drop is a large rock wall extending almost to the left bank which creates a large S-turn. This is easy in low water but formidable in flood.

Just downstream and around the corner is the most difficult rapids on the run. This rapids is affectionately known as Troll's Teeth. As the name suggests, this is a rock garden at lower water levels, and a mass of holes and keepers to eat you in flood. Approach cautiously and stop to scout on the left before the river disappears between several large rocks. A very large tree was found blocking the channel in the lower half of the drop (December, 1985); a portage is strongly advised. Portage if necessary along the left bank and put in about 100 yards downstream in a large pool.

The remainder of the rapids on this run are quite straightforward and can be boated without scouting by an experienced boater. A particularly long and enjoyable section of rapids at the Little North Fork County Park is preceded by a large curving undercut cliff on the left followed by a nice play-spot with a fast V with green waves and generous eddies.

Downstream you'll pass under a bridge. The next rapids deserves some attention. The river narrows to the left and drops sharply. The drop is straightforward except for a protruding rock to the left of the chute. Scout the rest of the drop from a large eddy on the left. The rest of this run bounces pleasantly along until meeting the North Santiam (turn right here, please!). Just before reaching the Mehama Bridge, go to the right for the more exciting chute around a large island. The left channel will take you through a few large haystacks before the take-out at the boat ramp under the bridge.

Difficulties: Everyone, regardless of experience, should scout Troll's Teeth. Logs and debris from floods frequently plug the channels.

Shuttle: The river is about 18 miles northeast of Salem on Oregon 22. To reach the put-in, turn left at the flashing light 0.7 mile east of Mehama. The boater can put in at Elkhorn Valley Campground or at a concrete bridge over the river at miles 9 and 6, respectively, from the turn-off. Take-outs include Little North Fork Park and the boat ramp under the Lyons-Mehama bridge over the North Santiam.

To miss the more difficult rapids on the upper run, put in at the Little North Fork Park or better yet, at a bend in the river 1.2 miles above the park. There is an easy trail to the river and some good water before the put-in in the park.

Gauge: Several days of hard rain or warm winter weather are needed to produce an acceptable flow for boating. A good spot to check this flow is at the bridge on Oregon 22 over the Little North Santiam, 0.8 miles east of Mehama. Look downstream, the visible rapids will indicate the condition of the shallowest rapids of the run. Also look at where the concrete arch connects with the pillar on the downstream side of the bridge. The water should at least reach the bottom of the concrete.

There is also a gauge on this river. Contact the River Forecast Center in Portland to obtain the flow. If there's not enough water to run the Little North Santiam, the North Santiam, which is just a stone's throw away, is always boatable.

Chapter 8. Lower Willamette Valley and Columbia Gorge Drainages

ABIQUA CREEK
Abiqua Falls to Abiqua Road
Hank Hays

Class	Flow	Gradient	Miles	Character	Season
2(3)	400+	80 C	7	forest houses	rainy

Description: Abiqua Creek is in the watershed between Butte Creek on the North and Silver Creek to the south. All are tributaries of the Pudding River, which flows into the Molalla just before the latter reaches the Willamette. Abiqua Creek's gradient and drainage area are similar to both sister streams, but it doesn't have as much action as either of them. The gradient is fairly constant with some pool-drop. Most rapids are rock gardens.

Above the recommended put-in, Abiqua Falls plunges over a 75-ft sheer drop into a pool. The gradient above the falls is steeper, up to 200 feet per mile, but there isn't a put-in far enough upstream to make the portage around the falls worthwhile. Walking around the falls would involve a carry up to the road then down the trail at the recommended put-in. About 1.8 miles below the recommended take-out (between mileposts 8 and 9), there's a dam that would be difficult to portage, mainly because of steep banks with barbed wire fences at the top.

The first 1.5 miles of this run is class 2 with a few strategically placed sweepers to liven things up. The first class 3, Hank's Mistake, has a large padded boulder near the bottom center. At the recommended flows, far right is advised as left of the rock is a narrow channel with a nasty, boiling eddy. The current pushes left, all the way from the top, and going right of the boulder at the bottom is easier said than done. There are some nice holes and wave action just after the next island.

A mile later is Pink Bridge Rapids. Pinky is a long boulder garden with a left bend half-way through, where the bridge comes into view. The left side should be clean, but a quick scout for logs by at least one of the party is prudent. From here down, cabins and homes are occasionally seen, rapids diminish, and in one place the left bank consists of a huge pile of sawdust.

Difficulties: Getting to the put-in is probably the hardest part of the run. On the river, Hank's Mistake and Pink Bridge Rapids are the most difficult between the recommended put-in and take-out.

Shuttle: On Oregon 213, about 3 miles north of Silverton, is a blinking yellow light at Abiqua Road NE. Take Abiqua Road NE east about 6.25 miles to a concrete bridge over Abiqua Creek. Just upstream is a rocky turnout which makes a good parking spot. To get to the put-in, continue upstream another mile to the end of the pavement at a green steel bridge. Proceed 2 miles from the green bridge, keeping right where the main gravel road swings left. In about another 0.2 miles, several driveways take off in all directions. Go straight on through on whatever looks like the main road. This is where the road gets bad. Three and one-half miles later, after a bone-jarring, oil-pan-crunching ride, is a grassy pull-out on the right. From here a well defined hiking trail takes off upstream, ending at the base of the falls in less than 0.5 mile. There are two short steep sections in the 0.25 mile down to the creek. You can continue up the road for a bit to the top of the falls, but the trails to it aren't as easy to find.

Gauge: None, but if you don't mind the rockiness of the boulder garden at the take-out, go ahead and try the run.

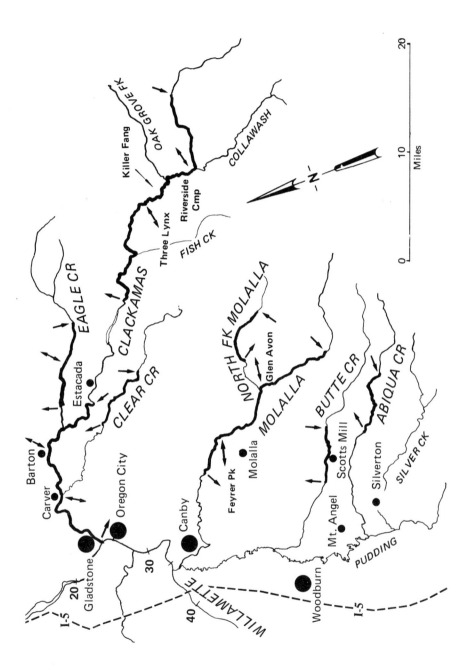

BUTTE CREEK
Fault Line to Oregon 213
Andreas Mueller

Class	Flow	Gradient	Miles	Character	Season
3(4-)T (P)	200- 800	60 PD	7.5	forest	rainy

Description: This section of Butte Creek flows through scenic forested mountain foothills that are in abrupt contrast to the rural countryside found near Mount Angel and Woodburn. It has considerable variety for a small stream: ledge drops, a few slots, S-curves, rock gardens, a gorge, one slide, a couple of log limbos, and two dams. An alternate take-out at the park in Scotts Mills shortens the trip by two miles.

Difficulties: A 5-ft drop on river right, which can be scouted by looking upstream from a green steel bridge one mile below the put-in, is a nose cruncher at low water. At higher water the drop is less of a problem, but a log directly below the bridge requires a difficult limbo. The local property owners let boaters walk this drop over their land on the left; in turn boaters leave their summer swimming hole log in place.

One mile below the bridge is a difficult rapid that should be scouted from the right bank. The rock garden at the top is taken on the right. The water immediately picks up speed, forms two large river-wide waves, funnels down to 20 ft in width, goes over a 4-ft drop, and bashes onto a rock on the right; stay left. The rock garden below is run anywhere at higher water. At low water the best route is down the left. Boaters who choose to walk these two sections should stay on the creek bank so that the property owners are not disturbed.

Two miles above Scotts Mills is a tight S-turn that goes left, then right, with a rock splitting the top channel. Stay to the left of the right channel and maintain a straight line course, ducking under a log at the bottom. Otherwise, portage on the right. Scotts Mills pond is a good take-out if boaters want a short run. The dam is a mandatory portage. The fish run is class 3 as is, but would only be a class 2 if all the brambles hanging overhead were eliminated.

A rapids with numerous large holes can be scouted by looking upstream from the Scotts Mills bridge. Midway between the Scotts Mills bridge and Oregon 213 is a second dam with a ramp on the left which makes an abrupt right turn. Here the water running down smashes head-on into a raised ledge before connecting with the main channel. Those who feel they must run the ramp should intentionally miss the right turn, run the ramp sideways while keeping the bow pointed downstream, and high brace at the bottom off the ledge. Otherwise, walk around on the left.

Shuttle: The take-out is at Jack's Bridge 1.4 miles southwest of Marquam on Oregon 213, or in the park at Scotts Mills. From there to the put-in drive 0.1 mile north of Scotts Mills bridge to Maple Grove Road, which runs east. Butte Creek Road angles off to the right 0.1 miles later. Follow it 4.5 miles to a turnoff on the right by some houses. This road crosses a brook and looks down on Butte Creek after 0.5 mile. Put in down the embankment by throw rope just below the "San Andreas Fault." The local residents prefer that scouting be done from the creek rather than from the road.

Gauge: Check the reading at the Monitor bridge gauge on the way to the river. A 5.5 ft reading on the bridge's downstream west bank side is a minimum flow. Also have a look upstream from the Scotts Mills bridge. If these rocks are slippery enough, the others upstream should also be wet. Usually 3 days of rain will fill the creek to a fair level.

MOLALLA RIVER
Introduction by Rob Blickensderfer

The Molalla River flows from the western slopes of the Cascade Mountains into the Willamette River. It drains the area between the North Santiam and Clackamas Rivers. The upper river flows through a steep valley with some fascinating slots through columnar basalt. As the river enters the Willamette Valley, the gradient decreases and rapids give way to gravel riffles. Many steelhead fishermen occupy this river in the winter, so be prepared to yield to their fishing holes.

MOLALLA RIVER
Nine Miles above Glen Avon to Glen Avon
Rob Blickensderfer

Class	Flow	Gradient	Miles	Character	Season
3 T	800	55 C	9	forest	rainy
4	2000			canyon	

Description: At the minimum flow of about 600 cfs, this section is a technical class 3; at higher flows it is a more enjoyable class 3; and at high water it becomes fairly difficult.

For the first mile or so below the put-in, the water is fast but fairly straightforward. At Shotgun Creek, where the creek shoots out of a rock high up on the cliff on river left, the action begins. In the next few miles, the rapids are close together and fairly steep. There are several 3-4 steep drops that can be seen from the road on the way to the put-in. When running the rapids, some eddy-hopping will be necessary to pick the correct route. Many of the run-outs are riffles leading to the next rapids.

Columnar Rapids, about 2 miles below the put-in, is the largest rapids. It leads into a fantastically picturesque gorge with moss-laden columnar basalt twisted into weird and wonderful shapes. Just below Columnar Rapids, the gorge is only 14 ft wide in places, and the water is deep, slow, and eerie. The gorge alone makes the trip worthwhile. In the second half of this section, numerous shallow boulder fields occur at 600 cfs, and the routes are not easily discernible. About 0.2 mile above the bridge at Glen Avon, the relatively small North Fork Molalla enters from the right. Take out on the right between the North Fork and the bridge.

Difficulties: The longest and most difficult rapids, Columnar Rapids, leading into the columnar basalt gorge, is about 2 miles below the put-in. It becomes solid class 4 at high water and can be clearly seen from the road on the cliff above. One long rapids, not seen from the road and about a mile from the take-out, has a sharp right turn at the bottom. Before becoming committed to any of the rapids, be alert for logs.

Shuttle: Go to the community of Glen Avon, where a concrete bridge crosses the river. To get to Glen Avon, see the following river description. Access to the river for a take-out is poor because of the steep banks. One possible take-out is about 0.1 mile upstream of the bridge, on the northeast side of the river. To get to the put-in, cross the bridge to the southwest side of the river and continue upstream. About 9 miles up, the road crosses the river, and a little farther up a pullout on the right gives good access.

Gauge: The flow is near the minimum runnable level when the gauge on the bridge pier at Feyrer Park reads 2.6 ft. At this level the flow in the upper section is estimated as 600 cfs. The most enjoyable level occurs at a gauge reading of about 3.4 ft. The flow is unregulated.

MOLALLA RIVER
Glen Avon to Feyrer Park
Rob Blickensderfer

Class	Flow	Gradient	Miles	Character	Season
2	1000-2000	30 PD	6	agriculture rural	rainy

Description: Several straightforward class 2 rapids and good play-spots alternate with class 1 stretches of fast water. The water is more interesting and not nearly as flat as it appears from the road on the way up to the put-in. Several attractive houses are visible from the river. About 4 miles below the put-in, a private bridge crosses the river. The take-out is at the next bridge at Feyrer Park, on the left. Depending upon the skill and mood, this short section could be combined with the section either above or below.

Difficulties: All of the largest rapids, class 2, occur in the upper half of the run. The waves can be relatively large, but the rapids are straight forward.

Shuttle: To get to the put-in, first go to the take-out at Feyrer Park. From Feyrer Park, (see next description) cross the bridge and drive upstream on the paved road on the east side of the river. About 5 miles up, in the community of Glen Avon, a road to the right crosses the river. This bridge is the put-in.

Gauge: The flow is uncontrolled. A gauge level of 2.6 ft on the bridge pier at Feyrer Park means ample water; estimated at 1000 to 1200 cfs.

MOLALLA RIVER
Feyrer Park to Oregon 213 Bridge
Rob Blickensderfer

Class	Flow	Gradient	Miles	Character	Season
1 +	1000-2000	21 C	8	rural	rainy

Description: This is an excellent section to take beginning kayakers on for their second river trip. It is relatively free of brush, has numerous riffles, and enough small rapids and speed to keep the boaters interested. The first bridge, after 2 miles, is the Oregon 211 crossing. The second bridge, after an additional 6 miles is the Oregon 213 crossing. Take out under the bridge on the left.

Difficulties: None in particular.

Shuttle: The put-in at Feyrer Park is about 2 miles southeast of the town of Molalla. From Molalla, follow Oregon 211 east and take the first right to Feyrer Park, as indicated by a sign. The take-out is the Oregon 213 crossing.

Gauge: A gauge level of 2.6 feet on the bridge pier at Feyrer Park means ample water.

NORTH FORK MOLALLA RIVER
Way above Feyrer Park to Above Feyrer Park
Harvey Lee Shapiro

Class	Flow	Gradient	Miles	Character	Season
5- T (P)	300-1200	200 PD	6	gorge logging	rainy

Description: Although the land has been logged in this magnificent canyon, the river has so much action that there is no time to think about it. In places the river is only about two boat lengths wide. It is recommended that this run be made with someone who is familiar with the river since there are many blind turns with technical and congested entrances and exits. The river consists of continuous class 4 + water, two rapids that are usually portaged, and blind turns that require scouting. The wild nature of the cliffs make scouting extremely difficult and time-consuming, if not impossible. The road high on the river left cliff would be difficult to reach if a walk out were necessary.

From the put-in at the bridge it is 0.5 mile to the first portage at a rapids known as Laughing Teeth of Death (LTD). The area around LTD can be scouted from the road on the way to the put-in. Just above LTD is a tricky drop around an island. The channel on the left side of the island has been blocked by a log which cannot be seen from the road. The route on the right side of this island consists of 3 very steep technical drops followed by 3 smaller drops, which are extremely difficult at lower water. Eddy out on the left for the carry around LTD. One may also eddy out on the right, carry to a creek confluence and carefully line boats over to the island. From there one may run the last drop of LTD. It is also possible to line boats down the bank and to put in below LTD.

The hardest rapid on this run is immediately below LTD. The rapid consists of three parts with a pool below. The river then flows between several islands. The main drop is on the left, but unfortunately it is choked with boulders and followed by a log blocking most of the channel.

After two short drops comes a rapid known as the Knotches. This rapid is probably one of the most dangerous drops on any river because it looks innocent from above. It consists of a large undercut rock in the middle of the river. Perfect alignment and momentum are needed to avoid being swept under this middle rock. Fortunately, there is an easy portage on the right. Be sure to eddy out high, especially in high water, since the water is fast and tries to push one into the main channel. The author does not know of anyone running this drop recently, although exciting adventures relating to this drop are told by early paddlers.

Following Knotches are several miles of class 4+ drops with at least three places where the river bends to the right, away from a cliff on the left. All of these have a technical entrance, a big drop, and then lots of action around a blind bend. One should probably run the first of these on the left and the next two right of center.

The river then narrows into a canyon which is about 2 boat lengths wide. The water here is not difficult and the scenery is beautiful. One last big drop appears around a bend to the left. In low water this drop is not particularly significant, but in high water there is a river-wide ledge which can hold an unsuspecting paddler. It can be punched left of center.

The remaining four miles to the main Mollala are runnable, but may be considered anticlimactic after the upper run.

Difficulties: Portage LTD and Knotches as described above.

Shuttle: From Feyrer Park cross the Mollala, turn right and continue upstream. (To get to Feyrer Park, see Mollala River description.) At Dickie Prairie bear right and continue upstream; cross the North Mollala about 6 miles above Feyrer Park. Turn left on the paved road (called Slais Road) shortly beyond the North Mollala river crossing. Continue along this road, past the end of the pavement and a gate and sign welcoming you to Crown-Zellerbach property. About 300 yards beyond this gate, turn left onto a road that crosses the river in a short distance. The take-out is above this bridge.

To get to the put-in, return to the main dirt road and turn left to continue upstream. Take the first road to the left, about 5 miles upstream, and cross the river in about 0.2 mile. Put in here at the bridge or return to the main road 0.5 mile downstream and line your boats down below LTD.

Remember that this is a private road and private property which is owned by Crown-Zellerbach. Log trucks use the road on weekdays.

Gauge: The river is runnable only a few times a year after heavy rains, usually when the Feyrer Park gauge on the Mollala River is between 3.25 and 4.75 ft. The river is probably runnable if the Breitenbush is between 1100 and 1600 cfs. The gauge at Three Lynx on the Clackamas should be 3000 cfs and rising or 4000 cfs and falling.

CLACKAMAS RIVER
Introduction by Hank Hays

The Clackamas system drains over 930 square miles southeast of Portland. With reliable class 2 to 3 + runs, the stretch below Three Lynx Power Station is heavily used. In season, though, there are many miles of water available to capable boaters in search of solitude.

Its proximity to the state's largest population center has lent the watershed the dubious distinction of claiming 109 lives between 1970 and 1980.

The Clackamas, with its deep forested canyon, offers many attractions: scenic sheer cliffs, several relatively undeveloped hot springs, excellent fishing and numerous campgrounds. Estacada is the dividing line between the upper white water runs and the lower Clackamas which is part of the state scenic waterways system.

As is the case with most Cascade rivers, man's attempt to harness the river is significant with 6 existing dams and impoundments and several potential sites listed. However, during the 1964 flood, the Cazadero Dam broke and sent a wave of water down the river, peaking the gauge at the river mouth at 120,000 cfs.

The Clackamas watershed has supported a diversity of uses: area water works, fisheries, power generation, logging, irrigation; and now recreational boating needs to take its place among the necessary services the Clackamas will provide for the future.

CLACKAMAS RIVER
Seven Miles above Collawash to Riverside Campground
Rich Lewis and Hank Hays

Class	Flow	Gradient	Miles	Character	Season
3 +	1600-	77 PD	8	forest	rainy
4	5000			hot springs	snowmelt

Description: Those who have never run a clear rocky stream should make this one of their first. The road parallels the river and if at any point the rocks start jumping in the way too often, a boater can readily take out. This river has 7 miles of very entertaining class 3 rapids. This quick river requires many eddy turns and a constant adjustment of boat angle. This run can be extended up or down the river. By driving upriver one can start on a flatter section and warm up for the rapids below.

There is an added advantage to running this river. Austin Hot Springs are right on the river bank about 2.5 miles above the Collawash confluence. These hot springs are worth stopping for, both when paddling downstream and driving upstream to pick up the shuttle car.

This is a rocky section of river and the clear water often makes the rocks appear to stick out more than they do. If the river looks like there just isn't enough water, there is probably plenty. If the river appears to have plenty of water the trip will be very enjoyable.

Difficulties: There are four rapids that are definitely steeper and harder than the rest of the run. From the road, scout the drop hidden by a big rock monolith about 0.5 mile below the hot springs. This drop (class 4) is easiest to run on the left. The other drops can be scouted from the boat although scouting from the shore is recommended for the less experienced. This section is narrow enough that trees could be a problem. Check before committing yourself.

The first two of the above four rapids are class 3 and present no real problem aside from the current pushing into the bank. The chutes are evident. The third rapids is at the above-mentioned monolith. The last one is a 200 yard long boulder garden (class 3+) with some nice action: waves, holes, and rocks to dodge. This fourth rapids occurs just above the Collawash River confluence. One further difficulty is the Austin Hot Spring. The warm pools tend to lengthen most trips. The main outflow can be very hot (150 Degrees or more) so don't burn yourself.

Shuttle: Oregon 224 east of Estacada runs along the river. The recommended put-in is at a bridge about 7 miles above the mouth of the Collawash. A take-out is possible at the Collawash junction or about one mile downstream at River Bend Campground on the right bank. As the road runs along the river a put-in or take-out can be arranged almost anywhere.

Gauge: Contact the River Forecast Center in Portland for the flow at Three Lynx on the Clackamas. This reading should be at least 1500 cfs.

CLACKAMAS RIVER
Collawash River to Three Lynx Power Station
Roger Van Zandt and Hank Hays

Class	Flow	Gradient	Miles	Character	Season
4(6)	1000-	43 PD	7.5	forest	rainy
P	3000			no road	snowmelt

Description: This secluded and scenic section of the river is also one of the most dangerous. A near perfect roll, reliable equipment, and a competent leader are prerequisites for this run. Boaters should always be wary of logs.

The first two miles have class 2-3 rapids, short drops with fun waves. The pace picks up during the next 2.5 miles. Gates Rapids, a line of big boulders blocking the river, is the first rapids. Just downstream is "Hole in the River," a large hole on the left. Several blind corners that could require scouting follow. About 4.5 miles below the Collawash put-in, is Rocky's Rapids, where the river bends right after slamming into a wall. Alder Flat Campground is just below and has a trail on the right up to the road. This campground is the easiest take-out before the nasty stuff begins downstream.

Immediately below the campground is a pushy class 4 rapids called Drop Stopper. Watch out for the large boulder in midstream at the bottom. Twice in the next half mile, the river bends right after slamming into high rock walls. Prelude Rapids, two narrow slots, is just to the right of the second wall. We recommend scouting from above Prelude, because Killer Fang (class 6) is 150 feet downstream, and out of sight. After running Prelude, land on river right for the MANDATORY PORTAGE around Killer Fang.

At flows under 1100 cfs, all the water in Killer Fang goes under three mega-boulders, which block the entire river. Logs are visible in the underground chutes. In the Spring of 1982, two rafts deliberately attempted to run Killer Fang at about 3500 cfs. Both rafts got caught in a dead-end whirlpool on the right. Throw ropes saved the rowers, and, after one raft lost a bottom and the other was deflated, the boats were pulled free.

Do not relax after Killer Fang. The next mile has two class 4 rock gardens. The first, the Sieve, has some undercut rocks left of center, so a quick scout is advisable. Next comes River's Revenge. Some fancy eddy hopping is required to maneuver through the narrow slots between large rocks. Class 2 rapids continue for about a mile until the take-out.

Difficulties: Due to the narrow slots and tight turns on this section, logs pose a real threat on any of the rapids. As always, scout if the bottom of a rapids is hidden from view. Definitely scout Drop Stopper, Prelude, and Sieve. Killer Fang is a MANDATORY PORTAGE at any water level.

Shuttle: Follow Oregon 224 out of Estacada to the take-out at Three Lynx Power Station. Continue up Oregon 224 and USFS 46 to the put-in at the intersection of USFS 46 and USFS 63, where the Collawash River meets the Clackamas. An alternate put-in, located 1 mile downstream at Riverside Recreation Site, allows the beginning flatwater to be skipped.

Gauge: The River Forecast Center in Portland has information on the flow of the Clackamas River at Three Lynx.

CLACKAMAS RIVER
Three Lynx Power Station to North Fork Reservoir
Bill Ostrand

Class	Flow	Gradient	Miles	Character	Season
3(4)	750 and up	43 PD	10	forest popular area	all year

Description: This beautiful and scenic Cascade River has taken a great number of lives. More than self-confidence, common sense, and minimal equipment are needed to run this river. As with any whitewater, proper training in boating skills, safety, and rescue are mandatory for a safe run. Most people who get into trouble on this stretch are inexperienced and un-trained boaters in unsuitable craft. These people have often been drinking alcohol. The river can be unforgiving, so beware!

Boaters who put in above Three Lynx should scout two large drops just above the power station. Immediately below Three Lynx Power Station the run begins with several class 2 rapids, then builds to class 3 at the narrows about 0.2 mile down. Roaring River Rapid is the next major rapids, located just above the confluence with the creek for which it is named. At lower water levels this is a real boat-cruncher. The cleanest channels are to the left. The Hole-in-the-Wall follows 0.2 mile downstream. It has been called the Toilet Bowl by the Forest Service and rescue squads in the past, and local boaters refer to it as the Head Wall. The "real" Toilet Bowl is farther down stream. Rescue teams are trying to standardize the name by calling it Hole-in-the-Wall. The next few miles are playful - many class 2 rapids. However, there is one noteworthy hole which often surprises boaters. It is found downstream of the second bridge, just after Fisk Creek flows in from the left. Here the river splits around an island. Usually both channels are runnable. If you decide to run left, remember that there is a sizable hole in the center down below, so plan your move ahead of time! A quarter mile below here is Carter Bridge Rapids (class 4). It is located just upstream of the third bridge on the run. Scout it during the shuttle. Run on the far left. If you've made it this far, nothing which follows should give you much trouble until the Toilet Bowl. This class 3 rapids, located 0.2 mile downstream of the Big Eddy Recreation Area, may at high water, contain the biggest waves in the Oregon Cascades. One quarter mile downstream is Bob's Hole, a favorite play-spot. The remaining river to the lake is generally easier than the described rapids.

Difficulties: The Hole-in-the-Wall is by far the most dangerous rapids on this section. Many lives have been lost here. At the approach most of the water is forced to the left where it forms a fast chute. This chute is obstructed by the wall which forces the current to split. Most of the water moves right and downstream, but a large portion of the flow turns left into an extremely turbulent eddy. The eddy is easily avoided at higher levels by running right. At lower levels the right becomes clogged with rocks except for a twisty route down the middle that is difficult to see. The more common low-water route is to run the left chute and turn right before reaching the wall. Should you find yourself out of your boat and swimming in the eddy you're in for quite a ride. Keep cool. As long as you have your life vest on and remember how to escape from the eddy, you'll be okay. Take advantage of the life vest and keep all parts of your body near the surface. The walls of the eddy are undercut and a submerged swimmer could be swept under the wall. The rock walls that border the eddy are too steep to climb except at the point where the walls form a corner. In 1984 a metal ladder was installed to enable swimmers to climb out. Needless to say, this self-rescue plan must be reviewed while scouting the rapids, not while swimming it. Carter Bridge Rapids (see Description) should be scouted.

Shuttle: Oregon 224 follows the Clackamas very closely on this run and allows for many possible put-ins and take-outs. The two most common put-ins are at the bridges immediately above and below the Three Lynx Power Station. Possible take-outs include Big Eddy Recreation Area, a road pull-off just below Toilet Bowl, several other recreation sites further downstream, or at North Fork Reservoir.

Gauge: For flow information contact the River Forecast Center in Portland.

CLACKAMAS RIVER
McIver Park to Barton Park
Bob Collmer

Class	Flow	Gradient	Miles	Character	Season
2 +	1000	17 PD	8	park lowlands	all year

Description: This beautiful stretch of the river may be run all year. The first 2.5 miles of the run are located entirely within McIver Park. For a short trip, boaters may take out at the lower end of the park. For those continuing on downstream, it is another 5.5 miles to the take-out at Barton Park.

The put-in at the boat ramp offers a view of the first and largest drop. A ledge across the river provides several good standing waves for surfing. The river twists through the park with more small rapids and goes into a rock garden. The rock garden is followed by a nice play-spot with more standing waves and eddies on both sides. There are more bends and small rapids on the way to the park take-out at McIver. This take-out is at the park's lowest picnic area. From here to Barton Park there are several more small rapids and play-spots. It is mostly class 2 water and is fairly flat. Barton Park also has both a boat ramp and picnic area.

Difficulties: In high water, the first drop should be checked for the boat-eating hole that develops. There is a headwall below the play-spot mentioned above which can circulate a swimmer at high water.

Shuttle: Be prepared to pay an entrance fee at both McIver and Barton Parks. To reach the Barton Park take-out, drive west from the Portland area on Oregon 224. The park closes at dusk. The put-in is reached by driving upstream to McIver Park. Once in the park, follow the road down the hill. The put-in is at the boat ramp. The take-out for the short (2.5 mile) run is reached by driving to the lowest parking lot (and picnic area) within the park.

Gauge: This section is runnable most of the year. Rocky runs have been made at levels as low as 750 cfs. Contact the River Forecast Center in Portland for the readings below Estacada Lake.

CLACKAMAS RIVER
Barton Park to Carver
Bob Collmer

Class	Flow	Gradient	Miles	Character	Season
2+	1000 and up	14	6	houses	all year

Description: This stretch of the river is an excellent training area for beginners. There are many small class 2 drops, usually with eddies close by. The rapids are clean and have good run-outs. The scenery is uncluttered even though some areas have housing on the river's edge. The river class rises to the 2+ level in the spring and drops to the 2- level in the summer. It is runnable all year and often run in the evening when daylight permits.

Difficulties: There are no major problem areas, although several rapids pick up speed and provide some bouncy places.

Shuttle: The put-in is at the boat ramp at Barton Park, which closes at dusk. Drive to Barton on Oregon 224 and proceed to Barton Park. The take-out is at the Carver boat ramp just upstream from the bridge.

Gauge: Contact the River Forecast Center in Portland for the flow.

CLACKAMAS RIVER
Carver to Clackamette Park
Kurt Renner

Class	Flow	Gradient	Miles	Character	Season
2	1000 and up	9 C	6.8	houses	all year

Description: This stretch of river is a fine run for canoeists of intermediate experience. The rapids are characterized by turns with standing waves on the outside to middle of the channel with a nice soft eddy on the inside. The most difficult rapids are a pair of right bends followed by a pair of left bends. The second pair has a central rock to avoid. High rocks and a trestle bridge are next. There is an easy riffle here, but several 17-ft aluminum canoes have been seen wrapped around the bridge piers. The run finishes with a nice long but not too tight S-turn. The waves here are irregular and can be fun. Clackamette Park is 0.8 mile farther down on the left. The Clackamas River then flows into the Willamette River.

Difficulties: Canoeists should know how to handle S-turns with high standing waves.

Shuttle: Carver is located 5.8 miles upstream of Oregon City on Oregon 224. The put-in is at the bridge that crosses the Clackamas at Carver. To reach Clackamette Park drive west on Clackamas River Road, on the river's south bank. At the intersection with Washington (Oregon 213) turn left. After 1 mile turn right to cross the railroad tracks and right again immediately after the tracks onto McLoughlin Blvd. Continue north 0.5 mile to Clackamette Park.

Gauge: Contact the River Forecast Center in Portland for the flow of the Clackamas at Clackamas.

EAGLE CREEK
Fish Hatchery to Snuffin Road
Hank Hays

Class	Flow	Gradient	Miles	Character	Season
2-3 T	300	62 PD	5.75	forest	rainy
(6)				cabins	

Description: Eagle Creek drains the Cascade foothills east of Estacada, and flows generally northwest into the Clackamas River about halfway between Estacada and Barton. It was named for the eagles that used to dip to catch the thousands of spawning salmon. The headwaters (nothing runnable) are in the Mt. Hood National Forest. The creek is small and seldom run by boaters, though fishermen abound. There are some cabins and homes along the creek. Although several bridges cross the creek, paddlers catch only glimpses of the road, and then only in the vicinity of Eagle Fern Park.

The first settler in the area, Philip Foster, was part owner of the Barlow road, the first real alternative to the dangerous rafting trip through the Columbia Gorge. The Fosters' house was a way station on the Road. Foster Road, between SE Portland and Damascus is named in his honor. The Philip Foster house is still standing and lived in.

At the put-in, the creek is narrow with overhanging shrubbery. If the water level is high, the current can be intimidating. Sweepers, logs and blind turns make the upper part of this run quite interesting, though rapids are usually not too complex. There are several logs spanning the stream that can be ducked at the recommended flow. As of 1984, the first one is in a pool immediately after a right bend in the river. Immediately afterwards is a blind left bend with the main current slamming into a small log jam, skirtable on the left. There were two negotiable log dams on this run in the Fall of 1984 that were not present in the Spring of 1981. An unnamed creek enters on the right about 1.5 miles below the put-in.

There is a 15 + ft waterfall at mile 3.5. Keep an eye out for the 4-ft high concrete fish ladder bypassing the falls. It's on the right bank past a sharp right-hand bend. Take out on the right in the slower moving water well before the concrete wall. There is a trail to a "road" that leads to the pool at the bottom. A boat can also be hiked down the fishladder, which is shorter, but probably not much easier. This falls can be reached from George Road by hiking in 0.8 miles from a locked yellow gate about 1.2 miles up the hill from Snuffin Road.

Delph Creek comes in on the left shortly past the falls. There are remnants of a footbridge that crossed here in the past. It's about a mile from the base of the falls to Eagle Fern Youth Camp--a large open area on the left with some sports facilities. Some of the best action on this run comes in the next mile, between the camp and the take-out. The creek goes around a right bend and into an interesting boulder garden. It gets worse near the bottom, after a left bend. In real high water there will be a large, river-wide roller here. There is a short respite, some more fun boulder gardens, then the bridge at the take-out.

Difficulties: The falls, logs and log dams, the boulder gardens between the Youth Camp and the take-out. The water is up into the bushes at the recommended flow so watch for sweepers and overhangs. Avoid fisherman as much as possible and watch for fishing lures in low, overhanging branches.

Shuttle: Oregon 211 crosses Eagle Creek about 4.5 miles north of the stoplight in Estacada. Just north of the bridge turn east, onto Wildcat Mountain Drive, which is marked by a sign pointing to Eagle Fern Park, the fish hatchery, and Dover District. Keep right at an immediate "Y" and then cross Eagle Creek Road. In less than 2 miles turn right onto Eagle Fern Road. Snuffin Road comes in from the right about 3 miles from this intersection. The entrance to Eagle Fern Park is 0.8 miles behind you. Either the Park or the Snuffin Road Bridge can be used as a take-out.

To reach the put-in, return to George Road which starts at the junction of Snuffin and Eagle Fern Roads. Follow George Road about 4.5 miles to a right turn onto Rainbow Road. A sign on the left points towards the hatchery, 2 miles away and 600 ft down. There is a marked parking lot next to a private bridge across the creek. The easiest put-in is across the bridge on the downstream side. This is private property; please respect it.

Gauge: None. Take a look from the Oregon 211 bridge.

EAGLE CREEK
Snuffin Road to Eagle Creek Road
Hank Hays

Class	Flow	Gradient	Miles	Character	Season
3 + (6)	300	55 C,PD	5	forest	rainy
P				houses	

Description: The character of the lower section of Eagle Creek is similar to that of the upper section, which is described in the preceding description.

About 0.5 miles below the put-in at Snuffin Road bridge is a low head dam (1 or 2 ft). A shallow slide in the center of the dam makes an easy run. A mile below the put-in, the North Fork of Eagle Creek emerges underneath a bridge at a left bend in the river. A half mile farther is "The Falls," preceded (200 yards, at least) by a sign on a cable across the river. There is plenty of action before the falls. Work towards the right after the sign and take out on the right in a very small eddy at the upstream end of the fish ladder retaining wall. Portage and put in about 100 yards downstream. Like the upper falls, this one can be reached from Eagle Fern Road by hiking in at the yellow gate about 0.5 mile below the North Fork bridge.

There are 1.5 miles of boulder gardens below The Falls. The first half mile drops at the rate of 125 feet per mile. There are also some strategically placed logs, so scout blind corners before attempting a run. The first hard right bend below The Falls quite often has logs on the left bank. They may be close to the best chute, which is left center. The drop is blind, but there is usually a big eddy upstream of the logs. Scout left.

About 0.5 mile below The Falls, on river left, at the beginning of a blind left bend, is a small island with shrubs on it. Just past the island there is a huge rock at left center. Several logs are wedged between the rock and the left bank, some reaching well into the right channel. Scout left, from the top of the island. A run can be quite dangerous, but, if the water isn't too high, boats can be lined down under the logs. Portaging this would not be easy as the banks are straight up on both sides. This is the last real nasty spot, but there are many more interesting drops and boulder gardens for about the next mile. There are also a couple automobiles in the creek.

The recommended take-out is the first concrete bridge. Land about 25 ft above it on the right for the easiest hike up to the road. There is a private bridge about a mile above here. The run could be continued on down to where Dowty Road crosses, about 0.5 mile short of the mouth, or even down to Barton Park on the Clackamas, but there is a lot of flat water involved. The gradient of the 3 miles between Eagle Creek Road and the mouth is 33 feet per mile.

Difficulties: Possible log jams and sweepers, steep-walled gorges, The Falls, the rapids at the right bend and at the left bend after The Falls. There are usually many fishermen in this section, so courteously avoid them.

Shuttle: Directions to a put-in at Snuffin Road or Eagle Fern Park can be found in the shuttle for the previous section. A car can be dropped off on the way in by taking a right onto Eagle Creek Road (the first crossroad after leaving Oregon 211), and parking in the pull-out on the east side of the road before crossing the bridge. Please don't block the driveway. The put-in can also be reached from Estacada by going east on Coupland Road (up the hill east of the High School) for 2 miles, turning left onto Currin Road, then a right after another 2 miles onto Snuffin Road. Follow the signs towards George and Eagle Fern Park.

Gauge: None. Take a look from the Oregon 211 bridge.

CLEAR CREEK
Oregon 211 to Redland Road
Hank Hays

Class	Flow	Gradient	Miles	Character	Season
2 + 3	500	41 PD	8	forest	rainy
T				houses	
				log jams	

Description: The main stem of Clear Creek drains the north face of Goat Mountain south of Estacada, then flows north between Estacada and Colton, through Viola and Fischers Mill, and into the Clackamas River at Carver. It's not a big stream. Several log jams were present on the exploratory run, primarily in the flatwater near the end of the run. Take a peek around blind bends in the river before committing yourself. There are stretches of flatwater with good current between drops and in the lower reaches of the run.

Quite a bit of the area has been logged, although a buffer has been left along most of the bank. Most of the land along both banks is private except for two small sections of Bureau of Land Management (BLM) timber and Metzler Park. Above the put-in at the Oregon 211 bridge, Clear Creek has no public access and gets awfully small as it breaks up into several main feeders. Below Redland Road the stream is runnable, but the land is used mostly for agricultural purposes, and one is likely to run into fences crossing the river.

Difficulties: Just downstream of the put-in is a left-hand bend with some logs and rocks to dodge. Watch for more stream-spanning logs between here and Metzler Park, about 0.8 miles below the put-in. Just above the park a footbridge crosses the river, and Swagger Creek comes in on the left. Below the footbridge is a small low-head dam that has a surfable roller at runnable water levels. Swimming is not recommended here as there are short rebar stakes in the shallow water below the dam. These can wreak havoc on bodies and boats. About 0.5 mile below the park, there is one good class 2 + rapids.

About 5 miles into the run is a gravel logging road which crosses the river. As of 1984, the poured asphalt in the riverbed provides a small surfable roller on the downstream side at the recommended flow. This marks the start of a half-mile long steep section. The creek goes around a sharp right bend with some shallow slides, and slowly curves left again before a 3-ft rocky dropoff. This last ledge is bumpy and hard to scout, but probably runnable almost anywhere. The rest of the run is moving flatwater, probably with log jams requiring portage. There are several private homes in this area, so be careful of trespassing.

Shuttle: To get to the put-in, follow signs for Oregon 211 from Estacada towards Molalla. Oregon 211 follows Dubois Creek up a long hill to the Springwater area then down the other side along Little Cedar Creek to the put-in at the bridge over Clear Creek. This bridge is 6.5 miles from the bridge in Estacada. The put-in is river right on the downstream side of the bridge; anything else is private property.

For the shuttle to the take-out, drive 2.5 or 3 miles back towards Estacada, turn left at the top of the hill onto either Tucker Road or Wallens Road, and then take the first right onto Springwater Road. About 5 miles farther, take Redland Road, the first left turn after the entrance to McIver Park.

If you're coming from Portland along Springwater Road and want to drop a car off, Redland Road is the first right turn after the Viewpoint Restaurant. Be careful as Redland Road takes a sharp right bend a half mile after leaving Springwater Road. The bridge at the bottom of the hill, 1.5 miles from Springwater Road, is Clear Creek. The shuttle can also be done on the west side of the river via Highland and Fellows Roads. Park on Mattoon Road (river right), a bit downstream of the bridge. Climbing up that steep embankment with a boat is loads of fun.

Gauge: None. Clear Creek rises and falls abruptly. The exploratory run was made in early April after three days of heavy rain, when the Clackamas at Three Lynx was at 5435 cfs. Check the river level at the bridges described above.

SANDY RIVER
McNeil Campground to Lolo Pass Road Bridge
Thom Powell

Class	Flow	Gradient	Miles	Character	Season
4 + T	600-800	200 C	5.5	wooded	rainy snowmelt

Description: There is only one rapids on this section of the Sandy. It begins at the McNeil Campground bridge and ends 5.5 miles later at the next bridge. It begins as a class 4, gets tougher around the middle (4 +), and lets up a little toward the end. The run takes about fifty adrenalin-filled minutes to complete (barring unforeseen problems) and is among the steepest runnable river sections anywhere in the state. The rather continuous rate of drop is what makes a manageable run out of an otherwise outrageous gradient. This also makes the drops rather uniform in difficulty, but occasionally a steeper or narrower passage is encountered. The first trip down this section is an unforgettable experience.

This section has a remote feeling to it, but the Lolo Pass Highway is usually less than a quarter mile through the woods on river right. The alders and underbrush are quite thick, but anyone who is experiencing early difficulty should quickly opt for the nature walk, for the maneuvering gets tougher before it gets easier.

The river begins with some very technical maneuvering and then eases up, giving one a false sense of accomplishment. Stay alert! The river will pick up again shortly, only this time with more force. It is useless to describe the drops in detail since there are just too many of them. Eddies are very scarce, but they offer the only chance to catch your breath. There are no pools to speak of.

The river's channel is split by islands in several places. When in doubt about which way to go, take the left channel. In all cases, the left is freer of branches and obstructions.

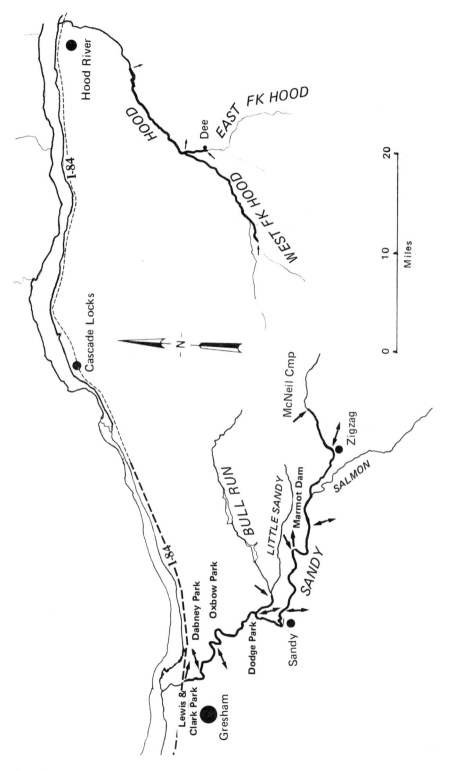

Worthy of mention are the tree stumps that have been driven into the river bed for some mysterious reason. They occur intermittently in the middle third of the run, and in two places they stand right in the middle of the river, appearing to block the channel. They look positively awful, jutting up out of the river with the water pillowing up against them. Experience indicates that they can be outmaneuvered with decisive moves.

Consider paddling past the take-out at Lolo Pass Road and down to Wildcat Creek, another 9 miles. It is a bit anticlimactic after the mill race down from McNeil, but the water is still quite swift and interesting.

Difficulties: Logs are a concern on any river this steep and narrow. At this writing (1985) a log spans the river downstream of the McNeil bridge, just out of sight. It is recommended that paddlers carry their boats down the road for 400 yards or so and put in just below the log, on river right.

In several places where the current splits around an island, the left is the best choice in all cases. Near the bottom of the run, there are a couple of houses on river right. This is the start of a development called Zigzag Village. It is imperative that you use the left channels in the vicinity of these houses, for one of the right channels is completely blocked by a log jam.

The class 4 + rating given to this section can be misleading. Much more than a reliable roll is needed here. It's the kind of place where you don't even want to think about tipping over. It's fairly tough to roll in most places, but it's even tougher to get a swamped boat ashore. In two past instances, swimmers were able to get to shore quickly, but their boats traveled quite a ways before being corralled.

It is important that boaters keep their distance from each other. There's usually only one good channel and not much room to maneuver. Rescue is difficult because your fellow boaters are usually too busy to be aware of anyone else's problems. The action demands total concentration and aggressive, continuous maneuvering. Also, protruding rocks in fast chutes provide countless opportunities to pin a boat, so the boater can almost never afford to get sideways to the current. If this discussion sounds discouraging, it should; this is expert class whitewater.

Shuttle: The take-out is near the town of Zigzag. To reach the take-out turn north off US 26 at the Zigzag store onto the Lolo Pass Road. The take-out is about a mile down this road at the second bridge. (The first bridge crosses Zigzag River). To get to the put-in, continue up the Lolo Pass Road. After 3.5 miles look for a sign that marks entry into the Mt. Hood National Forest. Just past this sign, turn right on USFS 1825, which leads to Ramona Falls. Continue up this road for one mile to reach the put-in at the bridge just before McNeil Campground.

Gauge: Three days of heavy rain are needed, even in winter, to bring this section up to a runnable level. The only way to gauge the flow accurately is to check the water level against some logs that are built into the river-left bank just below the McNeil bridge. When the water is halfway up the lowest log, it is a runnable flow, and if this same log is covered, it is too much. The river level drops rapidly as soon as the rains subside, providing about a three day period to run the river before it gets too low.

SANDY RIVER
Zigzag to Wildcat Creek
Bill Ostrand

Class	Flow	Gradient	Miles	Character	Season
2 T	700-	70 C	9	forest	rainy
	2000			houses	snowmelt
3	2000 +				

Description: The author had the pleasure of living along this section of the river and running it almost every day that water levels would allow. The river flows through a broad valley with rural housing development along the banks. It has an almost constant gradient and a sandy bottom covered with small to medium sized boulders which give the river its rapids. Areas without boulders form fast moving pools. The dynamic nature of this type of river bed makes the description of individual rapids pointless. Each minor flood will change the rapids somewhat and may change the locations of deep channels and the best paddling routes. A major flood may completely change the river.

The most difficult rapids are at the top of the run where the river is steepest. Farther downstream are more pools but still plenty of whitewater. After the confluence with the Salmon River (about 0.5 miles above the Marmot Bridge), the volume increases greatly and the water takes on more "big water" characteristics. There are many stationary, smoothly shaped waves in the lower rapids during medium and high flow levels.

The author has run the river at all levels and has found that even at the highest runnable flows, just short of flood, the river does not form dangerous features such as river-wide holes or exploding waves. The most difficult level is actually a bit lower at medium-high flows when the river is high enough to form holes behind the large boulders. When the river is so high that rocks and boulders can be heard crashing together on the bottom, one should consider another form of recreation for the day.

Difficulties: No rapids stand out as significantly more difficult or dangerous than the general pace of the river. Occasionally brush extending from the banks may cause problems.

Shuttle: From the Portland area take US 26 east to Zigzag. Turn north onto Lolo Pass Road, just east of the Zigzag store. Continue to the second river crossing, the put-in. To reach the take-out, return to US 26 and turn west. The take-out is approximately 8 miles downstream at Wildcat Creek. (Signs indicating Alder Creek or the Ivy Bear restaurant indicate that one has driven too far west.) At the Wildcat Creek sign there is a graveled parking area below the road level.

It is important to note that the water running by the parking area is not the main river channel. To ensure that one does not boat past the take-out, walk up the side channel far enough to pick out river marks. Below this point there is no public access until Marmot Dam.

Other points of easy access are the bridges at Brightwood and Marmot. To find additional points of access inquire locally at the Brightwood or Zigzag stores.

Gauge: A new gauge has recently been installed on the Sandy River (Spring 1985) and correlations between feet on the gauge and cfs have not yet been made. This section is runnable most of the late fall, winter, and spring. Especially warm spring days during years of good snow pack may yield excellent runoff paddling when many other rain-dependent rivers are low. If the river appears too low at the put-in, consider putting in farther downstream. The Zigzag and Salmon Rivers, as well as other side streams, add considerably to the flow.

SANDY RIVER
Wildcat Creek to Marmot Dam
Bill Ostrand

Class	Flow	Gradient	Miles	Character	Season
2(4)	700 and up	33 C/PD	4	forest, canyon houses	rainy snowmelt

Description: This is short section of the river is often run as a warm-up for boating the Sandy Gorge, which begins just below Marmot Dam. If the gorge is not to be run, it is possible to lengthen this trip to about 6 miles by putting in upstream at the Marmot Bridge.

The first mile of this section begins with a series of class 2 rapids followed by Alder Creek Rapids (class 4). Below Alder Creek the rapids become progressively easier until the water becomes completely flat at the impoundment behind Marmot Dam. The take-out is on the right.

Difficulties: Alder Creek Rapids can present a real challenge. The drop appears as a horizon line from upstream, with an A-frame house overlooking the rapids from the left. An easy scout or portage is on the right. The Dam is unrunnable. It is easily seen from above and easily avoided.

Shuttle: The lower put-in is about 10 miles east of the town of Sandy on US 26. Wildcat Creek is located just east of the small community of Alder Creek at the base of a very long incline. There is a parking area on the north side of the road near the Wildcat Creek road sign.

To reach, the take-out continue east to the second paved road on the north side of the highway, about 2 miles, and follow the road to the Marmot Bridge which crosses the Sandy. This is the alternate put-in. Cross the bridge and turn left immediately after crossing the river. Follow this road for a slow 6 miles, 5 miles of which will be on gravel. Turn left onto a private road which winds steeply 2 miles back down to Marmot Dam.

Gauge: A new gauge has recently been installed on the Sandy River (Spring 1985) and correlations between feet on the gauge and cfs have not yet been made.

SANDY RIVER
The Gorge from Marmot Dam to Revenue Bridge
Hank Hays and Rod Kiel

Class	Flow	Gradient	Miles	Character	Season
3 +	1200	40 PD	5.5	forest	snowmelt
4 +	3000			no road	

Description: For almost the entire length of this section the Sandy cuts a winding and often quite narrow canyon through a formation of compacted volcanic ash conglomerate. The walls of the canyon are deeply sculpted, sometimes overhanging, and rise to a height of 150 feet. A multitude of small waterfalls cascading down from both sides, plus lush vegetation consisting of both deciduous and evergreen trees, mosses and maidenhair ferns that cling to the ceilings of caves and overhangs make this stretch of river one of the most picturesque in Oregon.

For the first 3.5 miles the river drops with many short enjoyable rapids, and one longer class 3 rapids at about mile 1.5. In the last two miles there are four rapids that should be scouted. At the first one, Boulder Rapids, the canyon narrows dramatically, with a tremendous overhang and free-falling waterfall on the left and large boulders in the middle.

Difficulties: 150 yards below the recommended put-in is a major rapids which contains the remnants of a huge 1964 logjam. This should be scouted on the right. At moderate to upper levels most people portage this on the right. It is possible to pin on any number of vertical logs about halfway down on the left, especially at lower levels. At the bottom the current slams into the root system of a large downed tree on the right. If you decide to run it, start right and end up in the eddy on the left at the bottom. There are some holes about halfway down just to complicate the run a little.

Boulder Rapids is almost impossible to portage and is usually run on the left. The right chute has a log that can be seen at lower levels. Run the left chute, avoiding the huge undercut rock on the right. Eddy out under the overhanging left wall to avoid the big hole along the canyon wall which usually cannot be seen when scouting.

The difficulty of the next two rapids, Rasp Rock and Drain Hole, varies dramatically with different water levels. Rasp Rock Rapids is a furious 50-yard drop over conglomerate boulders with some big holes interspersed throughout. It is shaped like a funnel with a huge hole at the beginning of the neck and two big boulders at the end. This hole tends to surf you into the left wall. Scout and if desired, portage. Check for logs in the narrow chutes at the bottom before committing yourself. Any of the three possible chutes are narrow enough for a boat to wedge crosswise, so a swim might be recommended as an alternative to a delayed roll if you flip anywhere near the bottom.

Drain Hole looks like the end of the river. A rock jumble forces the water left, and from your boat it seems to be dammed by a shore-to-shore line of three megaboulders. The water slams into the left-most of these, and at lower water levels it can be seen to be dangerously undercut. There are logs in some of the other narrow chutes so try to slip between the right-most rock and the canyon wall, as that chute is usually open. Scouting on the right is recommended. Even most expert paddlers portage this one at moderate to high levels.

The last major rapids is Revenue Bridge Rapids, which is recognized from the top by glimpses of the bridge through the trees as one rounds the bend. One can try scouting from the cliff on the right shore but it is difficult to see much of the beginning of the drop. The last half is easily scouted from the rocks on the left. The usual plan is to go far right against the cliff and then eddy out on the left before the two big holes near the bottom. Take the first one on the right and try to get left for the second river-wide stopper. At lower levels it can be run anywhere, but the slightest angle can create problems. Use your own judgment at higher levels. It can be portaged on the left. Take out almost under the bridge on the left. A steep trail winds up to the road.

Shuttle: From the junction of US 26 and Oregon 211 in Sandy, head east for several blocks and turn left towards Bull Run and Oral Hull Park. This road switches back down into the Sandy River Canyon (take a hard left at the first "Y") and goes across Revenue Bridge, the take-out. To get to the put-in, continue across the bridge and follow the pavement until it ends in about 5 miles, keeping right at all paved intersections. About 0.2 mile farther take a right road through a gate that is usually open, onto PGE property, and continue about 1.3 miles down to the second turnout on the right. Carry boats down a steep trail past the diversion canal tunnel to the river.

Gauge: Flow information is not directly available. An approximation for the flow on this section is to deduct 600 cfs from the River Forecast Center's figure for the Sandy.

Looking upstream from Revenue Bridge one sees a rock halfway between the bridge and the bottom of Revenue Bridge Rapids. The flow for the run is most ideal when enough water splashes over this rock to create a good visible souse hole.

SANDY RIVER
Revenue Bridge to Dodge Park
Bob Collmer

Class	Flow	Gradient	Miles	Character	Season
2 +	1200-3000	40 C	5	houses	rainy snowmelt

Description: This run starts at Revenue Bridge with a crawl down the hill to get to the river. The upper part of the run is class 2 with many small rapids. Things pick up where a long slide area is visible on the left. Below here drops are steeper, more frequent, and sometimes rocky. This is a pretty run, but a little more open and populated than the lower run.

Difficulties: The lower drops should be run with caution. Follow the main current and be very careful of rocks in the drops. At very high water this is a hazardous run as the water goes into snaggy banks and eddies disappear. There also may be logs in the river at high water.

Shuttle: Drive to Sandy on Oregon 26 and turn off at Glos Ford. Follow the road down the hill until it crosses the river at Revenue Bridge. The take-out is at Dodge Park.

Gauge: Flow information can be obtained from the River Forecast Center in Portland.

SANDY RIVER
Dodge Park to Oxbow Park
Bob Collmer

Class	Flow	Gradient	Miles	Character	Season
2 +	1200-3000	23 PD	6	forest no road	rainy snowmelt

Description: The river is very beautiful in this area. It is mostly wooded canyon and is a designated scenic river. It is pool-drop with most of the drops clean and many surfing waves scattered along the entire stretch.

The scenery remains almost primitive in the canyon. The lower stretch opens up some, but remains wooded and remote. Wildlife is often seen. The run ends at Oxbow Park boat ramp and there is always the feeling of a great trip. The run is nicest on a sunny day but neither rain nor snow hurt this run. Spring is the best running time but the river is runnable usually through July.

Difficulties: Pipeline is 0.5 mile from the put-in and should be scouted as some rocks are in the drop. Pull off in the eddy on the left above the visible pipe across the river. There is always the possibility of trees in the river after heavy run-offs. About 3 miles into the run is a long rock garden.

Shuttle: Put-in is at Dodge Park which is reached by driving to Powell Valley Road and following signs to Dodge Park. The take-out is at Oxbow Park boat ramp.

Gauge: Flow information can be obtained from the River Forecast Center in Portland.

SANDY RIVER
Oxbow Park to Dabney Park
Sarah Ostrand

Class	Flow	Gradient	Miles	Character	Season
1 +	700	8	5.5	wooded	rainy
	and up			no road	snowmelt

Description: This mild run is a favorite among rafters for summer outings. The majority of the rapids are within Oxbow Park. Beginning kayak classes use the park area frequently. No rapids are more difficult than class 1 + and there are plenty of eddies to catch.

After leaving the park there are a few more rapids and a number of riffles. Continued opportunities to view wildlife add to the pleasure of this trip. Sightings include osprey, bald eagle, great blue heron, and various species of waterfowl. The gentleness of the river and the beautiful scenery beckon many boaters to the river.

Difficulties: The only potential hazard occurs near the end of the run. There is a sharp right turn and the current tends to trap trees on the outside of the bend.

Shuttle: Dabney State Park, the take-out, is located on US 30 (The Scenic Columbia Gorge Highway) east of Portland. Follow Stark Street east from Portland and take a right after crossing the Sandy River. The park is located approximately 0.2 mile from the bridge. For an optional route to the take-out, follow I-84 east from Portland to the Lewis and Clark State Park Exit, and then follow the road along the river to Dabney (about 3 miles).

The put-in is at Oxbow County Park. From Dabney cross the bridge over the Sandy and follow signs. After entering the park, continue to the furthest upstream boat launch. There is an entrance fee during the summer. You may also put in on the north side of the river. To reach this put-in area continue east on the Scenic Highway from Dabney and turn right onto Hurlburt Road. Follow Hurlburt and turn right onto Gordon Creek Road. There is a sign at the parking area.

Gauge: A new gauge was installed on the Sandy River (Spring 1985), but correlations between feet on the gauge and flow have not yet been made.

SANDY RIVER
Dabney Park to Lewis and Clark Park
Bill Ostrand

Class	Flow	Gradient	Miles	Character	Season
1	500	6 PD	3	canyon	all year
	and up			houses	

Description: This is one of the most frequently floated sections of river in the state. Fishermen float the river all winter and rafters and innertubers drift during hot summer days. The run is not completely flat; there are several class 1 riffles.

Difficulties: As with most Oregon rivers, the water is extremely cold. Most of the year boaters will encounter fishermen in drift boats or along the shore, so look out for lines in the water.

Shuttle: Take the Lewis and Clark exit off of I-84 just east of Troutdale. The take-out is at the boat ramp within the park. To reach the put-in, follow the road along the river upstream to Dabney Park.

Gauge: A new gauge has recently been installed on the Sandy River (Spring 1985) and correlations between feet on the gauge and cfs have not yet been made.

BULL RUN RIVER
Bull Run Road to the Sandy River
Thom Powell

Class	Flow	Gradient	Miles	Character	Season
3	700 +	30 PD	2.5	canyon	all year

Description: Portland's municipal water supply is drawn from the Bull Run River about six miles above the bridge at Bull Run Road. Consequently, the entire watershed is closed to public access. There is only a 2.5 mile section from this bridge to the confluence that can be run. The upper section was supposedly run in 1984 and rumored to be class 4(5). However, this could not be verified because of the restricted access.

This brief run offers six class 3 drops beginning just below the bridge. The last of these drops is Swing-set, so named for the cable and basket arrangement that is strung across the river just below the drop.

The river mellows to class 2 for the final half mile or so to the confluence with the Sandy. Within sight of the confluence is an inviting take-out beach on river left. The beach can be reached on a road that leads through Dodge Park from Lusted Road.

Those who are interested can continue down through Pipeline Rapids on the Sandy. Pipeline is a fitting finale for this trip but it complicates the take-out. Running Pipeline means either running all the way down the Sandy to Oxbow Park or taking out on river left below Pipeline, amidst a tangle of fishermen's lines. This mandates a carry of about 0.3 mile along a trail to get back to the highway.

Difficulties: None in particular, with the possible exception of the very steep put-in. The passages are narrow at lower flows, increasing the difficulty slightly. At higher flows, Swing-set has an impressive wave. Running through Pipeline increases the difficulty to a 3 + .

Shuttle: The take-out at Dodge Park, east of Portland, is reached via Powell Valley Road by following the signs to Dodge Park. To get to the put-in, go to the east end of the bridge at Dodge Park, head east and bear left on Lusted Road. Proceed 1.8 miles then turn left again on SE Ten Eyck Road toward Aims. Turn left again on Bull Run Road and descend to the bridge over the Bull Run River. Basically, take every paved left after leaving the east end of the Dodge Park bridge and you will arrive at the put-in bridge in less than three miles.

The Portland General Electric (PGE) employees at the powerhouse just below the put-in have been friendly and willing to allow gear to be left on their lot and out of harm's way while dropping a car at the take-out.

Gauge: Not available. The flow is augmented by the PGE powerhouse at the put-in with water which has been diverted from the Sandy River at Marmot. Consequently, this section can be run most of the year.

WEST FORK HOOD RIVER
White Bridge Park to East Fork Hood River
John Karafotias

Class	Flow	Gradient	Miles	Character	Season
4(5) P	800 +	100 PD	6.5	forest	rainy snowmelt

Description: The first 1.5 miles of this run are pool-drop with some nice play waves. But as Branch Creek flows in on the left, the river widens and the gradient increases. The most demanding drops are on the next section of the river. About 2.0 miles downriver from Branch Creek is a new fishladder, where there was once a beautiful 13-ft waterfall. The fishladder is a mandatory portage on the left. The next major rapids is a 50-yard long boulder garden which should be scouted on the right. The last drop, Punchbowl Falls, should have been scouted from the take-out. The take-out is at the confluence of the West Fork with the East Fork, less than 0.5 miles downriver from Punchbowl Falls. This run at normal flows is a solid class 4. At flows above 3,000 cfs, be ready for some class 5 water!

Difficulties: The drops mentioned above are more demanding than the rest of the run. The fishladder is a mandatory portage on the left. The boulder garden is a technical rapids at low flows and a maze of holes at high water. The last drop, Punchbowl Falls, is a large powerful drop. Here all of the water pours over an 8-ft ledge. Some good boaters get eaten here, so run the drop with plenty of momentum. At low water, scouting can be done from the ramp near the falls.

Shuttle: From I-84 in the city of Hood River, take exit 62 (West Hood River - West Cliff Drive). Follow the signs to Odell and Parkdale, then follow the road towards Dee and Parkdale. Turn right at the sign for Dee - Lost Lake Road. After crossing the E. Fork of the Hood River at Dee, turn right onto Punchbowl Road. Continue on Punchbowl Road, and take a right onto a road just before the bridge over the W. Fork of the Hood River. This is the take-out. The river is about 500 ft down a trail. To scout Punchbowl Falls continue across the bridge and up the road to a turn-out on your right. A hike down the stairs brings you to the falls.

To get to the put-in, backtrack to the three-way intersection near the bridge over the E. Fork of the Hood River; keep right at the intersection and follow the Lost Lake signs. Continue upriver on Lost Lake Road. After crossing the second bridge, continue upstream another 1.5 miles then turn left into White Bridge Park, the put-in. The shuttle is 6.9 miles.

Gauge: Call the River Forecast Center in Portland and ask for the flow on the Hood River. Two thirds of this flow is a good estimate of the flow on the West Fork. There is also a gauge at the lower take-out, under the bridge. This reading should be about 5.0 ft for optimum conditions.

HOOD RIVER
Dee (E. Fork Hood River) to Bridge below Tucker Park
Stan Jacobs and Jay Nigra

Class	Flow	Gradient	Miles	Character	Season
3 (4)	700	66 PD,C	7.5	forest	rainy
4	2500			houses	snowmelt

Description: The first 1.6 miles are on the East Fork, which is pool-drop and runs through a beautiful narrow canyon. At the confluence with the West Fork, the water volume doubles, and the gradient drops off and becomes more uniform. The river is wider, but no less challenging than the upper section. At lower flows the upper section is class 3, with a couple of technical class 4 ledge drops. At higher flows it becomes continuous class 4.

Difficulties: Two rapids should be noted. Approximately one-half mile from the put-in is a technical class 4 drop. Another class 4 drop occurs just above Tucker Park and is identified by an island with most of the river on the right.

Shuttle: From I-84 in the city of Hood River, take the first or second exit and follow the signs to Parkdale and Odell on Tucker Road. After several turns, cross the Hood River, where the take-out is on river right, under the bridge. To reach the put-in, follow the signs up the river past Tucker Park towards Parkdale. Stay right on the paved road until reaching the mill at Dee. Cross the bridge and enter a large parking lot on river left. The put-in is about 50 yards downriver, down a steep bank.

Gauge: A gauge is located at the take-out. A reading of 4.5 to 6 ft is ideal. Gauge information is also available from the River Forecast Center in Portland.

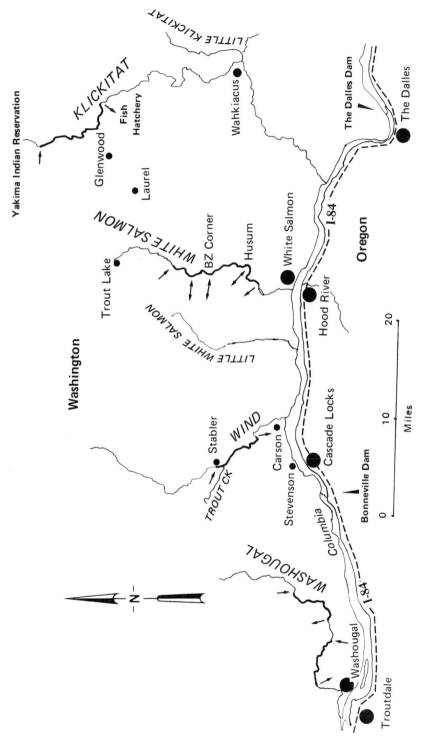

Chapter 9. Southern Washington Rivers

KLICKITAT RIVER
Indian Reservation to Fish Hatchery
Frank Furlong and Bill Ostrand

Class	Flow	Gradient	Miles	Character	Season
3 +	800 and up	35 C,PD	13	pine forest no road	snowmelt

Description: This is a predictable class 3 + river with many good play-spots and small eddies. The best water is within the first 3 miles, making the alternate take-out desirable for those who have previously taken in the scenery downstream. The remainder of the run is class 1-2.

There is a real sense of isolation on this run. Even on the busiest summer holiday weekends, it is very unlikely to encounter other people on the river. Because of the extremely long, steep, and difficult put-in, only the most die-hard rafter should consider this run. The scenery features beautiful exposed rock cliffs intermixed with open park-like ponderosa pine forests.

Difficulties: As with all northwest rivers, trees can be a problem. The put-in is a major difficulty. Care should be taken to prevent falls and injuries during the descent. It may be wise to keep your helmet on for the hike down. Use care to keep your boat under control so it will not fly down the hill and injure someone down below.

Shuttle: From I-84 in Oregon cross the Columbia River at the city of Hood River. Take Washington 141 to B-Z Corner. Turn right and proceed to Glenwood, then turn east. Follow the sign indicating Klickitat Salmon Hatchery - Washington Department of Fisheries. This leads to the take-out.

To get to the put-in return to the main road at the Klickitat Salmon Hatchery sign and turn right. About 100 ft from the sign, turn right onto the first road going west. Continue 11 miles until you reach a large sign: Yakima Indian Reservation - Road Closed to the Public. Park here. The put-in is reached via a class 4 trail, 100 + ft "down" to the river.

An alternate take-out is at the gauge one third of the way down the river from the Indian Reservation to the fish hatchery. From the road to the put-in, take K1400 then K1410 to the river.

Gauge: Flows can be obtained by calling the River Forecast Center in Seattle.

WHITE SALMON RIVER
Green Truss Bridge to Zig-Zag Canyon
Andreas Mueller

Class	Flow	Gradient	Miles	Character	Season
4T,P 5-,P	400-1000	135 PD	2.7	forest canyon	snowmelt

Description: The upper Upper White Salmon is always at least a solid class 4, even in early fall when the snowfields on Mt. Adams that feed it have nearly melted down. When every other good run in summer has dried up, this section is still guaranteed to keep the adrenalin bubbling. It is mostly pool-drop, with some drops being so concentrated in portions that it is like boating down a flight of wet stairs without ever scraping bottom. When the water is down it's not as pushy, but still thrilling in a different manner. There is less horizontal flow out away from the drops, which results in boaters getting more tail stands.

A similar run to warm up on before doing this stretch is Upper Quartzville. This water is absolutely for experts only. Walking out at any point between put-in and take-out is extremely difficult. At high water during spring run-off, pools disappear and the run becomes a mad dash downhill with three class 5 rapids and one mandatory portage. First timers should boat the river in early fall to get familiar with the portages around the unrunnables.

Difficulties: One-half mile below the put-in, at a point where the guard rail from Washington 141 is visible, there is a double S curve that goes from right to left to right to left. Eddy-hopping down, rather than running it in a straight line, lessens the risk of plowing into the boulder at the bottom.

One-quarter mile below this rapids is Bob's Falls. It is about 12 ft high and has an enormous boil one and one-half boat lengths away from its base that gushes up just to the right of center. At high water, nothing short of a hang glider will allow a boater to sail over the falls and land downstream of the boil; it is a guaranteed swim. Portage it on the right. At low water, Bob's Falls can be run successfully on the left. The pool below is plenty deep, according to Bob's underwater darkness and inner ear pressure tests. If you still don't want to run it, portage on the left.

One-eighth mile below this is an unrunnable 30-ft falls. Take out in the left-side pool, portage up the embankment, across the plateau, and down the next ravine by throw rope to the base of another falls similar in appearance to Bob's. During portages watch out for yellow-jacket and hornet nests.

The river eases up and changes character from this point down to Zig Zag Canyon, the take-out. You'll need to line your boat up the steep embankment at Zig Zag Canyon on the right.

Shuttle: The take-out is 2.1 miles above B-Z Corner on Washington 141. (See the B-Z Corner to Husum write-up on the White Salmon River for directions on how to reach B-Z Corner.) It is at the end of a dirt road 0.15 mile long with overhanging brush; it first turns left and then sweeps right 180 degrees, paralleling the river. Please note that this is private property.

The put-in is 4.7 miles above B-Z. Turn and drive 0.1 mile down a paved road to a green truss bridge. A leaking water pipe crosses the river on sagging supports just upstream and parallel to the truss bridge. Line your boat down the embankment less than 50 yards from the bridges on the river's west side. Eat your Wheaties; there is no warm-up.

Gauge: The White Salmon receives considerable ground water and often runs ten times clearer at the take-out than at the put-in. Stop at Husum Falls on your way to the put-in and have a look. As a general rule, only about 40 % of the water cascading over Husum Falls will be found flowing at the put-in. The percentage will be greater during periods of high snowmelt and less when the ground water is the major contributor. Flow information is available from the River Information Center in Seattle.

WHITE SALMON RIVER
Two Miles above B-Z Corner to B-Z Corner
John Karafotias

Class	Flow	Gradient	Miles	Character	Season
4 + T(6)	900	90 C	2.2	forest	snowmelt
P	and up			canyon	

Description: If after numerous runs on the B-Z to Husum section of the White Salmon a boater feels the need to really challenge his skills and abilities, he will find some excellent opportunities on the upper two miles. Not only does this section offer some class 4 + water, but also a somewhat annoying put-in and one significant portage. The boater also needs to be aware of where the road is in case a carry-out is necessary.

Two rapids are definitely more difficult than the rest. The first is the drop just below the put-in, which should be scouted on the left. Precise boat handling is mandatory on this drop. The second major drop appears less than a mile below the first; scout on the left. Although this drop is not as technical as the first, the penalty for a swim here is much more severe, for less than a few hundred yards downriver lies a 14-ft waterfall, the only portage on this quick run.

Difficulties: The falls that lie two thirds of the way down the run are recognized by a sweeping right turn in the river and should be portaged on the right. There are many different and exhilarating runs on the White Salmon, with varying degrees of difficulty. Boaters must recognize their abilities and limitations when considering this run and those upstream.

Shuttle: The take-out on this run is the put-in on the B-Z Corner to Husum run (see following write-up). To reach the put-in, drive north from the take-out 1.8 miles on Washington 141. Look to the right for a small roadside turnout. Park here and begin the walk to the river. When you reach what is left of an old log bridge, lower or carry your boat to the water. This is best done with some rope and a few friends. Once you are in your boat and ferrying across for the eddy on your left, look upstream and get an idea of what the upper few miles are like!

Gauge: See B-Z Corner to Husum.

WHITE SALMON RIVER
B-Z Corner to Husum
John Karafotias

Class	Flow	Gradient	Miles	Character	Season
3 + (4)	900	90 C	5	forest	all year
	and up			canyon	

Description: This run is an exciting class 3 + with two class 4 drops, which may be portaged if desired. On a hot afternoon the cold, clear water, nice lunch spots, and a good ender hole draw both rafters and kayakers to this river canyon. The rapids are fairly continuous, especially during the first few miles. If, at the end of the run, you decide to run Husum Falls, you might receive the added pleasure of running the slalom course for the Husum - White Salmon Slalom and Wildwater Race, an annual event held here in July.

Difficulties: The first and last drops are by far the most intense. B-Z Rapids, the first rapids, can be scouted on the right while putting in. The river is very narrow and one must move from one side of the river to the other and back again. This first rapids can be portaged on the right by

carrying boats down the rock shelves to the last possible put-in area. The last drop, Husum Falls, is a 15-ft vertical drop generally run near the center. Scout this drop from the take-out in Husum. Take out about 50 ft before the falls on river right if you've decided not to take the plunge. Also, keep a sharp eye for logs spanning the river. If you can't see through an entire drop, scout it first.
Shuttle: From the Portland area, take I-84 east to Hood River. Cross the Columbia River at the White Salmon Bridge, turn left onto Washington 14, then turn right onto Washington 141 just before you cross the mouth of the White Salmon River. Follow the signs to Husum. The take-out is on Washington 141 at Husum, either 500 ft below the falls on river left or 50 ft above the falls on river right.

To get to the put-in, continue north on Washington 141 to B-Z Corner, go past the town about 0.2 mile, and turn right at the sign indicating the put-in. Currently (1985) there is a charge for putting in here. This is private land and should be treated as such.
Gauge: The flow should be approximately equal to the release from the Pacific Power and Light station at Northwestern Lake, which is downstream from Husum. However, at present (1986), PP&L does not make the release figures generally available.

WHITE SALMON RIVER
Husum to Northwestern Reservoir
Bob Collmer

Class	Flow	Gradient	Miles	Character	Season
2	900 and up	25 PD	3	shallow canyon	all year

Description: The very scenic lower section of the White Salmon winds its way through a shallow, wooded canyon. It is short, yet beginning boaters will enjoy the class 1-2 rapids and may even stop to play at a few spots. The upper end of the run gives opportunities for practicing eddy turns and surfing small waves. The lower end of the run near the take-out is flat-- great for "paddle-in-a-straight-line" practice.
Difficulties: At high water some of the play-spots develop good class 3 holes. The water is always very cold.
Shuttle: See the previous description for directions to Husum, the put-in for this run. The take-out is found by driving back down Washington 141 from Husum. Take the first road to the right that crosses a bridge; go over the bridge and turn left into a small park. There is usually a landing fee charged during the summertime.
Gauge: The flow should be approximately equal to the release from the Pacific Power and Light station at Northwestern Lake, which is downstream from Husum. However, at present (1986), PP&L does not make the release figures generally available.

WIND RIVER
Stabler to High Bridge
Harvey Lee Shapiro

Class	Flow	Gradient	Miles	Character	Season
5	300-1500	90 PD	6	forest gorge	rainy snowmelt

Description: This river has an extremely long season, being runnable from the start of the rainy season until late May or June. The river flows through beautiful scenery approaching that of a rain forest. One has the feeling of being deep in an isolated gorge. However, the road is always relatively close on river left and is accessible from almost anywhere along the run.

Because of the power and pushiness of the water, and the continuity of the rapids in the two miles below Rock Creek, the author believes that this section of the Wind River is among the most difficult runs in the area. At medium level the river is calm at the take-out and at the put-in the river appears to have minimum water. Since the biggest rapids are extremely close together during the first third of the trip, it is strongly advised that boaters new to this river initially run it in the company of experienced boaters who are familiar with the river. The lower two thirds of the run seem anticlimactic, although the rapids would be considered significant on most other rivers.

Put in at Stabler and enjoy the 0.8 mile of technical class 3- warmup before the first big rapid, Initiation. Look on the left for a house above a cliff and on the right for the confluence of Rock Creek to mark the beginning of Initiation. This is a long rapids that can be scouted from river left.

Following Initiation are four tightly spaced rapids, which become a single mile-long rapids in medium high water. The last one culminates in a noticeable wave on river right. Just past this wave, eddy out on river left in order to scout the next major drop, Ram's Horn. A run on the far right side of Ram's Horn is quite exciting, requiring that the paddler punch a hole at the bottom. An easier route is found to the left of center at the top, and through the wave at the bottom.

Below this rapids is the first real pool since Initiation. Looking downstream from the pool, one can see a 30-ft waterfall entering the Wind River on the right, in the middle of the next rapids. Several drops of moderate difficulty follow. A class 3+ approach leads to the next big rapids, which is against the cliff on the right. It consists of 4 large waves with a pool at the bottom.

After a few more slightly easier drops, Climax, the biggest drop on the river, is reached. Eddy out high and on river left (although right handed C-1 paddlers have found eddies on the right as well). This drop is easier than it looks. After Climax, the rapids continue to ease up, though they are still significant in difficulty. Take a breather and enjoy the scenery!

Difficulties: Initiation, Ram's Horn and Climax are the most difficult and are all within the first third of the trip.

Shuttle: The Wind River is near the town of Carson which is about 7 miles east of Bonneville Dam, off Washington 14. From Carson continue north on Wind River Road. To get to the take-out turn left onto High Bridge Road which is about 300 yards south of High Bridge across the Wind River. There is a sign for a scaling station on the right just north of High Bridge Road. From High Bridge Road make the first right onto Old Detour Road and follow this dirt road down to the river and the take-out.

To reach the put-in return to Wind River Road, turn left, cross the Wind River and continue north to the town of Stabler. Make a left onto Hemlock Road and immediately cross the Wind River. One can put in at this bridge or make the first right and then bear right for an alternate put-in.

If there is enough water one might want to run Trout Creek, which enters the Wind from the right just above Initiation. This will give the paddler 0.6 mile of very technical warmup before reaching the Wind. To get to Trout Creek continue west on Hemlock Road from Stabler and turn at the first left which is Trout Creek Road. Follow this road south until it crosses Trout Creek, the put-in for this stretch. (Alternately one may continue on Hemlock Road and put in about one mile higher on Trout Creek. This alternate put-in is not recommended since there are no significant rapids between the upper and the lower bridges.)

Gauge: There is a gauge on the river near Carson, but no known correlation exists at this time. The river is usually runnable when the gauge at Three Lynx on the Clackamas reads 1900 cfs or more.

WASHOUGAL RIVER
Dougan Falls to Salmon Falls
Maryann McCormick and Susan Seyl

Class	Flow	Gradient	Miles	Character	Season
3-(4),P	700+	42 PD	6	wooded fishing	rainy

Description: Although it is less than an hour from the Portland-Vancouver area, the upper Washougal is not often run. This apparent lack of popularity may be due to the dramatic changes in character of the river over the 6-mile stretch. In the upper section the long stretches of flat water, with occasional class 2 or 3 drops would appeal to intermediate boaters, but the class 4 gorge is long and difficult to portage.

The beginning of the heavy water at river mile 4.5 is marked by a green trailer on a hill, river right, at a spot where the bank is washed out. Just downstream is a class 3+ entrance rapids. If the class 4 water below is to be portaged, it is necessary to get out above this entrance rapids, on the right, and carry along the road high above. (The return to the river after this portage involves a class 5 hike through blackberry bushes.)

Below this entrance rapid, the river passes through a pool and then drops out of sight. Scout from the right bank at low to medium water, but from the left at high water. The rapids are about 200 yards long with several distinct parts at low water. At high water it is class 5 with huge holes and little room for error.

The river broadens again for the last mile before the take-out above Salmon Falls. Be sure to have scouted the landmarks here, because the falls come up fast around a blind curve. Although Salmon Falls has been run at some levels, it has a dangerous rocky keeper at the bottom.

Difficulties: There are two dangerous but easily avoidable obstacles in the first three miles. The first is a concrete weir, one and one half miles from the put-in and just downstream from a short class 3 drop. It is marked by a wire across the river. Portage right. The second is a wooden dam just beyond the highway bridge. From December 1 through September 15, sections of the dam are removed for migrating salmon, and it can be run on the left. Otherwise portage on the right. Both portages can be scouted on the way to the put-in.

Remember that the banks are private property above the high water line. Be respectful of private property.

Shuttle: Take Washington 14 east from Vancouver to Washington 140 at the town of Washougal. Follow Washington 140 upstream 8.4 miles and continue straight where 140 turns right across the river. Continue 1.5 miles from this point to the Salmon Falls Fish Hatchery. Pull off on the right side of the highway near a dirt road (with a locked gate) which leads down to the river. This is the take-out. To get to the put-in, follow the highway upstream 5.7 miles to the second bridge. Dougan Falls will be on the right. The put-in is on either side of the bridge or upstream from the falls.
Gauge: There is no gauge on the Washougal. The flow is unregulated. Like many coastal streams it is runnable only after a heavy rainfall.

WASHOUGAL RIVER
Below Salmon Falls to Above Washougal
Stan Jacobs and Jay Nigra

Class	Flow	Gradient	Miles	Character	Season
3(4)	800 +	33 C	7.3	forest houses agriculture	rainy

Description: This pleasant run is close to Portland. It has several different types of drops, ranging from wide open clean rapids to a class 4 boulder garden. A flow of 1500 cfs is estimated to be optimal.
Difficulties: A major rapids, a class 4 boulder garden, is located 4.7 miles upstream from the take-out, and can be scouted on the way to the put-in. A short distance downstream is a steep class 3 rapids with a large hole midstream.
Shuttle: Take Washington 140 north at the town of Washougal and go upstream approximately 2.5 miles to the take-out (two toilets and an unimproved boat ramp). The put-in is 7.3 miles farther upstream. Cross at the bridge, turn right, and proceed down a gravel road to a public access across the river from the store.
Gauge: There is no gauge and the flow is unregulated.

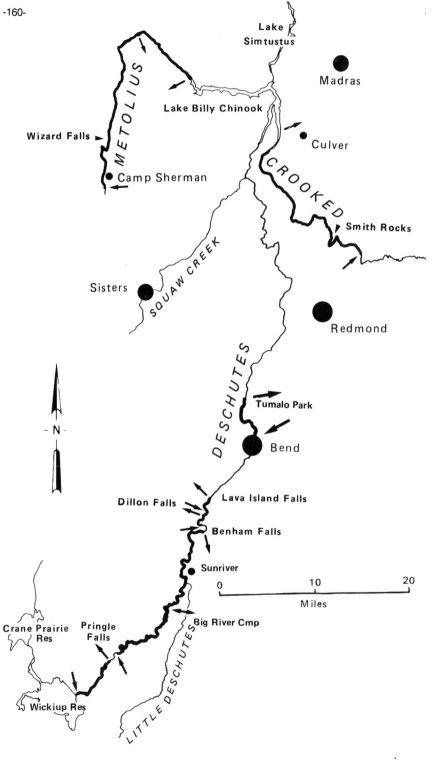

Chapter 10. Central Oregon Rivers

DESCHUTES RIVER AND TRIBUTARIES
Introduction by Rob Blickensderfer

The Deschutes River, Oregon's second longest river, drains the east side of the Cascade Mountains from Diamond Peak to the Columbia River. Near the source the river has stretches of class 1 or easier water with an occasional class 4 to 6 waterfall. The lower regions of the river have considerable whitewater, up to class 3. The literal translation of the French name "Riviere des Chutes" (river of falls), should not be overlooked, as there are several unrunnable cascades and waterfalls. The Warm Springs River which enters below Lake Billy Chinook is no longer runnable. (The Warm Springs Indian Reservation Council has decided to close off access to the river. Please respect their property rights.) Much of the upper Deschutes water is diverted into a large irrigation canal near the city of Bend. Bend boaters sometimes set up a class 2 or 3 slalom course in the canal.

DESCHUTES RIVER
Wickiup Dam to Pringle Falls
Carl Landsness

Class	Flow	Gradient	Miles	Character	Season
1(4)	500 +	4 C	9	forest, osprey sanctuary	dam controlled

Description: This is one of the author's favorite flatwater runs in Oregon. Many things combine to create a stimulating and often exhilarating experience--high mountain air, clear blue water, ponderosa pine, abundant camping sites, and great fishing are but a few. Perhaps the strongest asset of this region is the dense population of osprey. The sound of an osprey calling and the sight of a vertical dive to pull a 12-inch trout from the water near your canoe are experiences not soon forgotten.

The majority of boaters on this stretch take out at Wyeth Campground on river left. Pringle Falls, a class 4 drop, lies just below here. Only expert kayakers should consider this drop, and only after scouting. It is definitely not a rapids for open canoes.

For those who wish to continue on downstream without running the falls, a portage is possible. The portage around Pringle Falls is long but easy walking. From Wyeth Campground, follow the entry road to Road 43; turn right and cross the river. Continue about 0.3 mile to the second road on the left and follow it to Pringle Falls Campground. The portage is about 1.5 miles long. Unfortunately, the land on both sides of the falls is private; thus the long portage.

The falls start with 200 yards of class 2- whitewater above the Road 204 bridge. Experienced class 2 boaters could eddy out on river right just above the bridge and save almost half the portage distance. The next 100 yards of class 3 + water lead into a class 4 drop with a potential keeper just above a footbridge. The remaining 200 yards are a bouncy class 3.

Difficulties: The portage around Pringle Falls.

Shuttle: Most people will reach this river section from US 97. At a sign to Wickiup Reservoir turn west onto USFS Road 43, about 2 miles north of La Pine, or about 4.5 miles south of the entrance to La Pine State Recreation Area. In 9 miles USFS 43 crosses the Deschutes River just above

Pringle Falls. The first left after the bridge, USFS 4370, leads to Wyeth Campground, the take-out, in a few hundred yards. Take out on river left at the Wyeth Campground boat ramp. There are signs warning of the upcoming falls.

Reach Wickiup Dam by continuing west on USFS 43 another 2.5 miles. Take a left onto USFS 4380, which runs to the reservoir levee. Turn left again to follow the levee to the put-in on the north (river-left) side of the dam. There is a 200 yard carry from a locked gate to the water. Refer to the recent (1982) edition of the Deschutes National Forest Map for details on roads and campgrounds, since the roads have been completely renumbered since the previous map.

Gauge: This river is regulated by Wickiup Dam. From late spring until early fall, the flow is generally very consistent at 1200-1600 cfs to supply the many irrigation canals near Bend. Outside of these periods, the flow can be severely and abruptly reduced. For information on water release from Wickiup Dam, contact the State Water Resources Department watermaster for the Bend region, (503) 388-6669.

DESCHUTES RIVER
Pringle Falls to Big River Campground
Carl Landsness

Class	Flow	Gradient	Miles	Character	Season
1 (2)	500 +	2.5 C	16	forest	dam controlled
				marshgrass	
				waterfowl haven	

Description: The first 7 miles of this section are similar to the pine-forested section upstream. Near the La Pine Recreation Area, the river begins to slow considerably and meander through wide open areas of marsh grass. The river takes on a very serene nature, disturbed occasionally by the sounds of fish and water fowl. Views of the nearby hills and distant mountains further enhance the enchanting nature of this section.

Difficulties: Tetherow Log Jam blocks the river 4 miles below Pringle Falls. Several signs warn of its presence. The portage is an easy 200-yard walk along the right bank. It is often possible to sneak the logs on the right bank and then run 100 yards of class 2 waves.

Shuttle: Put in at Pringle Falls Campground, below Pringle Falls on river right. (See portage description in the preceding write-up.)

Take out at Big River Campground, on river right, at the USFS Road 42 bridge. Reach Big River from Pringle Falls by driving west on USFS 43 one-half mile, and going right onto USFS 4350 for 2 miles. Turn right onto USFS Road 42 and follow it 8 miles to Big River Campground.

To reach Big River Campground from US 97, drive 2 miles south of Sunriver, turn west onto USFS 9724, follow it to USFS 42, thence to Big River.

Alternate take-outs are at the Tetherow Log Jam boat ramp on river right or at La Pine State Recreation Area. Check the Deschutes National Forest Map for Details.

Gauge: See previous section.

DESCHUTES RIVER
Big River Campground to Benham Falls
Carl Landsness

Class	Flow	Gradient	Miles	Character	Season
1 (5 +)	1000-3000	1 PD	18	forest houses resort country	dam controlled

Description: The first 7 miles to Harper's Bridge wander very slowly, with houses lining the banks for most of the length. The next 6-mile section passes Sunriver Resort with a noticeably stronger current and a large contingent of leisurely drifters.

Below Sunriver, the Deschutes makes a rather dramatic geological transition as it passes around and over the many lava flows of this region. After miles of absolutely mirror-like water the river is suddenly and violently churned into a frenzy at Benham Falls, a spectacular series of class 5 + ledges, holes, and froth, cascading more than 100 ft in 0.5 mile.

The normal take-out is on river right at the Benham Falls boat ramp, just above a footbridge over an impassable logjam. Boaters who wish to continue on downstream must portage the logjam and the falls. To portage, take out at the boat ramp, cross the footbridge, and follow a small jeep road 0.3 miles to the start of the falls. The portage leaves sight of the river and continues another 0.8 mile or so. Several paths lead down to the river.

The exact put-in depends on the skill of the boater. About 200 yards from the base of the steepest part of the falls, the river becomes a series of class 3 + ledges and waves, flowing through several channels and continuing for about 0.5 miles. The final few hundred yards are class 2. Scout it, enjoy the view, and take your choice. Also, experienced boaters might save 0.2 miles of walking above the falls by attempting a quick but tricky portage around the upstream logjam and paddle the 0.2 miles to the falls. However, the take-outs above the falls on river left are small and tricky to catch. Do not miss them!

Difficulties: The Benham Falls portage (1.5 miles)

Shuttle: Put in at Big River Campground, on river right, by the USFS Road 42 bridge. See the shuttle description for the previous section. Reach the take-out at Benham Falls from US 97 just south of Lava Lands Visitor Center. Take USFS 9702 west 5 miles to Benham Falls. Alternate take-outs are at Harpers Bridge and Besson Camp. Refer to Deschutes National Forest map for roads and campgrounds.

Gauge: The flow on this section is generally consistent between 1500 and 2500 cfs from spring to early fall. In fall, Wickiup Dam drops its release dramatically. Flow data at Benham Falls may be obtained from the State Water Resources Department in Bend, (503) 388-6669.

DESCHUTES RIVER
Benham Falls to Dillon Falls
Carl Landsness

Class	Flow	Gradient	Miles	Character	Season
1 (6)	1000-3000	2 PD	2.5	forest meadows lava flows	dam controlled

Description: This short section can be a lovely diversion on a warm summer afternoon if you're in the Bend area. The nearby resorts use this section heavily for their guests. Don't let its short length prevent you from giving it a try.

Several signs warn of Dillon Falls, another lava flow over which the river cascades. Don't miss the take-out on river left! After careening over a 15-ft class 6 ledge, Dillon Falls continues with almost 0.5 miles of exciting class 4 rapids. It is possible for advanced kayakers to put in at the base of the falls and run this class 4 rapids. Scout it first. The film "Up the Creek" was filmed here.

A 1-mile portage around Dillon Falls is possible on the left bank.

Difficulties: Don't miss the take-out.

Shuttle: To reach the put-in drive south on USFS Road 41 from Century Drive. Turn left at the Dillon Falls sign. Shortly before reaching Dillon Falls, turn right and continue past the Slough Camp (an alternate put-in) sign. Put in below Benham Falls, a moderate walk from the road. The take-out is located at the campground just above Dillon Falls.

Gauge: See previous section.

DESCHUTES RIVER
Dillon Falls to Lava Island Falls
Carl Landsness

Class	Flow	Gradient	Miles	Character	Season
3	1000-3000	16 PD	2.5	forest rafting freeway	dam controlled

Description: This is the famous "Big Eddy" run. The nearby resorts run an incredible number of visitors down this whitewater mini-run in the summer. One curler here has captured more rafts for film than any other in Oregon.

This section begins with a quiet mile between Dillon Falls and Aspen Campground, where most people put in to avoid the 0.8 mile put-in walk at Dillon. The next mile offers a few class 2 rapids before the river makes a sharp right turn through a quiet pool above Big Eddy. Big Eddy consists of several curlers. These can be great play-spots or potential keepers, depending on the flow. Scouting is advised (left bank). One hundred yards farther downstream is a class 2+ drop with a nice play wave at the top. Catch the small eddy on river right in order to play here. For the ambitious, it's an easy 300-yard carry back upstream to do Big Eddy again.

The take-out is on river left above Lava Falls. It is clearly marked with warning signs. Lava Falls is 0.5 miles of class 4-6 rapids where several drownings have occurred. The portage is equally hazardous. Don't attempt either.

The 9-mile section from here to Bend consists of several knarry class 4-6 rapids, some of which have been run by expert boaters from the Bend region. The author is personally unfamiliar with this section.

Difficulties: Scout Big Eddy Rapids.

Shuttle: Put in at Dillon Falls (a 0.8 mile walk), or 1 mile downstream at Aspen Camp. See the previous description. To reach the take-out, take USFS Road 41 south from Century Drive. Turn left at the sign to Lava Island Falls. Follow the river road upstream to Aspen Camp and Dillon Falls. Refer to the Deschutes National Forest map for details.

Gauge: See previous section.

DESCHUTES RIVER
Bend to Tumalo State Park
Carl Landsness

Class	Flow	Gradient	Miles	Character	Season
4	500-1500	57 PD	5.5	basalt canyon wooded, houses	dam controlled

Description: This short action-packed run is very convenient for Bend boaters. However, its primary drawback is that the local irrigation districts turn off the valve which feeds the river from mid-April until mid-October. Because of the 3500-ft elevation, December through February tends to appeal mainly to polar bears. The author recommends ordering a nice sunny day in March or April. When the morning ice on the windshield freezes one's boating enthusiasm, head for the ski slopes of Mt. Bachelor. When the snow turns to slush at noon, head for the river, because 3 to 4 hours are sufficient to complete this outstanding run.

A class 2+ rapids in front of the Riverhouse Motor Inn at the put-in allows a nice warmup. A footbridge about 0.5 mile downstream at Sawyer State Park marks a short class 3- drop. At the first bridge below Sawyer Park, Upper Rockefeller rapids begins, named for the value of the homes along the river. This is a bouncy, class 3+ drop with a few noteworthy holes; scouting is optional.

Just above the next footbridge, take out on river right and scout Lower Rockefeller from the bridge. Stay alert for a large square log with nasty nails that may be lodged on the left side (noted in Spring 1985).

Farther downstream look for a pier on river right and take out for the next scouting. At some levels this drop can be rather difficult. The possible routes are tight and surprisingly difficult to hit just right. Use your judgment and portage if necessary.

Soon the houses disappear as the river descends into a moderate-sized basalt canyon with pine trees that enhance the scenery. When the river suddenly narrows and disappears from view, stop and scout from river right. This class 4 drop requires some technical maneuvering for about 150 yards and ends with a pillow on the left. At lower levels, this section may be very difficult.

A short class 3 drop which soon follows is difficult to see from a boat. Trapped logs are a possibility, so one person from the group should scout the drop.

A short way downstream, talus, blasted from an irrigation canal, is evident high on the left bank. A sharp bend to the right announces The Slot. This class 4 drop warrants scouting on river left. The first 100 yards is a fairly straightforward paddle on river right. A big eddy on the left just above the final drop could be used by confident boaters to check out the last drop.

Another bouncy class 3 drop leads into the last class 4 drop of the run. When the river bends to the right and gets difficult to see, eddy out on the right and take a look. This drop has several holes, strong hydraulics, and a few well placed boulders. Its nature changes dramatically with the flow. This section concludes with 1-2 miles of enjoyable class 3 drops and play-spots. Be alert for a couple of low bridges and logs.

Difficulties: See description. Several scouts are required.

Shuttle: Put in just above the bridge at Riverhouse Motor Inn on US 97 in Bend. Take out at Tumalo State Park, which is northwest of Bend just off of US 20.

Gauge: Flows for the Deschutes River below Bend may be obtained from the State Water Resources Watermaster in Bend. The phone number is (503) 388-6669.

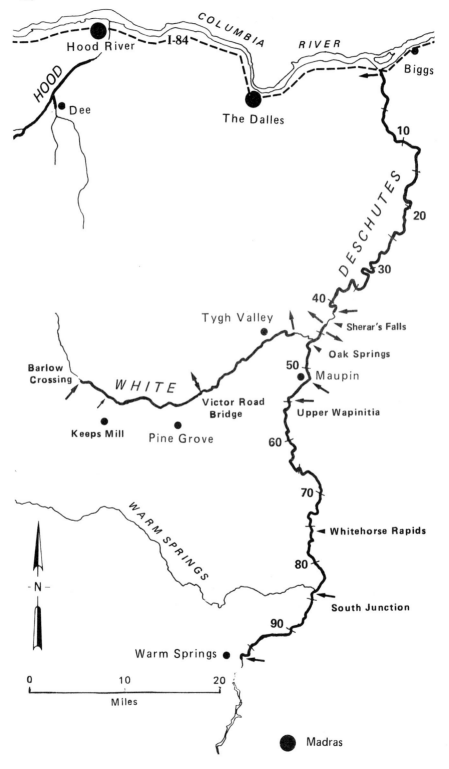

DESCHUTES RIVER
US 26 Bridge to Sherar's Falls
Rob Blickensderfer

Class	Flow	Gradient	Miles	Character	Season
3	3000-8000	12 PD	54	popular desert canyon	all year

Description: The lower Deschutes is a large desert canyon with an active railroad along the river. Rattlesnakes, chukars, and deer live here. The bottom of the canyon can become oppressively hot in the summer. Stiff up-canyon winds are normal in the afternoon. This section is a designated Scenic Waterway.

The first 20 miles below the US 26 bridge are fairly flat with only one significant rapids, Trout Creek Rapids. For this reason most boaters put-in at South Junction, 13 miles downstream. The river has numerous class 2 play-spots, good sharp eddies, and several class 3 rapids. The tempo is faster from Maupin to Sherar's Falls. The water is clear, fishing is usually good, and campsites are plentiful; but watch out for poison oak. The Warm Spring Indians own the land along the left.

Difficulties: Whitehorse Rapids, class 3, drops 25 feet in 300 yards. Upper Wapinitia Rapids has probably the fastest chute on this section. Lower Wapinitia Rapids, class 3, (sometimes called Boxcar Rapids, where a boxcar fell into the river in the late 40's) requires going over a 2-4 ft ledge and maneuvering around some large boulders. Oak Springs Rapids, a class 3 rapids which becomes more difficult as the water drops and rocks become exposed, is considered the most difficult on this section. Take out above Sherar's Falls. Look for a lumber shed and the road coming down to the river on the left.

Shuttle: The upper put-in is at the east end of the bridge where US 26 crosses the Deschutes, 11 miles north of Madras. The alternate put-in is at a place called South Junction, which is not a town. The turn-off to South Junction is on US 197 about 22 miles north of Madras. It is a fairly slow 12 mile drive over a dirt road to the river. The second alternate put-in, or take-out, is just below the bridge at Maupin on the right at the City Park. Recently, however, the caretaker has been assessing boaters a fee. Boaters may also put in at Upper Wapinitia Rapids by following a dirt road out of Maupin on the east side of the river. Maupin is on US 197. The take-out at Sherar's Falls is above the falls on the left along OR 216; an alternative take-out is at a sandy beach on river right about 1 mile above the falls. A paved road follows the east bank from the falls to Maupin. The run from Upper Wapinitia to Sherar's Falls is a common one day run.

Gauge: Contact the River Forecast Center in Portland. The flow is controlled by Pelton Dam, and adequate flow is maintained all year. Note: The railroad mileposts are approximately 4 miles greater than the river miles.

Watermarks:
Miles from the Mouth

'98	US 26 Bridge, put-in. Elevation is 1370 feet.
'96	Pioneer wagon road winds down east rim to old ferry crossing and washed out bridge at Mecca Bridge pier.
'94	Gorge of dark basalt.
'89	Large island, whitewater begins.
'88	Trout Creek Rapids begins on a right turn. Class 2. Next 8 miles are open valley. First sighting of railroad, on right, where it leaves the canyon. Dirt access roads on both sides.
'85	South Junction on right. Warm Springs River enters on left.
'78	Kaskela, a group of summer homes on the right.
'77	Small island.

'76   Whitehorse Rapids, class 3. Identified by a sharp pinnacle on the right, and a steep bank leading up to the railroad on the right, at the end of a stretch of slack water, which ends in a short plunge. Land below here on right to scout Whitehorse. The rapid begins on a sweeping right bend.

'75   Take left channel because right channel runs onto rocks. Enjoyable water through here.

'73   Davidson or North Junction. Railroad crosses to the left bank. Not much white water for next 10 miles. River passes through the Mutton Mountains, very scenic.

'68   Windows in colored stone, eroded by wind.

'65   Dant. Perlite mine high on the left.

'64   Buckskin Mary Falls. Run straight down the middle for a fine roller coaster ride. Good whitewater next 3 miles.

'55   Upper Wapinitia Rapids. After a left bend, spot a steel railroad bridge on the left crossing Wapinitia Creek. The rapid begins there on a right turn. Run right.

'54   Lower Wapinitia Rapids, class 3. Scout the first time through from either bank. The rapid begins with an abrupt left turn, then curves right with a very fast current. Next is a ledge across the entire river, with a 2-ft drop on the left and 4-ft drop on the right. A huge boulder with a dangerous hole behind it lies just below the ledge.

'52   Maupin Bridge. Possible take-out at City Park on right. Fine whitewater from here to Sherar's Falls.

'47   Oak Spring Rapids, class 3. Look for green growth on the left side of the canyon and mossy tanks of the Oak Springs fish hatchery. Whitewater begins 200 yards above the hatchery. The lower rapid is made difficult by the two ribs of basalt that divide the river into three channels. At high water the left channel can be run easily, but at low water the middle channel should be run; it's rocky.

'46   The White River enters on left. Nice chute just below.

'45   Osborne Rapids, a 4-ft drop in a short distance. Identified as the second drop below a protruding rock near midstream.

'44.5   Sight a shed and the road to Tygh Valley, both on the left. Land on the left as soon as the highway is reached and take out. Elevation 720 feet.

'44   Sherar's Falls, class 6, a 15-ft waterfall. Do not miss the take-out above the falls.

DESCHUTES RIVER   *Michael Becerra*

DESCHUTES RIVER
Sherar's Falls to the Mouth
Rob Blickensderfer

Class	Flow	Gradient	Miles	Character	Season
3	3000-8000	12 PD	44	popular desert canyon	all year

Description: See the previous section for the general description of the river. This section has more horseshoe bends and fewer rapids, but the current is brisk.

The Indians have treaty rights to fish for salmon at the base of Sherar's Falls. During the spring and fall they stand on flimsy scaffolding to dip salmon from the maelstrom below. From early times, the Indians had a bridge across the narrow gorge below the falls. In 1826 Peter Skene Ogden lost five horses into the river while attempting to cross the bridge.

Difficulties: There are five class 3 rapids. Bridge Rapids, just below the upper put-in, is difficult to see as it is approached. It can be avoided by using the put-in 1 mile downstream. Three other major rapids, Gordon Ridge Rapids, Colorado Rapids, and Rattlesnake Rapids, come within the last 6 miles. See Watermarks for description.

Shuttle: There are two possible put-ins near Sherar's Falls, where Oregon 216 crosses the Deschutes. The first is just above Sherar's Bridge on the right bank. To reach the alternate put-in drive downstream along the right bank on a secondary road about 1 mile, then run left to get to the boat ramp. The take-out is at Deschutes River State Park, just off I-84. The Park is visible from the interstate.

Gauge: Contact the River Forecast Center in Portland. The flow is controlled by Pelton Dam, and adequate flow is maintained all year.

Watermarks:

Miles From the Mouth

'44	Sherar's Falls. Fascinating to look at.
'44	Bridge on Oregon 216. Possible put-in is just above the bridge on the right bank. Bridge Rapids, class 3, is just below this put-in. Most difficult in low water.
'43	Better put-in, 1 mile down the access road along the river right past Buck Hollow. This road continues to mile 23.

'41	Railroad crosses to the right bank, goes through a tunnel, and back to the left bank.
'40	Island.
'39	Wreck Rapids, class 3 +. The extreme right is clean; the center is runnable but has some concealed rocks. There are no major rapids for the next 30 miles, but the river moves at 5 mph. Many small rapids are present.
'31	Cedar Island. Near the end of a large horseshoe bend is a dramatic basalt cliff. Automobile campground is on the right.
'26	Sinamox Island.
'26	Hill's ranch; abandoned buildings on both sides.
'25	Ferry Canyon with railroad bridge on the left.
'24	Island.
'20	Two islands after a right bend in the river.
'12	Harris Canyon and old water tank are on the right. Tall over-hanging reddish basalt cliffs.
'8	Freebridge. Old piers remain. Kloan, a railroad shed on left.
'6	Gordon Ridge Rapids, class 3. After the river makes an abrupt right turn, it drops over a 3-ft shelf followed by heavy whitewater for one-half mile.
'4	Colorado Rapids, class 3. The rapids is located above Gordon Canyon on the right, identified by the old wooden trestle across the mouth. Colorado Rapids is a long series of large standing and breaking waves. Rafts are sometimes capsized here.
'3	Green Narrows. A maze of rock ridges covered with grass divides the river into numerous channels. The right side is deepest. This leads directly to Rattlesnake Rapids.
'3	Rattlesnake Rapids, class 3. This is the most powerful rapids on this section. The rapids can be scouted from either bank. Most of the river flows over a very narrow upper ledge. The fierce hole below must be avoided. Normally run on the left.
'2	The skyline across the Columbia Gorge in Washington can be seen.
'1	Moody Rapids, class 2. Standing waves where the fast Des-chutes encounters the pool caused by The Dalles Dam.
'0.5	Take out on the left at the Lower Deschutes River Boat Ramp.

METOLIUS RIVER
Riverside Forest Campground to Lake Billy Chinook
T.R. Torgersen and Rob Blickensderfer

Class	Flow	Gradient	Miles	Character	Season
3(4)	1300-2000	24 C	28	forest fishing	all year

Description: This very unusual river originates in the high Cascades. Within a distance of several hundred feet, the river wells up from the ground in a series of gushing springs and becomes 30 feet wide. Within one-half mile, the river swells to an average flow of 1500 cfs, from which it deviates little throughout the year. Because the water comes from underground, the water is always frigid. The river level fluctuates little so the banks are overgrown by heavy vegetation throughout the entire length. The vegetation, uniform gradient, and lack of sizable eddies make landing spots hard to find. From the source, which is not accessible to boaters, the first few miles of river flow through meadowlands. At the first bridge in the community of Camp Sherman most visitors pause to look for the huge trout that lie waiting to be fed. Throwing a few salmon eggs into the water makes the fish suddenly appear as the bait disappears.

The character of the Metolius can be divided into two sections. The upper section from the source to Lower Bridge, about 11 miles, has a resort atmosphere with private camps, forest campgrounds, and picnic areas. Because this section has also been designated for fly fishing only, it is a favorite area for fishermen, so respect their fishing rights. The 17 mile section below Lower Bridge is primitive. A very poor road extends 8 miles along the river. Below the road is wilderness with no access for 7.5 miles until Lake Billy Chinook. Along the lower road are numerous primitive campgrounds with access to the river.

From the river's source to several miles below Camp Sherman the river is fast and replete with snags, but no significant whitewater. The tempo increases towards the Gorge, a fast class 3 rapids about a mile below Gorge Campground. Immediately downstream private land exists on both sides of the river and one or more of the very low bridges may require a portage. Kayakers commonly run some of the bridges "bottoms-up" and roll up once the passage is made. Wizard Falls, site of one of the low bridges, is not a true falls but a turbulent region through narrow channels in the riverbed. The 3 miles from Wizard Falls to Lower Bridge are class 1. Below Lower Bridge the tempo gradually increases again for 1 mile; thence a long class 3 rapids begins. From here to the end of the road are numerous shorter rapids with truly beautiful whitewater. Below the end of the road the water is similar to the upper stretch. About 3 miles below the road's end is the largest rapids on the river. The river continues at a fast pace to Lake Billy Chinook, where the change to flat water is like a gentle awakening from a pleasant dream. Take out on the right at campgrounds either above or on the lake.

Difficulties: The greatest danger is the potential of a ponderosa pine completely blocking the river. A short distance below the Gorge Campground is The Gorge, a relatively long fast class 3 rapids with rock dodging required. The second long fast class 3 rapids is located about 1 mile below Lower Bridge, also known as Bridge 99. The lower end of this rapids cannot be seen from the top. Therefore, check for possible tree blockage during the shuttle. This rapids is visible from the dirt road below Lower Bridge. The most difficult rapids on the Metolius is an easy class 4 located about 3 miles below the end of the dirt road. It is in a straight section of river and can be identified by the boulder and large holes at the top, which is the most difficult part. The water is very cold, about 43 degrees F at most.

Shuttle: Take US 20 or Oregon 22 east across the Santiam Pass or west from Sisters. Turn off to Camp Sherman about 5.5 miles east of Suttle Lake. If you want to see the origin of the river, take a minute and follow the signs to "Head of the Metolius." This unusual sight is well worth seeing! The paved road from the Head of the Metolius essentially parallels the river on the east side to Lower Bridge, where a poor secondary road continues along the east side for another 8 miles and dead-ends at a trail. The shuttle to Lake Billy Chinook is about 35 miles, mostly on gravel roads. The turn-off is about midway between Head of the Metolius and Lower Bridge. Follow the signs.

Put-ins are available at any of the campgrounds. If you put in at the Gorge or Wizard Falls, for example, the take-out can be at any of the unimproved campgrounds below Lower Bridge or at the end of the road. Lake Billy Chinook could be reached on the second day. If the take-out is one of the camps along the river, be sure to find a good landmark because this region all looks about the same from the river.

Gauge: Information on the flow is unnecessary on this run because discharge fluctuations are minimal. Throughout the year the discharges range from 1250 to 2500 cfs with a 58-year mean of 1500 cfs.

CROOKED RIVER
Lone Pine Bridge to Crooked River Ranch
Ron Mattson and Scott Russell

Class	Flow	Gradient	Miles	Character	Season
3 (4)	800	40 PD	18	inaccessible	snowmelt
4 (5)	4000			desert gorge	dam controlled

Description: The Crooked River has many big rapids and runs through a spectacular gorge. There are few good put-ins or take-outs on this hair-raising run. This run is for advanced to expert boaters. Much equipment has been lost in the Crooked River gorge. The next lost paddle or boat could be yours if you decide to run this river! Although the Crooked was run only by decked boaters in the past, expert rafters ran it in April 1979. This run requires quality river rafts and expert rafters able to run technical drops of 10 to 25 ft.

There are two possible put-ins for this run, one 4 miles above Smith Rocks State Park and the other 1.5 miles above the park. Boaters who opt for the put-in just 1.5 miles above the park will have no warm-up for the 1.5 miles of continuous class 4 rapids just above the park. Beyond this first stretch of very busy class 4 is a long loop of very slow water around Smith Rocks State Park. Rock climbers flock to this area year-round for some of the best climbing in Oregon. Boaters who paddle around Smith Rocks hear cries of "crazy" from above. The "crazy" may well apply to the small speck hundreds of feet above the river.

About a mile beyond the park is the first of a series of rapids, simply called Number One. Number One is a very steep short drop with a boulder in the center and more boulders and holes in the left channel. Scout right. About a mile farther is Number Two, which may be run on the left or right side of Lava Island. This drop is difficult to approach and should be scouted from the left.

The next rapids is a series of waves called the Bumps, located about 0.2 mile beyond Number Two. The Bumps are a prelude to Wap-te-doodle, a very long drop with powerful hydraulics and a very large hole at bottom center. This can be scouted from the left; note the log on the left. There are a couple of lesser rapids between here and the US 97 bridge that crosses high above.

From the bridge to the next major rapids, called No Name, the river is a very busy class 3 to 4. No Name is a very long and rough rapids with many boulders and a large hole at the bottom. No Name is scouted on the right. This drop is followed by several shorter and easier rapids.

The next major rapids is Chinese Dam, located at the end of a stretch of flatwater below sheer cliffs. This was the site of mining activity years ago. The river broke through the dam, leaving the center and the left of the river bed very shallow and rocky. The rapids are runnable, but only after scouting. Chinese Dam can be quite difficult at lower levels. The broken rocks are sharp.

It is possible to take out just above Chinese Dam Rapids on the left at the access road from the Crooked River Ranch. This take-out requires a very steep climb to the access road. An easier take-out is about 200 yards below Chinese Dam. Facilities are available at the ranch for camping.

Difficulties: This run presents many difficulties that demand special attention. See Description above for details. Retreat from the river due to equipment loss or injury is very difficult in most of the canyon.

Shuttle: The put-in is 3 miles east of Smith Rocks State Park at the Lone Pine Bridge. The state park is 3 miles east of Terrebonne, which is on US 97 between Redmond and Madras. An alternate put-in is 1 mile east of Smith Rocks State Park at the aqueduct.

CROOKED RIVER   *Smith Rocks*   *Lance Stein*

The take-out is at Crooked River Ranch, a resort community. Follow the signs off US 97 north of Terrebonne, to Crooked River Ranch and the clubhouse. Drive past the clubhouse and turn right just before the little white church. Continue on the gravel road to a graveled lot. Drive through the gate on Hollywood Road, a very rough, steep (four-wheel drive) road down 1.3 miles to Chinese Dam.

Gauge: This section is runnable for only a short time each year, usually in late April. In years of low snowfall there may be no water released. For information on planned releases contact the Oregon Water Resources Department Watermaster in Bend or the Ochoco Irrigation District in Prineville.

CROOKED RIVER
Crooked River Ranch to Lake Billy Chinook
Scott Russell and Hank Hays

Class	Flow	Gradient	Miles	Character	Season
3(4)P	1000	35 PD	9	inaccessible	all year
	5000			desert gorge	

Description: This part of the Crooked River is not quite as intense, and only half as long, as the previous section. Even with a flow of only 100 cfs at Prineville Dam, numerous springs increase the flow to 1000 cfs within 5 or 6 miles, making the river runnable year-round. One may opt to put in either above Chinese Dam, a difficult rocky rapids, or about 200 yards downstream. At normal summer flows (low), Chinese Dam is not runnable. Put in below it. One mile past Chinese Dam is The Wave, which, at flows above 3500 cfs, has a steep V-wave that envelops the boater with water converging 4 ft overhead.

Four miles farther is Opal Springs Dam. A 0.2 mile portage on the right is required at the dam as the river disappears into a power tunnel. Below Opal Springs Dam is Opal Springs itself, followed by a gauge; both are on the right. Several easier rapids follow. The last whitewater before Lake Billy Chinook is long and heavy with some big holes. About 3 miles of lake paddling brings the boater to the take-out at the bridge over the Crooked River arm of the lake.

Difficulties: The Wave, a mile below Chinese Dam, is steep; at really low water, the left looks most promising, but it may not be runnable. It is rocky on top left and even worse on bottom right. At higher water, center to right is better. Opal Springs Dam is recognized by the concrete structure on the left. Portage on the right. Beware of sharp and slippery rocks.

Shuttle: For the put-in at Crooked River Ranch, see the take-out of the previous section. The take-out bridge crosses the Crooked River arm of Lake Billy Chinook about 6 miles west of Culver, which in turn is a few miles west of US 97, south of Madras. Follow signs to Cove Palisades State Park. Pass the park and continue to the bridge.

Gauge: Located below Opal Springs Dam, on right. It is not telemetered. At 2.0 ft the flow is nearly 1200 cfs, and at 3.0 ft, 1700 cfs.

WARM SPRINGS RIVER
Fish Hatchery to Lower Bridge

Description: The Warm Springs Indian Reservation Council has decided to close this river to the public. Please respect their property rights!

WHITE RIVER
Barlow Crossing to Victor Road Bridge
Harvey Lee Shapiro

Class	Flow	Gradient	Miles	Character	Season
3+	400	78 C	18	forest, canyon	snowmelt
4-	1400			wilderness	

Description: This magnificent run starts on the east side of Mount Hood amongst the trees (and often snow), continues through a wilderness gorge, and ends in a desert. The change in scenery en route is spectacular.

The first 2.5 miles below the put-in at Barlow Crossing are class 1+. The river gradient then increases and there are many blind turns. The first significant drop is 4.5 miles below Barlow Crossing. It consists of two big ledges, which should be scouted on river left.

From here to the take-out, the river is a continuous class 3+ with a beautiful rhythm of its own. At medium levels eddies and play-spots are abundant. There are 3 or 4 places where the river drops more steeply. They can be recognized by the highest cliffs on river left. All of these drops are runnable and can be scouted by eddy hopping.

Keeps Mill is an alternate put-in, 7 miles below Barlow Crossing. Here the river flow increases about 30% as Frog Creek enters from the right. About two thirds of the way through the trip, hanging metal gates mark the National Forest boundary. A short way below here the river gains more volume, and at higher water levels becomes pushy.

Difficulties: The first drop around a blind right turn at mile 4.5 is a major difficulty. Also, the White is susceptible to log jams. One can almost always be assured of some log jams that will require portaging. Most paddlers underestimate the speed of the current, and there is usually at least one log-jam-related story on every trip. Fortunately, there have been no fatalities on this river as of this writing (1985). Please use extreme care when approaching log jams.

Shuttle: If the road is open, the easiest way to the put-in from the Portland area is to take US 26 and turn left on Oregon 35. Follow Oregon 35 until it crosses the White River. There will probably be about 50 cfs in the river at this point. Turn right on Road S408, a paved road that follows the river on the river left side. Take the first dirt road on the left after crossing the bridge. This is the historic Barlow Road. In about one mile is another bridge marking Barlow Crossing, where the pioneers crossed the White River. Put in here.

An alternate put-in, at Keeps Mill, should be used if the river is below 550 cfs at Tygh Valley. To get to Keeps Mill take US 26 east, turn left onto Oregon 216 toward Maupin. After 3 miles and about 1 mile before Bear Springs, look for a sign to Keeps Mill and Road S483. Turn left and continue about 2 miles on the main road down to the river. Road conditions change frequently due to logging activity, thus the last 1.5 miles is extremely slow.

To reach the take-out from Keeps Mill, go back to Oregon 216 and to Bear Springs (see below). To reach the take-out from Barlow Crossing, continue south on the paved road which is now S448. When S448 ends, turn left on US 26 and continue east. Take Oregon 216 toward Maupin and continue past Bear Springs to Pine Grove.

Continue about 2 miles. There will be a small green sign on the right saying Victor Road - White River. Turn left onto this dirt road and follow it as it jogs right and then left. Shortly after it turns right again, take the first road to the left. There is a sign to Wamic. After making the left turn, note the sign about the road being extremely hazardous, especially in winter. Have faith and continue to the river and the take-out at Victor Road bridge, river left side, a total drive of 17 miles from Barlow Crossing.

Gauge: Contact the River Forecast Center in Portland for the Tygh Valley Gauge on the White River.

WHITE RIVER
Victor Road Bridge to Tygh Valley
Harvey Lee Shapiro

Class	Flow	Gradient	Miles	Character	Season
2 + (3)	700-	40 PD	11	forest, canyon	snowmelt
	2000			wilderness	

Description: This is an easy run through some of the most beautiful scenery in Oregon. There are a few rapids at the start followed by a narrow canyon with steep walls on both sides. The water is moving but there are no real rapids in the canyon. Farther along is one significant rapids that should be scouted on river left. There are usually log jams which must be portaged. Do not underestimate the speed of the river when approaching a log jam. The take-out is along the roadside in Tygh Valley. About 2 or 3 miles below Tygh Valley there is an unrunnable 90-ft waterfall. Two miles below the falls the White River flows into the Deschutes River.

Difficulties: Log jams are the major hazard. See the discussion of difficulties in the previous section.

Shuttle: From the put-in, return by Victor Road and turn left onto Oregon 216. Continue to Tygh Valley. See the previous section for directions to Victor Road bridge.

Gauge: Tygh Valley on the White River.

Chapter 11. Eastern Oregon Rivers

JOHN DAY RIVER

Introduction by Rob Blickensderfer

The John Day runs a course of over 250 miles from the headwaters in the Blue Mountains to the confluence with the Columbia River in north central Oregon. Three of the longer scenic and more isolated sections are described here. These sections provide a good combination of easy whitewater and fine camping and hiking. The upper section on the North Fork is the most difficult and is not recommended for open canoes except for the very experienced and well prepared. The lower sections are excellent for open canoe and beginning kayak trips. The countryside changes from pine forests in the upper regions to semi-arid treeless desert, complete with small cactus, in the lower region. For the most part the scenery is superb. The countryside is open range, and cattle visit the river for drinking water, especially in the lower sections. They are not a problem in camp, however.

DO NOT drink the river water; it is polluted and turbid. Carry about 2 to 3 gallons of drinking water per person. Creeks in the lower section are normally dry; if not, they are polluted. The sun can be very intense. Bring proper protective clothing and sun lotion.

N. FK. JOHN DAY   *Rob Blickensderfer*

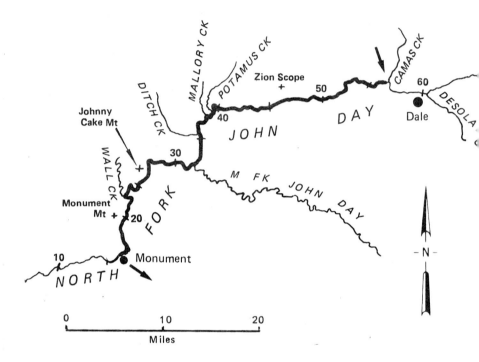

The John Day is fed primarily by snowpack in the Blue Mountains, so its flow is very seasonal. The peak flow is usually in April and at Service Creek can be as high as 20,000 cfs or higher, although the mean peak is 6,000 cfs. The minimum flow in August to October can be less than 200 cfs. The best time to run the North Fork is in April or May when the flow is near its peak. The summary hydrograph indicates the mean flows.

Although the lower sections are runnable at the higher levels around 6,000 cfs, the combination of cold and big water could kill the ill-prepared. Wetsuits should be required for all persons in April and May. The lower sections are more enjoyable at flows around 2,000 cfs when the water and air are much warmer. At this time, usually early June, the river is one of the few in Oregon that swimmers can enjoy. Bass can also be caught then.

Additional information can be found in books by Arighi, Campbell, and Garren.

NORTH FORK JOHN DAY RIVER
Dale to Monument
Rob Blickensderfer

Class	Flow	Gradient	Miles	Character	Season
2 +	800-5000	21 C	40	forest canyon	snowmelt

Description: This section marks the transition between the foothills of the Blue Mountains and the high desert country typical of Eastern Oregon. The terrain is mountainous with open forest of ponderosa pine and little evidence of civilization. Wildflowers are abundant in the spring, and walks into the hills above camp are well worthwhile. The open vegetation makes walking easy and enjoyable. Good campsites are common. Before the midpoint of the trip two bridges cross the river, and farther on, the Middle Fork of the John Day merges from the left.

Difficulties: From the put-in the river is relatively fast and straightforward. About 3 miles below Camas Creek, the first of the three largest rapids occurs. The first rapids, class 2+, can be rocky and require some maneuvering. Many will wish to scout it; the portage is on the right. The approach to the rapids is rocky at low water, and the water flows along a small cliff on the left at the lower end. The run-out is good.

Two additional rapids quite similar in character to the first rapids occur in the next seven miles. The river gradually flattens out over the next 30 miles, but several long class 2- rock gardens and some large standing waves make it interesting. At higher water the river takes on a class 3- character. At any water level the North Fork is definitely more difficult and much faster than the lower John Day, described in the next section.

The water is quite cold from the snowmelt, and the remoteness from civilization must also be considered. The weather can turn cold unexpectedly with the possibility of frosty nights or snow flurries into June. Thus a smashed boat with lost gear and cold weather could combine to threaten one's survival.

Shuttle: There are several put-ins in the vicinity of Dale. To reach Dale, take US 395 either south from I-84 at Pendleton or north from US 26 at Mount Vernon. Several automobile campgrounds are within a few miles of Dale. US 395 follows the north shore of the North Fork for 2 miles between the bridge over the North Fork on the east and the bridge over Camas Creek on the west. There are several river accesses along US 395 or at the second bridge across the North Fork, 3 miles upstream from Camas Creek. From the west end of the Camas Creek Bridge an unimproved road along the north shore of the North Fork provides a choice of put-ins as well as unimproved campgrounds.

To reach the take-out, follow US 395 south for 26 miles to the town of Long Creek, then turn west to Monument, another 21 miles. Take out near the bridge in Monument.

Gauge: Contact the River Forecast Center in Portland for the flow at Monument. The gauge includes the flow of the Middle Fork, which usually carries less than half as much water as the North Fork. The flow at Monument is normally 60 to 70% of the flow at Service Creek (see next section).

Watermarks:

Mile

'0.0	Camas Creek on right. Elevation 2700 ft.
'3.0	Grandstand Rapids, class 2 +. House on right at mid-rapids can be seen straight ahead before reaching rapids. Rapids begin with a wide curve to left. To scout, land on right at curve. The straight fast drop ends with a curve to the right as a wave rolls off cliff on the left. A small pool below rapids is followed by a fast class 1 + rapids.
'3.5	A-frame house on right.
'3.8	Class 2- rapids.
'4.0	Cabin on right.
'4.5	Surprise Rapids, class 2 +. The approach is not obvious. Large waves are at the bottom of this relatively short rapids. A hole on left, near the small cliff, may surprise you.
'6.0	Chainsaw Rapids, class 2. Good eddy on right, ahead of rapids, provides a landing. Upper section of rapids has large standing waves between relatively narrow steep banks. A pool with an eddy and a cabin on the right precede the lower section, a straightforward 500-ft long rapids.
'10.	Zipper Rapids, class 2 +. The approach is an S-curve. The main rapids, at the end of the S, quite similar in character to Grandstand Rapids but more demanding, can be scouted from either side.
'11.0	Zion Scope. This dominant symmetrical mountain ahead on the right is visible for the next 2 miles.
'12.0	Stony Creek on right. Wooden bridge across creek.
'12 +	Devils Backbone. Dominant on right past Zion Scope.
'13.8	Upper Bridge Rapids, class 2-. A 1000-ft long fast boulder garden begins just as bridge becomes visible.
'14.0	Concrete bridge.
'14.5	Lower Bridge Rapids, class 2-. A 1000-ft long boulder garden.
'16.5	Old homestead on right in a clearing. Creek.
'18.0	Potomas Creek on right.
'18.5	Concrete bridge. Road to Ritter up Wrightman Canyon on left.
'19.0	Mallory Creek on right.
'21.0	Ditch Creek on right.
'23.0	Class 2- rapids on gentle curve to left.
'24.0	House on right.
'24.5	Middle Fork John Day enters from left. Several campsites below here.
'28.5	Cabin and barn on right. Cabin Creek on right.
'29.0	Johnny Cake Mountain, elevation 3606 ft, is the dominant feature to the west for several miles. The horizontal layers of basalt look like a layer cake.
'31.0	Class 2- rapids in a narrow basaltic channel. Neal Butte, prominent mountain just southwest of Johnny Cake Mountain.
'31.5	Coyote Canyon on right, between Johnny Cake Mountain and Neal Butte.
'32.0	Two Cabin Creek on left, followed by class 2- rapids.
'34.0	Barn, cabins, and house on right.
'34.2	Wall Creek, a major tributary, enters from right, seen straight ahead, before river makes a sharp 180-degree turn to left.
'36.0	Two class 2- rapids. Monument Mountain, with fire lookout, is dominant on right.
'37.5	House on right. Canyon opens, powerlines and irrigation pumps are passed as Monument is approached.
'40.0	Bridge in Monument. Possible take-out on right on gravel bar above bridge. Elevation 1865 ft.

JOHN DAY RIVER   *Rob Blickensderfer*

JOHN DAY RIVER
Service Creek to Clarno
Rob Blickensderfer

Class	Flow	Gradient	Miles	Character	Season
2	1200-	8 PD	44	desert canyon	snowmelt
1 + (2)	6000				

Description: This section of the John Day is a favorite for open canoeists, drift boaters, and beginning kayakers who want a fine desert wilderness experience. Although there are a number of ranches and cultivated fields at several places along the river, other stretches are uninhabited and cut off from civilization by the towering walls of the canyon. The view around each bend seems more beautiful and inspiring than the last. The sculpture of nature in the twisted basalt canyons present forms never before imagined. The most scenic stretch has been preserved by the designation as a Scenic River. The other stretches have seen ever-increasing pressures of man's relentless efforts to cultivate any land which has water available. Thus the many irrigation pumps flooding alfalfa fields leave the boater with the uneasy feeling that the river may be pumped dry before he reaches his take-out.

Campsites are quite plentiful, often with sandy beaches below and juniper trees farther up. There are no campsites near the ranching area of Twickenham or along the last eight miles to Clarno. There are no stores in either settlement.

Below the put-in at Service Creek the boater has several easy class 1 rapids and riffles as he feels himself slipping away from civilization.

Difficulties: Open canoeists should scout the three class 2 rapids in this section, although kayakers with class 2 experience will not have difficulty. About 1 of 4 open canoes will swamp in Russo rapids. Therefore, less experienced canoeists may wish to portage. At lower water levels the portage is easiest on the left, but at higher water it becomes impossible because of the cliff, the portage must be on the right. Wreck Rapids, with its side-breaking wave off the cliff on the right, can also swamp an open canoe. Schuss Rapids is the shortest and easiest of the three, but can swamp open canoes at flows above 3000 cfs. In several places the river drives headlong into cliff walls. At high water the rolling waves off the cliff, as well as the eddy on the inside of the bend, can give the unwary boater problems.

Afternoon up-canyon winds are normal and occasionally strong with erratic side gusts. Rattlesnakes and scorpions are present but seldom seen.

Shuttle: The take-out is at Clarno where Oregon 218 crosses the river. Parking and a boat landing are located at the east end of the bridge. The put-in at Service Creek is about an hour drive from Clarno via the town of Fossil. Service Creek consists of a small store on Oregon 19. The owners will shuttle a car to Clarno for $35 (1985). The put-ins are down the road from the store at either of two access points, both within 0.2 mile of the junction of Oregon 19 and 207 from Mitchell.

Gauge: Contact the River Forecast Center in Portland for the flow at Service Creek. If the gauge at Service Creek is broken ask for the flow at Monument and the flow at the town of John Day. The total of these flows is nearly equal to the flow at Service Creek.

Watermarks:
Mile

'0	Put-in at Service Creek, 1/4 mile above or below bridge.
'2	Abandoned cabin on left.
'6	Russo Rapids, class 2. Approach is at a curve to left. Rapids is straight with cliff at bottom left. At low water canoes can portage on left; at high water, on right.
'10	Approach ranches above Twickenham.
'12	Twickenham bridge.
'15	Wreck Rapids, class 2. Approach is a slight curve to right. Can land on left to scout or portage. The rapids has a side-breaking wave off the cliff on the right at the lower end.
'17	Greenish fossil beds and red earth on right.
'19	Class 1 + rapids.
'21	Burnt Ranch, ranchhouse on left.
'23	Schuss Rapids or Burnt Ranch Rapids. Large rock in center at head of rapids below 3000 cfs. Can scout from left or right.
'24	Rock pinnacle on right.
'25	Cherry Creek on left. Some parties take out here.
'27	Big Bend region. River makes several sweeping bends in beautiful deep canyon. Fine beaches and campsites. Numerous class 1 rapids.
'30	Rattlesnake Canyon on right toward end of Big Bend Region. A back road comes in here.
'34	Ranches. A secondary road on right connects to highway near Clarno.
'38	Cave on hill on left.
'44	Clarno Bridge. Take-out on right.

JOHN DAY RIVER
Clarno to Cottonwoods
Rob Blickensderfer

Class	Flow	Gradient	Miles	Character	Season
2-(3)	1200-6000	11 C	70	desert canyon	snowmelt

Description: This section of the John Day is a favorite for open canoeists, drift boaters, and beginning kayakers. Because the gradient here is steeper than it is in the preceding section, the river moves faster and has more wave action. There are fewer ranches and one feels more isolated in this section. It has been designated a Wild River under the Oregon Scenic Waterways System. Many magnificent canyon walls exist in isolation unseen by all but river runners. As on the preceding section, the spring weather can range from snow flurries to sunny with temperatures over 100 degrees F within a few days. Similarly, beware of strong up-canyon winds in the afternoons, rattlesnakes, and the lack of potable water. See Description of preceding section.

Difficulties: Clarno Rapids, class 3, is 4 miles below the bridge at Clarno. Class 2 water leads around a left curve and into the main drop. The rapids can be scouted from the left by landing above the class 2 drop. Most open canoes will swamp in Clarno Rapids, but they can be lined on the left. Below the main class 3 drop enjoyable class 2 rapids continue for about 0.5 mile. Basalt Rapids, class 2, is at mile 15. Below 3000 cfs the rounded black basalt rocks are exposed in the rapids and some maneuvering is required. The main rapids is fairly short and curves to the left. Enjoyable rapids, with some rock dodging, follow for the next half-mile.

Shuttle: The put-in is at the bridge in Clarno where Oregon 218 crosses the river. The take-out is at the Cottonwood Bridge where Oregon 206 crosses the river. To get from Clarno to Cottonwood follow Oregon 218 to Fossil, Oregon 19 to Condon, and Oregon 206 to Cottonwood.

Gauge: Contact the River Forecast Center in Portland for the flow at Service Creek.

Watermarks:

Mile	
'0.0	Clarno. Put in at bridge on right.
'3.2	Red bluffs and green formations seen ahead (on river left).
'3.5	Large riffle. Big holes in middle at high water; rocky at low water.
'4.4	Clarno Rapids. Island ahead of rapids, take left channel. Trees on left bank are followed by an eddy on the left with a small landing spot just above the main chute. Heavy fast water leads to the major drop about 300 ft downstream. It may be scouted or portaged on the left from the landing. Lower Clarno, class 2, continues for 0.3 mile. Rocky at low water.
'5.3	Mulberry camp on right below Clarno Rapids. Last camp and beach not on private land for 6.5 miles.
'7.2	Old cabin on right. Bill's place.
'7.7	Powerlines cross river.
'8.5	Cabin on left. Farquer McRay place, 1894. Island just below.
'10.5	Powerlines cross river again.
'11.3	Powerlines cross river, followed by old ranch buildings on right, followed by 0.3 mile of 1+ to 2- rapids.
'11.9	Butte Creek on right.
'13.5	Buildings on right, visible straight ahead from far upstream. Watermark for nearing Basalt Rapids.

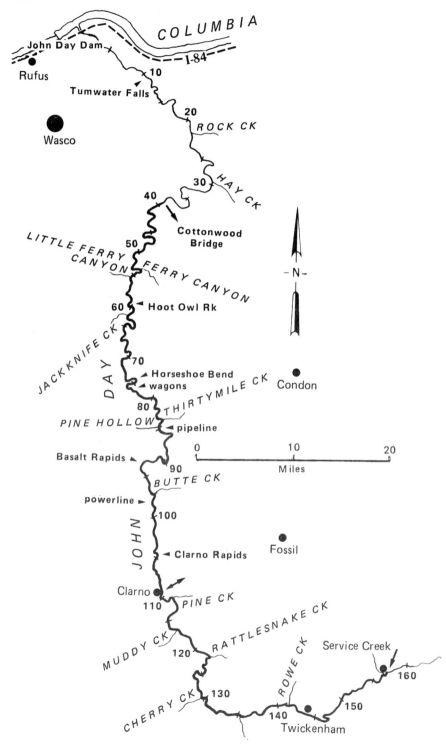

'15.9 Basalt Rapids, class 2 +. The approach is not obvious but can be identified by fast water leading around a slight curve to the right. Land right to scout. The main rapids, replete with basalt boulders, curves left. Lower Basalt Rapids, with large black basalt boulders in the river, continues for 0.5 mile. Good campgrounds here and in Great Basalt Canyon for the next 4 miles.

'20.0 Arch Rocks on right. Look back; two large arches appear high on cliff. One arch has large cave with excellent spring, but the climb is arduous.

'24.4 Sign and markers identify pipeline crossing. Natural gas line from British Columbia to San Francisco, built in 1963.

'25.3 Thirty Mile Creek on right. Habitations and access road to civilization.

'33.0 Old wagons on low land on right. Used in a 1928 movie, the rims were stolen once but returned by the Bureau of Land Management.

'33.5 River begins a sweep to the right (the Saddle ahead is only 300 feet wide followed by Horseshoe Bend, a 320-degree, 2-mile turn to the left.

'36.5 Indian paintings on right along road at Potlach Canyon.

'37.3 Two springs come out of hillside on left amidst vegetation, identified by a dirt bank on left and distorted columnar basalt on right, near river.

'39.0 Cave Bluff, a small cave at water level on right. Island just above here.

'42.4 Stairstep Palisades on left as river makes a sharp 180-degree turn to right. Farther downstream are more palisades on left.

'43.5 Kock Rock on right. A horizontally projecting column of basalt.

'45.0 Southbound Rapids. Straightforward class 1 +, headed due south, large gravel bar on left.

'49.3 Hoot Owl Rock on right. A 3-ft high owl against the skyline, about 50 ft above the river. Gravel bar on left. Citadel Rock, a fairy-tale fortress, formation dominates the view downstream. River makes a sharp 180-degree turn to the right.

'53.8 Little Ferry Canyon on left. Two flat islands just downstream. Red bluffs ahead to the left are the Gooseneck.

'54.5 The Gooseneck. River first curves sharply right, then makes a long 200-degree curve left around the Gooseneck.

'55.5 Ferry Canyon on right, with large delta about midway around the Gooseneck. A ferry ran here from 1893-1920. The George Owens cabin is up the canyon 0.3 mile. Ferry Canyon Rapids. Straightforward class 1 +.

'56.0 Charlie Owens cabin on right. It nearly collapsed in 1984.

'61.3 McCaleb cabin on left. Built in 1899, it nearly collapsed in 1982.

'63.4 Powerlines are visible on distant ridge.

'64.2 Ruggles pack grade is visible on hill on left.

'69.0 Cottonwoods bridge. Take-out on the right, just below bridge.

Note. These mileages are believed to be accurate. The mileages in Campbell's book are in error as much as 1.8 miles.

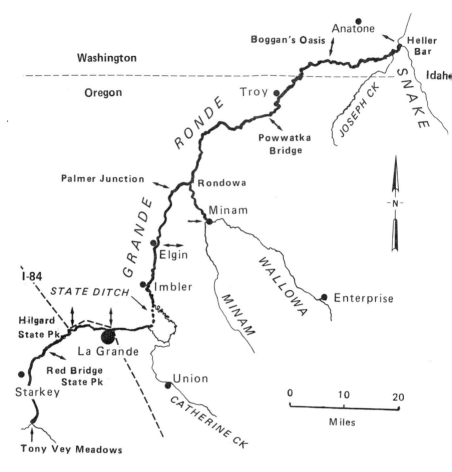

GRANDE RONDE RIVER
Introduction by T.R. Torgersen

The Grande Ronde and its main tributaries, the Minam and the Wallowa, drain about 4,000 square miles of northeastern Oregon. The drainage includes portions of the Elkhorn, Blue and Wallowa Mountains. Originating in the Elkhorns, the Grande Ronde River descends through nearly 50 miles of forest and rangeland. Near LaGrande it changes character abruptly to become a pastoral river in a broad, agriculturally dominated basin. Here the river is flanked on the west by Mount Emily at the crest of the Blue Mountains, and on the east by Mount Harris at the edge of the Wallowas.

Once past Elgin, the river strikes northeastward where it has carved a deep canyon. This canyon takes the river through nearly one hundred miles of forests and grasslands. Much of this latter part of the river and a short portion of the Wallowa River are under consideration by the State of Oregon for designation as a State Scenic Waterway. These river sections are uniquely qualified for protection under the Scenic Waterway Act.

Fine sport and commercial fisheries are spawned by this river system. Wildlife abounds in the canyon, which supplies critical range for Rocky Mountain elk, whitetail deer and mule deer. The riparian zone is also home for bald eagle, a diversity of waterfowl, otter, beaver, mink, raccoon, black bear and cougar. A diverse flora exists here, and several rare and endangered plants grow in the protection of canyon wall and forest glade. Recreationists use the river and its canyon for fishing, hunting, hiking and berry picking.

Several guide services hold permits to float the Grande Ronde, and many local boaters use the river. Thus, vacant campsites are sometimes difficult to find. In general, the river is not a highly technical one for floaters. The rapids which must be scouted from shore are expressly described in the following pages; all of the other rapids on the river can be scouted from the water. The only exceptions might be at some low flows, or at excessively high volumes. The gauges that supply pertinent flow data are at LaGrande, Rondowa, and Troy.

For other than the most detailed topographic features shown on USGS quadrangle sheets, US Forest Service maps portray the Grande Ronde river system and access roads best. River sections above LaGrande are shown on the Wallowa-Whitman National Forest / South Half map. Sections below LaGrande and extending about 10 miles below Boggan's Oasis are shown on the Umatilla National Forest map.

These maps are available at National Forest offices at Pendleton, Baker, and LaGrande. Or write to the Wallowa-Whitman National Forest, Box 907, Baker, OR 97814, (503) 523-6391; or Umatilla National Forest, 2517 SW Hailey Ave., Pendleton, OR 97801, (503) 276-3811.

GRANDE RONDE RIVER
Tony Vey Meadows to Red Bridge State Park
T.R. Torgersen

Class	Flow	Gradient	Miles	Character	Season
3(4 +)T	250-800	54	17	forest	snowmelt

Description: This section is near the upper limits of navigation. Above the put-in the river meanders through meadowlands for about 8 miles. Barbed wire fences are potential hazards and detract from the appeal of the above run; nonetheless it provides an easy and attractive float for canoeists and fishermen.

The put-in for the downstream whitewater section begins near an old splash dam at the edge of Tony Vey Meadows. The river changes character abruptly here and quickly becomes narrow, rocky and swift. Fairly steep, well timbered slopes and generally dense streamside vegetation border this section. There are several campgrounds and picnic sites affording comfortable rest stops.

Difficulties: The generally narrow channel and rapid descent of this section create a run that is potentially hazardous; water rescues will be difficult! Anticipate the need to react quickly to newly fallen trees blocking the channel.

The Stygian Steps are a series of drops that require scouting. They can be scouted from the road during the shuttle, about 3.5 miles upstream from Utopia Campground. On the river, they are about 0.3 miles below the River Picnic Site. At this writing (1985), a barbed wire fence and collection of debris forms an obstruction at Starkey. This is about 2.5 miles below Bikini Beach Campground, and 2 miles below a former bridge site. The latter is an optional take-out.

Shuttle: Take Hilgard State Park exit off I-84 and proceed about 12 miles on Oregon 244 to junction with Route 51 to Starkey. Put-in is at the junction of Forest Road 200 to Johnson Rock, and Route 51, 11.5 miles above Starkey Trading Post. Take-out is at Red Bridge State Park, 7.5 miles from I-84 on Oregon 244.

Gauge: An acceptable level for running this section can be estimated from the LaGrande gauge; a volume of 900 to 1100 cfs there is a boatable level from Tony Vey Meadows. Safe minimum and maximum flows are unknown.

GRANDE RONDE RIVER
Red Bridge State Park to Hilgard State Park
T.R. Torgersen

Class	Flow	Gradient	Miles	Character	Season
2	850-	22	8	forest	snowmelt
2 +	5000				

Description: The river canyon broadens considerably on this section and is bounded by open forest and some rangeland. A modest gradient and easy riffles make this a fine float for beginners in almost any craft.

Difficulties: Rapids constitute little hazard on this section, but beware of barbed wire fences across the river. A rifle club shooting range is situated on the river about 4.2 miles below Red Bridge Park. A sign, "Caution: Entering rifle range impact area," hanging on a wire crossing the river, warns the boater of potential hazard. Make your presence known to shooters who may be at the benches when you reach this spot!!

Shuttle: Red Bridge State Park is on Oregon 244 about 7.5 miles from the I-84 exit at Hilgard State Park. The take-out is on river left at Hilgard State Park either above or below the bridge.

Gauge: LaGrande gauge readings are used to designate flows for this section.

GRANDE RONDE RIVER
Hilgard State Park to Riverside City Park, LaGrande
T.R. Torgersen

Class	Flow	Gradient	Miles	Character	Season
2(3 +)	4500-6000	26	9	road	rainy
3(4)	7000 +				snowmelt

Description: This is a favorite conditioning and play run for local boaters. An annual raft race on this section attracts a flurry of floaters in every imaginable type of craft. The river is wide and gentle at first, giving way to several long rapids and good play-spots.

Difficulties: There are an initial few miles of easy warm-up. A ledge called Snoose Falls nearly spans the river and forms a good surfing wave. It also marks the beginning of intermittent rapids. The first significant rapids begin when the tall I-84 bridge comes into view. Below the bridge is a series of splendid standing waves as the river veers to the right. Two bridges beyond is Vortex, a fine play-spot and well known spectator vantage point to watch rafters and others get "eaten" in the curl.

At the Riverside City Park take-out is Riverside Rapids, known by kayakers as Baum's Swimmin' Hole. Scout this one before the run when you park the shuttle vehicle. On the river, the sound of the rapids and the presence of the Spruce Street bridge forewarn of the two closely spaced drops and the large curl at the bottom on river right.

GRANDE RONDE RIVER   *Minam Roller*   *Gary Lane*

Shuttle: The put-in is at Hilgard State Park immediately off the I-84 exit for the Park. The take-outs are at or near Riverside City Park on Spruce Street, located within the LaGrande city limits. Take LaGrande exit 261 off I-84. Proceed left toward town, and turn right at the 5-way intersection regulated by a traffic signal. Travel one block and take another right onto Spruce Street and continue for about a mile to Riverside City Park.

An alternate take-out which avoids the Riverside rapids is on river left, about 300 yards upstream from the Spruce Street bridge. A short gravel road on river left, immediately off the north end of the bridge, gives access for shuttle cars.

Gauge: LaGrande gauge readings are used to designate flow for this section. The gauge is near Perry on river right, between the road bridge and the railroad trestle.

GRANDE RONDE RIVER
Riverside City Park, LaGrande to Elgin
T.R. Torgersen

Class	Flow	Gradient	Miles	Character	Season
1	600 +	4	29	agriculture	rainy snowmelt

Description: This gentle, slowly flowing section has appeal for leisurely day outings. The borders of the river abound with wildlife, including small mammals, waterfowl, and songbirds. In its meandering course through the broad, fertile Grand Ronde floodplain, the river is crossed intermittently by numerous county roads and lanes that grid the valley. This abundance of crossings permits an almost limitless variety of trip lengths.

Difficulties: Be on the lookout for obstructing debris and barbed wire.

Shuttle: Riverside City Park is on Spruce Street within the city limits of LaGrande. It is accessible via Oregon 82 from both I-84 LaGrande exits. See previous section for directions to the park. The main route to Elgin is northward on Oregon 82 from the I-84 exit. USGS topographic maps entitled LaGrande SE, Conley, Imbler, and Elgin, and a US Forest Service map for the Umatilla National Forest show road details for alternate put-ins and take-outs on this river section.

Gauge: Flows for this section may be difficult to estimate because of water diversions for agricultural use. The nearest pertinent gauge is the LaGrande station.

GRANDE RONDE RIVER
Elgin to Palmer Junction
T.R. Torgersen

Class	Flow	Gradient	Miles	Character	Season
2(3)	5000-	21	13	agriculture	all year
2(4)	8000			hills	

Description: Initially this section retains the agricultural and rangeland character of the previous section from LaGrande. Within five miles from Elgin, the river descends into a deeper, narrower V-shaped valley that characterizes the river's course for much of its remaining length to the Snake River. Optionally, the boater may bypass Palmer Junction in favor of continuing downstream to the confluence with the Wallowa River at Rondowa. Please note that the road bridge at Rondowa is not passable. Also, because of a road closure on the south and private land at the north end of the bridge, Rondowa is no longer a suitable point of access or egress.

Difficulties: Andy's Rapids occur 4 miles from Elgin. Everyone is encouraged to scout this one. Scout, portage or line on river left; run on river right.

Shuttle: The put-in is on Oregon 82 at the north end of the town of Elgin. If Palmer Junction is to be the take-out, the shuttle is north from Elgin on the Palmer Junction Road. Get on the latter road from Oregon 204 a few blocks west from Oregon 82. The take-out is about a half mile below Palmer Junction at the campground on river left.

Gauge: Use readings from the LaGrande gauge to estimate relative flows for this section. Although the Rondowa gauge measures flow for both the Wallowa and Grande Ronde, its readings can be used to estimate levels.

GRANDE RONDE RIVER
Minam, on the Wallowa River, to Powwatka Bridge
Gary Lane

Class	Flow	Gradient	Miles	Character	Season
2	1200-	22 C	37	forested	all year
	3800			canyon	
3	6000 +				

Description: This log is dedicated to Tuk-eka-kas and Hin-mah-too-yah-lat-kekt, who along with their Nez Perce people respected the land and had the wisdom never to wish that they could stop a river from flowing. They called the Grande Ronde River Welleweah--"River that flows into the far beyond."

The put-in at Minam is at the confluence of the Wallowa and Minam rivers. The first 8.5-mile stretch of the run is on the Wallowa, which merges with the Grande Ronde at Rondowa. A rolling plateau makes up the top part of the canyon's rim. The canyon walls present tiers of horizontal lava flows that occurred during the Miocene epoch. These stratified formations are the oldest exposed rocks in the canyon, and contain pillars, spires, window-holes, and caves. Abstrusely dikes and columnar basalts add more geological variety.

From Minam the river can be floated any month of the year. May normally has the highest mean flows, while September sees the lowest flows. In low water (700 to 1400 cfs) anticipate encounters with rocks and seemingly endless shoals. Rafters and driftboaters should be prepared to do a lot of pushing, tugging and cursing. Kayakers would find low flows boring.

Flows of about 5000 cfs are optimum kayaking levels. At this level waves become surfable and still retain eddies for reentry. As flows increase, eddies diminish and many surfing waves become one-shot events, even if you're lucky. Flows of about 2000 cfs are optimum for open canoes. Weather begins to warm up in June, but snow and rain are good possibilities in late May and early June. December, January and February are very cold. The river can freeze during these months, but they are good times for observing winter populations of bald eagle and big game animals. In summer, shorebirds like sandpipers nest in the same areas that people use for camping. Please be on the lookout for nests, and be sure party members know their locations to avoid destroying them. Bear Creek seems to have the highest incidence of rattlesnake sightings, and rarely a scorpion has been found.

Treat or boil drinking water; streams originating beyond the canyon rim may be contaminated. These lower river sections receive heavy use. Though some outhouses have been erected at a few major campsites, we encourage the carry-out method for solid human waste. This method would greatly benefit this increasingly impacted river. It is a superior method for popular recreational rivers and the most responsible one.

Difficulties: The first 6 miles below Minam contain the best section of nearly continuous rapids on the lower river. A mile and a half below the Minam put-in is the Minam Roller or Hatchery Hole. The roller develops at about 3000 cfs, and becomes a great surfing and ender hole at about 5000 cfs. Beyond this volume the roller becomes a boat-eater and thrasher because of the pronounced backwash. This hole consumes swimmers, who usually experience blackwater and may not surface for 30 ft downstream. This rapids is located on the first major righthand bend in the river, and is recognized by several large basalt rocks on river left. Open boats should avoid the Roller at flows exceeding 5000 cfs by holding to the right bank.

This, and all other rapids, can be scouted from a boat. Most routes require a minimum of maneuvering. There are few potential keeper holes (with the exception of Vincent Falls in low water), but some rocks create obstructions that many novices have decorated with twisted and broken canoes, and wrapped with rafts. This section is reasonably well suited to novice boaters except at high flows. From 10,000 to 15,000 cfs, eddies become rare, the current fast, and large standing waves develop into great rides for dories, rafts, kayaks, and expert canoeists. At these volumes a swimmer would experience a long, cold endeavor to gain shore or reenter a craft. Remember that this river is born of snow and ice from the nearby Wallowa, Blue and Elkhorn Mountains.

Shuttle: The put-in is near the store on the south (left) side of the river bridge at Minam at Oregon 82 between Elgin and Wallowa. An alternate put-in is at Minam State Park about 1.5 miles downstream. This campground is accessible via a good dirt road along the left bank of the river.

The route to the Powwatka bridge take-out is a little tricky. Try to obtain a Wallowa-Whitman National Forest (North Half) map at one of the Forest Service offices in Pendleton, LaGrande, Baker, Wallowa, or Enterprise The seat-of-the-pants route is to go east from Minam toward Wallowa on Oregon 82. In about 8 miles go left onto Smith Mountain Road for about 2 miles to a junction with the Promise/Troy road. Go left and proceed for about 12 miles to a junction indicating Troy to the right; this will eventually get you to the bridge take-out. This is about 8 miles upstream from Troy. Total shuttle mileage by this route is about 41 miles. The take-out and parking area are at a primitive picnic area on river right immediately below the bridge.

Alternate shuttle routes are via County Road 500 to Powwatka (50 miles); via Palmer Junction and Troy on Forest Road 62 (62 miles); or via Enterprise, partly on Oregon 3, to Flora and Troy (80 miles). Most of these routes get rough in spring and summer, slick when wet, and snow-covered in winter. Shuttle service is available at the Minam Motel (503) 437-4475; ask for Mel.

Gauge: All flow data for this river section are based on the Troy gauge. This is the instrument monitored by the River Forecast Service for flow information. Accurate flow for the Wallowa between Minam and Rondowa can be computed by subtracting the Elgin gauge reading from the reading at Rondowa. The latter gauge will give a more definitive flow reading for the Grande Ronde below Rondowa. Interpretation of flow data: low, 700-1400 cfs; medium, 1400-5000 cfs; high 5000-12,000 cfs; very high, 12,000+ cfs.

GRANDE RONDE RIVER
Powwatka Bridge (Troy) to Boggan's Oasis
Gary Lane

Class	Flow	Gradient	Miles	Character	Season
2	3500	17	26	canyon, road	all year
2 + (3)	6000 +				

Description: Below Troy the stringers of trees spilling over the canyon rim begin to withdraw from the more arid sideslopes. The vegetation in the canyon takes on a drier grassland character. Here, the brushy draws and rimrock country are frequented by mule deer, which largely replace the elk that were the dominant big game upriver. Rattlesnakes are more common on this section. There are a few ranches along the river and a gravel road parallels the run for the entire distance from Powwatka ridge to Boggan's Oasis. A small park with outhouses, a tiny store with a cafe and gas pumps, and the immediate proximity to paved highway make the latter a good place to begin or end a trip.

Difficulties: The canyon becomes progressively steeper along this section. High flows create some interesting waves and strong headwall cross currents. Such places are accompanied by surging boils and large whirlpools that may require some heavy stroking to avoid.

Shuttle: See previous section for detailed instructions to the Powwatka bridge and Troy put-ins. The take-out is at Boggan's Oasis store and cafe on Oregon 3 (which becomes Washington 129) between Enterprise, Oregon and Lewiston, Idaho. This highway winds steeply down to the bridge which crosses the Grande Ronde at the store. The infamous Rattlesnake Grade claws its way tortuously out of the river canyon from here. A good all-weather route to Powwatka and Troy strikes westward immediately off the north end of the river bridge. Shuttle services are available at the Minam Motel (503) 437-4475; ask for Mel. Total driving distance from Minam is 75 miles.

Gauge: Use Troy readings. Consider flows below 1400 cfs as low; 1400 to 5000 cfs as moderate; and 5000 to 12000 cfs as high to very high.

GRANDE RONDE RIVER
Boggan's Oasis to Hellers Bar on the Snake River
Gary Lane

Class	Flow	Gradient	Miles	Character	Season
2(4)	3500	17	26	valley	all year
3(4)	6000 +			desert	

Description: Below Boggan's Oasis the canyon becomes increasingly arid and devoid of coniferous forest. Semi-desert vegetation, characterized by hackberry trees and prickly pear cactus, becomes common. This river section is not known for its inviting campsites. Overnighters in the canyon rarely fail to encounter a rattlesnake, scorpion or black widow spider. Be on the alert for rattlesnakes when scouting the Narrows.

In high water, there are several class 2 and 3 rapids, and some very large, powerful eddies on this river section. Only the Narrows demands scouting.

Difficulties: The Narrows is aptly named for low water only. Located about 4.5 miles below Slippery Creek, which enters on river left, the approach to the Narrows is marked by a big natural "X"-like form in Mazama ash soil on river left, one bend above the rapids. Some imagination must be used to see the "X". Look a little above eye level on an open hillside near the apex of the bend. This rapids is created by a constricted channel of irregular ledges and formations of volcanic debris that contort the river as it flows through a cut in solid basalt. The river pours through one of the lava flows, and in extremely low water a person might jump across it! High water covers much of the lava flow and the river then is quite wide.

There are normally two sections to this drop. The upper part is a roller-coaster ride on a long set of irregular waves. About 100 to 150 yards farther downstream, most of the river channels left and funnels into a large cresting, back-curling, standing wave. The magnitude of this roller varies widely depending on water level, but it has eaten many a craft. At flows above about 10,000 cfs, a third series of waves develop immediately below the above curler. Large cresting waves can be generated here, and this can become the nastiest portion of the Narrows.

Shuttle: Put-in is at Boggan's Oasis. See shuttle description for previous river section for detailed directions to put-in. To reach the take-out at Hellers Bar, drive north on Washington 129 to within 1 mile of Anatone. Turn right onto Montgomery Ridge Road and follow the sporadic signs to the Snake River. At the junction with the river, turn right (upriver) to the Hellers Bar boat launch ramp.

Gauge: Use the Troy gauge readings to plan trips on this section. Low flows are considered as less than about 1400 cfs; moderate flows are 1400 to 5000 cfs; and high flows from about 5000 to 12,000 cfs and greater.

SNAKE RIVER
Hells Canyon Dam to Hellers Bar
Ron Mattson

Class	Flow	Gradient	Miles	Character	Season
3(5)	8000	9 PD	78	desert, canyon	all year
				no road	

Description: The Snake River, largest tributary of the Columbia River, begins its westward journey to the Pacific Ocean from Yellowstone Park in Wyoming. The upper stretches of the river are very popular with fishermen and rafters alike, especially the sections around Jackson, Wyoming and the Birds of Prey area in southern Idaho. Farther westward, along the Oregon-Idaho border, rapids that were considered to be bigger than those in the Grand Canyon of the Colorado have been transformed into a series of reservoirs by Brownlee, Oxbow and Hells Canyon Dams.

Spared many times over from the Army Corps of Engineers' grandiose plans for dams, Hells Canyon is now protected as a National Recreation Area. Most boaters float through this mile-deep canyon in four to six days. Permits are required from the Friday preceding Memorial Day weekend through September 15. For permit information contact Hells Canyon National Recreation Area, 3620 B Snake River Ave., Lewiston, Idaho 83501.

Hells Canyon, rich in cultural history, was inhabited by Shoshone and Nez Perce Indians because of the abundance of fish and game and the mild winters. In the late 1870's fertile streamside canyons and meadows were used to raise sheep, cattle and hay while miners scoured the country for gold, copper and other valuable minerals. After its classification as a National Recreation Area, the Forest Service acquired most of the remaining homesteads. For further reading see the book by Carrey et al. (1979).

Although the Snake can be a vicious river at high levels and does contain two big class 5 drops, it can usually be negotiated by the average boater. Typically a pool-drop river, the Snake allows plenty of time to retrieve flipped boats and swimmers below the major rapids, Wild Sheep and Granite, if the water flows are in the 8000 to 16,000 cfs level.

Above these levels, skilled river runners will find tremendous challenge as the big drops become bigger, the water pushier, and the flow much faster. Biggest water is encountered at about 20,000 cfs; above this level the rapids begin to wash out slightly while strong eddy lines and currents begin to develop. Flows in the spring and early summer can easily reach 60,000 cfs at the put-in and may double after the Main Salmon enters at river mile 61.

Late spring trips are a real treat; the canyon is still green, the weather is usually pleasant. Summer is paradise: hot days and 70-degree water. Into late September and early October the weather remains pleasant, the water cools a bit and quick squalls can pop up. Year-round upstream winds can be encountered; it's best to row in the morning to avoid them. Camping and hiking opportunities abound with large sandy beaches, over 200 archeological sites, and good trails. As this area is protected by federal law, do not disturb archeological sites.

The two major rapids on the Snake can be run by intermediate boaters with a little guidance from skilled boaters. The first rapids is Wild Sheep, located not quite 6 miles from the put-in. Look for a large lone pine tree on the left to pull out. A trail located up the bank will lead to a good scouting point. At low water, work either left or right of exposed rocks at the top before working to the center of the river for the final drop. The large diagonal waves from the left at the bottom can flip an 18-ft raft easily if not hit straight on.

Downstream about 2 miles is Granite Creek Rapids. The best scouting is from river right where one can see the best view of the proper route--a tongue just right of center. Depending upon skill and size of boat, there are many optional routes. After Granite Rapids, many lazy miles of river with a few class two or three rapids, towering canyon walls, and possible wildlife sightings lie ahead.

An alternative to running the lower section of the Snake, which some people find uninteresting, is to take out at Pittsburg Landing and shuttle to Whitebird, Idaho for a Lower Main Salmon trip that ends at Hellers Bar on the Snake. Best bet is to hire a shuttle for cars to Hellers Bar and arrange a truck shuttle from Pittsburg to Whitebird. If the water is low on the Salmon, this plan is not recommended.

Difficulties: Wild Sheep and Granite Creek are the only rapids that will give the average boater any problems. Scout these two. Watch out for poison oak along the upper river. Jet boats will be encountered on the river, especially during the fall hunting season.

Shuttle: The put-in is located just below the Hells Canyon Dam where a Bureau of Land Management (BLM) ranger will check permits. The BLM can supply permit holders with a list of people that run shuttles, or you can run your own. The standard shuttle route to the take-out is to Clarkston, Washington via Joseph, Oregon, then upstream along the Snake about 30 miles to Hellers Bar. The take-out is a very convenient concrete ramp with food and telephone available.

Gauge: The Snake is runnable at all flows. Contact the River Forecast Center for the discharge from Hells Canyon Dam.

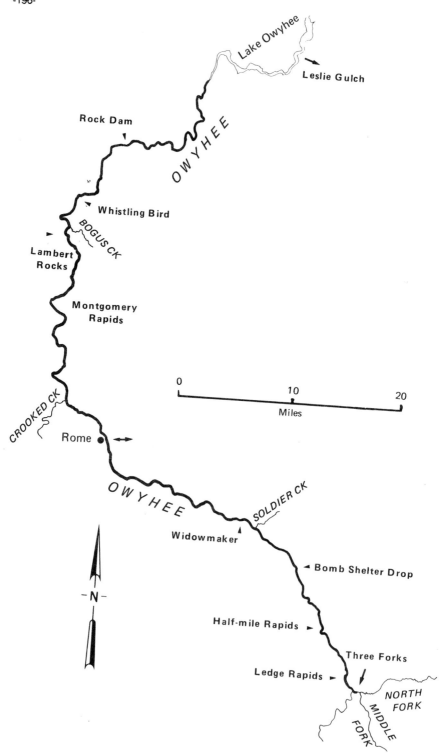

OWYHEE RIVER
Three Forks to Rome
Rob Blickensderfer

Class	Flow	Gradient	Miles	Character	Season
4(5)	1200-8000	22 PD	35	inaccessible gorge, desert	snowmelt

Description: This section of river is the most isolated and inaccessible in Oregon and among the most isolated in the US. The river has cut a canyon as deep as 3000 feet through basalt. The countryside is arid with little vegetation and no inhabitants. There are no access roads or trails between the put-in and take-out, although there are places where one could climb out of the canyon in an emergency. The steepness of the cliffs and narrowness of the canyon provide a fascinating experience.

In contrast to the pastoral scene at the put-in, the numerous rapids range up to class 6. Ample time should be allotted for the necessary scouting of rapids, and for savoring the experience of isolation. One may find hot springs, petroglyphs, and large caves that make unusual camp shelters.

The weather in the bottom of the canyon can be oppressively hot in April and May, when this section is normally high enough to run. However, one should also be prepared for cool weather, cold water, and even snow flurries. The canyon has one of the densest rattlesnake populations in Oregon, so one may feel more at ease sleeping in a tent. Camping areas are not nearly as plentiful here as on the lower section or on most other Eastern Oregon rivers. This river is becoming more and more popular.

Difficulties: This pool-drop river is much more difficult than the gradient of 22 feet per mile implies. A number of class 4 rapids of varying length and one class 5 rapids await the boater. Because of the remoteness of the canyon and extreme difficulty of hiking out, river conquerors must be conservative on this section. Some rafts have been known to get wiped out at Ledge Rapids, the first major rapids below Three Forks; others have never reached beyond Halfmile Rapids, which approaches class 5 and is nearly 0.5 mile long. Raft Flip Drop can be snuck on the left by kayaks, but rafts will find a deceptively powerful roller at the bottom of the main chute. The Widowmaker approaches class 6. It is possible for medium-size rafts to thread the chutes on the right. Although it looks very tempting to kayakers below 1800 cfs, a portage is highly recommended. The late Walt Blackadar portaged here.

As the flow of this section approaches 3000 cfs, the power and surging of the river can be felt; the Widowmaker appears ominous. At flows much over 3000 cfs, the river becomes very fast but some of the rapids wash out. For comparison, the Middle Fork of the Salmon, at the same flow, is considered easier than the Owyhee.

The road to the put-in can become impassable after a rain. When scouting along the riverbank, be alert for rattlesnakes. Further information can be found in Arighi and Arighi (1974).

Shuttle: From Rome head east across the river on Oregon 78. About 16 miles east of Rome take an unnamed dirt road on the right. Travel 35 miles to Three Forks. The dirt road, especially the last mile, can be muddy and impassable. The take-out is located about 0.2 mile upstream from the Rome bridge on the east bank. A large parking area, boat ramp, and toilets are here; but no drinking water (1980). Shuttle service can be obtained in Jordan Valley. See the shuttle description of the following section of river for details.

Gauge: Flow information may be obtained from the River Forecast Center in Portland. This river is unregulated and therefore runnable only in the spring as the snowpack melts from the mountains.

Watermarks:

Mile

'0	Three Forks, the put-in at a slow flowing pool.
'1.5	Ledge Rapids, class 4. As canyon narrows and water picks up to class 2, the ledge is approached. The ledge consists of several narrow chutes between boulders. Land near base of large rocks on left and scout from the left. About 400 yards of class 4 boulder garden follows the ledge.
'2.5	Sheepherders' abandoned cabin on right. Warm spring just downstream. Hot spring on left 100 yards down.
'4	Canyon narrows. Spring on the left.
'5	Cabin ruins on right. Several class 2 rapids.
'8.5	Halfmile Rapids, class 4+. After several class 2 to 3 rapids, look for a bend to the right. Stop before bend and scout. The rapids have an upper section and a lower section with a short class 2 pool in between. Scout from the right. At low water the lower section becomes extremely rocky; at any level there is a tendency for rafts to get swept too far right and lodged against boulders. It is only 100 yards to Raft Flip Drop.
'9	Raft Flip Drop, class 3 to 4. Big roller at the bottom of main chute can flip a raft. Kayaks may sneak small left channel at high water levels.
'10	Small spring on right.
'11-13	Several class 3- rapids.
'14	Subtle Hole, class 3+. Longer than Raft Flip Drop.
'14+	Bombshelter Drop, class 3. Large cave on the left, just above river level.
'16	Fast class 3 rapids.
'17	Finger Rock Rapids, class 3. A small and a larger rock stick up at the head of the rapids.
'18	Several class 2 rapids.
'19	Soldier Creek from the right. Extensive gravel bar.
'20	Springs on right. Several class 3 rapids in a steep canyon.
'20.5	Widowmaker Rapids, class 5. The approach to Widowmaker is identified by a 200 yard stretch of straight narrow canyon. The river seems to disappear among boulders ahead. On the right a talus slope extends down to the river. At Widowmaker are large boulders on both sides and in the river. A class 3 rapids, also among boulders, is located 100 yards above Widowmaker, with class 2 water leading to Widowmaker. Very strong parties at flows below 2000 cfs may run the class 3 rapids before stopping to scout, but all others should land on the right above the class 3 rapids. The drop from here to the bottom of Widowmaker is about 20 feet with Widowmaker itself being about a 10 foot drop. The portage is difficult on either side, but usually done on the right. A good spring flows from the boulders on the left about 40 feet above the big drop. Skilled rafters have been running the right series of two chutes of the big drop.
'21	Numerous class 2 and some class 3 rapids for next 8 miles. Small beaches occasionally dot the river banks.
'29	Springs on right and left, class 2+ rapids. Below here the canyon begins to open up. Several camping beaches and flat water for the next 2 miles.
'31	Last rapids, class 2. Flat water to Rome, as canyon rim fades away.

OWYHEE RIVER
Rome to Leslie Gulch
Dan Valens and Lance Stein

Class	Flow	Gradient	Miles	Character	Season
3(4)	1000-4000	15 PD	63	no road desert	snowmelt

Description: This section of the Owyhee has an interestingly diverse landscape. The canyon in general is broad and shallow although there are several stretches with narrow steep-walled inner canyons. The predominant basalts found in the upper canyon are interbedded with rhyolitic ash and sediments, which add various shades of white, red, green, and black to the canyon walls. Lambert Rocks are a colorful badlands eroded from these sediments.

This is arid country covered by sagebrush with some hackberry and juniper trees found along the river. Wildflowers and grasses add their color to the surroundings. So does poison oak, so beware! The canyon also supports a large population of birds and rattlesnakes, which may inhabit the numerous camping sites. Drinking water may be found in springs along the river, but these become sparse as the season wears on and typically are not located near campsites. Boaters should carry enough water for a day's use and fill their containers whenever they can. Often the springs are mere trickles; an extra U-shaped tent stake placed in the trickle to form a pouring spout can be indispensable. If river water is used for cooking or drinking it must be boiled. The river water may contain farm chemicals unaffected by boiling.

The Owyhee is a very isolated river. There is no access for one stretch of 35 miles, and even where there is access it is still a long hike to summon help. Boaters forced overland unexpectedly in this inhospitable country could be in serious trouble.

The rapids on this section are mostly class 2, making it a nice river for intermediate kayakers and rafters. However, the few class 3 rapids and the remoteness of the river demand that experienced boaters or extreme caution accompany a weak group.

Because the Owyhee is unregulated above Rome and depends on snowmelt the boating season is short and variable. It is usually runnable during April and May. Some years the season may extend into early June, while other years it may end by mid-May. The weather also is undependable, with temperatures ranging from freezing to 100 degrees and above. Be prepared for rain or drought. Further information can be found in Arighi.

Difficulties: Whistling Bird Rapids at mile 29.5 should be scouted on the left by those unfamiliar with it. The current washes into a large slab that has fallen from the canyon wall. This should be avoided by pulling to the left. Whistling Bird is preceded by a large rock wall on the left 0.5 mile upstream. A dry wash on the left, the rock face and slab on the right and the noise of the rapids mark its location.

Iron Point, also referred to as Montgomery Rapids, may be tricky for unsuspecting rafters at low water levels. It is located at mile 32.5 in a steep-walled canyon after a left turn followed by a pool. The river drops and turns right, pushing boats towards a rock on the left. At high water there is plenty of room to maneuver.

Rock Dam at mile 39.5 should be scouted on the right. A small gully enters the river on the left just above it, and part of an old concrete diversion dam is visible on the right. The noise of the rapids at the broken dam alerts you to its presence.

Possible routes are on the left or in the center at high water. At low water rafters may choose to line this rapids on the right.

Lake Owyhee is the toughest run on this section. It is an 8-mile long stretch. In light rafts without a headwind, expect a minimum of four hours to cross it. Lazier folks (some might say smarter) may wish to arrange beforehand for a tow (see Shuttle).

Shuttle: Shuttle service may be obtained from two local sources:

Eva Easterday	Kenneth Haylett
Jordan Valley	Jordan Valley
(503) 586-2352	(503) 586-2406

Haylett can also arrange to tow you to the Leslie Gulch take-out. Those wishing to run their own shuttle should take US 95 to Jordan Valley and then north to the Succor Creek-Leslie Gulch turnoff about 18 miles north of Jordan Valley. To keep trip expenses down obey the speed limit in Jordan Valley. From the turnoff follow the signs to Leslie Gulch (approximately 26 miles). An optional take-out on private property at Hole-in-the-Ground Ranch may no longer be available. Inquire locally.

Gauge: Contact the River Forecast Center in Portland for the flow at Rome. A flow of 1000 cfs is considered minimum.

Watermarks:

Mile

'0	Rome put-in.
'5	Crooked Creek on left; start of canyon.
'6.5	Canyon opens.
'14.5	Vertical wall on left with springs.
'17.5	Artillery Rapids, straightforward class 3.
'20	Abandoned stone cabin above river on right.
'22	Lambert Rocks, badlands, on left.
'24	Bogus Creek Falls, small falls from rimrock, on right.
'29	Red rock gorge begins.
'29.5	Whistling Bird Rapids, class 4-. See Difficulties.
'30.5	Steep-walled canyon begins.
'32.5	Iron Point, class 3 rapids. See Difficulties.
'34.5	Canyon opens.
'39.5	Rock Dam, class 3 to 4. See Difficulties.
'40.5	Hole-in-the-Ground Ranch on right. Private property.
'44.5	Small stone building on right. Start of scenic rugged canyon.
'49	Irrigated hayfield on right.
'50	Birch Creek Ranch and waterwheel on right.
'53	Deserted ranch on left.
'54.5	Waterwheel on right.
'55	Slack water.
'63	Leslie Gulch on right where lake bends left. Rooster Comb Rocks just uplake on left.

OWYHEE RIVER　　　*Half Mile Rapids*　　　*Lance Stein*

Appendix A. River Regulation Agencies

River Forecast Center U.S. Department of Commerce National Oceanic and Atmospheric Administration Portland, Oregon	(503) 249-0666
Reservoir Control Center U.S. Army Corps of Engineers Portland, Oregon	(503) 221-3741
Northwest Water Resources Data Center U.S. Department of Interior Portland, Oregon	(503) 231-2024
Watermaster Oregon Department of Water Resources Bend, Oregon	(503) 388-6669
Recreation Information Pacific Power and Light Company Portland, Oregon	(800) 452-9912
River Information Center U.S. Department of Commerce National Oceanic and Atmospheric Administration Seattle, Washington	(206) 526-8530
River Information Center California Department of Water Resources Eureka, California	(707) 443-9305
Cougar Dam U.S. Army Corps of Engineers Blue River, Oregon	(503) 822-3344
Detroit Dam U.S. Army Corps of Engineers Detroit, Oregon	(503) 897-2385
Foster Dam U.S. Army Corps of Engineers Sweet Home, Oregon	(503) 367-5124
Lookout Point Dam U.S. Army Corps of Engineers Lowell, Oregon	(503) 937-2131

Appendix B. River Stages (ft) and Flows (cfs) for Selected Gauges

ALSEA RIVER — near Tidewater

FT	3.0	3.5	4.0	4.5	5.0	5.5	6.0	6.5	7.0	8.0
CFS	645	900	1160	1460	1780	2120	2490	2890	3310	4260

CLACKAMAS RIVER — at Estacada

FT	1.5	2.0	2.5	3.0	3.5	4.0	4.5	5.0	5.5	6.0
CFS	1180	1780	2280	3350	4100	5400	6240	7700	8790	10,600

ILLINOIS RIVER — near Kerby

FT	3.0	4.0	5.0	6.0	7.0	8.0	9.0	10.0	11.0	12.0
CFS	380	655	1040	1480	2000	2600	3260	4000	4850	5780

McKENZIE RIVER — near Vida

FT	1.0	1.3	1.6	2.0	2.3	2.6	3.0	3.5	4.0	5.0
CFS	1800	2280	2790	3530	4130	4790	5700	6950	8200	11,200

NEHALEM RIVER — near Foss

FT	4.0	4.5	5.0	5.5	6.0	6.5	7.0	7.5	8.0	8.5
CFS	1810	2320	2890	3510	4170	4880	5630	6420	7240	8110

NESTUCCA RIVER — near Beaver

FT	4.3	5.0	5.3	5.6	6.0	6.3	6.6	7.0	7.3	7.6
CFS	716	1280	1560	1860	2300	2660	3050	3600	4010	4420

NORTH SANTIAM RIVER — at Mehama

FT	3.0	3.3	3.6	4.0	4.3	4.6	5.0	5.3	6.0	7.0
CFS	1260	1590	1980	2600	3140	3730	4580	5290	7200	10,600

NORTH UMPQUA RIVER — at Winchester

FT	2.0	2.5	3.0	3.5	4.0	4.5	5.0	6.0	8.0	10.0
CFS	957	1390	1930	2640	3460	4400	5410	7700	13,200	20,000

ROGUE RIVER — near Agness

FT	2.0	3.0	3.5	4.0	4.5	5.0	6.0	7.0	8.0	10.0
CFS	1150	2330	3060	3870	4810	5900	8320	11,100	14,200	21.600

SANTIAM RIVER — at Jefferson

FT	2.0	2.5	3.0	3.5	4.0	5.0	6.0	7.0	8.0	9.0
CFS	1510	1980	2620	3350	4200	6270	8900	11,800	15,200	18,900

SILETZ RIVER — at Siletz

FT	4.0	5.0	5.5	6.0	6.5	7.0	7.5	8.0	9.0	10.0
CFS	775	1440	1850	2290	2790	3320	3900	4510	5810	7160

SIUSLAW RIVER — Near Mapleton

FT	7.0	9.0	11.0	13.0	14.0	15.0	16.0	17.0	18.0	19.0
CFS	3260	5950	9100	12,400	14,100	15,900	17,800	19,800	21,800	24,100

UMPQUA RIVER — near Elkton

FT	4.0	6.0	8.0	10.0	12.0	15.0	18.0	21.0	24.0	27.0
CFS	2340	5560	10,100	15,400	22,000	32,600	45,300	60,500	75,500	92,300

WILLAMETTE RIVER — at Corvallis (Synthetic rating)

FT	2.0	4.0	6.0	8.0	10.0	12.0	14.0	16.0	18.0	20.0
CFS	7400	12,600	18,900	26,100	33,600	41,600	50,500	60,600	71,900	84,800

WILLAMETTE RIVER — at Salem

FT	5.0	6.0	8.0	10.0	12.0	14.0	16.0	18.0	20.0	22.0
CFS	6450	9100	15,600	23.600	33,000	43,900	55,600	68,000	81,500	96,800

WILSON RIVER — near Tillamook

FT	4.5	5.0	5.5	6.0	6.5	7.0	7.5	8.0	8.5	9.0
CFS	870	1120	1400	1710	2090	2520	3000	3530	4130	4850

Appendix C. Newspapers Reporting River Gauge Readings

Bend - The Bulletin
Crooked - Below Prineville Res.
Deschutes - Below Wickiup Res.
Deschutes - Below Crane Prairie Res.
Deschutes - At Benham Falls

Corvallis - Gazette Times
Alsea - Tidewater
Clackamas - Estacada
Nehalem - Foss
North Santiam - Mehama
Santiam - Jefferson
Siletz - Siletz
Siuslaw - Mapleton
Willamette - Albany, Corvallis

Eugene - Register Guard
Alsea - Tidewater
McKenzie - Vida
North Umpqua - Winchester
Siletz - Siletz
Siuslaw - Mapleton
Umpqua - Elkton
Willamette - EWEB Steam Plant
Willamette - Harrisburg

Grants Pass - Courier
Rogue - Grants Pass

Medford - Mail Tribune
Illinois - Kerby
Rogue - Lost Creek Dam Release
Rogue - Gold Ray Dam Release
Rogue - Agness

Portland - Oregonian
Oregon River Forecast

Roseburg - News Review
North Umpqua - Winchester
South Umpqua - Winston
Umpqua - Elkton

Salem - Statesman Journal
Alsea - Tidewater
Nestucca - Beaver
North Santiam - Mehama
Santiam - Jefferson
Siletz - Siletz
Willamette - Salem
Wilson - Tillamook

Appendix D. Books on Oregon Rivers

Arighi, Scott, and Margaret Arighi, 1974: Wildwater Touring - Techniques and Tours. MacMillan Publishing Company, New York.

Campbell, Arthur, 1980: John Day River - Drift and Historical Guide. Frank Amato Publications, Inc., Portland, Oregon.

Carrey, Johnny, Cort Conley, and Ace Barton, 1979: Snake River of Hells Canyon. Backeddy Books, Cambridge, Idaho.

Garren, John, 1979: Oregon River Tours. The Touchstone Press, Beaverton, OR.

Jones, Philip N., 1982: Canoe Routes of Northwest Oregon. The Mountaineers, Seattle, WA.

Quinn, James, M., James W. Quinn and James G. King, 1979: Handbook to the Deschutes River Canyon. Educational Adventures, Inc., Medford, OR.

Quinn, James M., James W. Quinn and James G. King, 1979: Handbook to the Illinois River Canyon. Educational Adventures, Inc., Medford, OR.

Quinn, James M., and James W. Quinn, 1983: Handbook to the Klamath River Canyon. Educational Adventures, Inc., Medford, OR.

Quinn, James M., James W. Quinn and James G. King, 1978: Handbook to the Rogue River Canyon. Educational Adventures, Inc., Medford, OR.

Schwind, Dick, 1974: West Coast River Touring: The Rogue River and South including California. The Touchstone Press, Beaverton, OR.

State of Oregon, Oregon State Parks and Recreation Branch, 1976: Willamette River Recreation Guide. Willamette River Greenway. Oregon Parks Dept., 525 Trade St., S.E., Salem, OR 97310.

Appendix E. Maps for Oregon Rivers.

Getting Around in The State Of Oregon

Getting between a put-in and a take-out on a river, not to mention finding the river in the first place, can sometimes be very difficult.
For finding routes between watersheds, The Official State of Oregon Road Map, the Rand McNally Road Atlas, and American Automobile Association (AAA) maps are fine. They show the larger rivers and even some of the shuttle routes, but detail is lacking for smaller streams and Forest Service roads. The Rand McNally Road Atlas has more small towns than the AAA map of Oregon, though it is harder to read. The Official State Road Map can be obtained from local offices of the State Division of Motor Vehicles (DMV). AAA maps are available for AAA members.
Oregon's U.S. National Forest maps are indispensable to boaters, no matter what part of the state you're in. Some rivers are in sections of Oregon that aren't on National Forest maps, but the vast majority of whitewater streams are covered thoroughly. The editors recommend that you buy a complete set and never leave home without them, even for a quick jaunt to the grocery store. All of the roads in the National Forests in Oregon and Washington were renumbered in 1982. The maps have been republished, so, if you have an old one, road signs probably won't match the numbers on your map. National Forest maps are available from the Pacific Northwest Region Field Office, 319 SW Pine Street, Portland, OR 97208, or from any of the National Forest Headquarters offices throughout the state.
U.S. Geological Survey (USGS) Topographical maps are indispensable for exploratory boating. More casual paddlers can also use them for locating prominent geographical features. However, coverage of Oregon's whitewater country by topographical maps is not extensive, and many of the maps are at least 20-30 years old. The best boating country is mapped in 15-minute quadrangles with 80-ft contour intervals. This large scale limits their usefulness to applications such as finding roads and figuring overall stream gradient, but they're better than nothing. There are some 15-minute maps with 40-ft contours. The newer 1/250,000 maps are good for marking put-ins and take-outs, and defining watersheds for exploratory purposes. The 7.5-minute maps are the ones to obtain if they are available. The detail is terrific and the reliability very good if they are recent.
USGS topographical maps are available from many sports stores and some bookstores. Most libraries have the maps that cover the local area; both Oregon State University in Corvallis, and the University of Oregon in Eugene, have complete collections covering the entire mapped state.
Most counties in Oregon publish a road map. Quality of coverage varies considerably. Some have all roads, some have only main roads, and others have mapped only a portion of the county. Check at the county courthouse for maps and prices.
Privately published maps of small, county-size areas abound. The quality and usefulness of these maps vary considerably; caveat emptor! Examples of these maps are the Thomas Brothers Maps, the Pittmon Maps, the Metsger's Maps, the Big Sky Series of maps, and Phillip Arnold's Maps. Most of these maps are available from bookstores and department stores.
If you really want to get a good look at an area before entering it, aerial photographs are available for almost the whole country. Finding the company that has the negatives can be a real chore. Inquire at the County Assessors office for aerial photos. In the end, it might be easier to hire a plane and pilot to go up for your own look.

For most purposes, the editors of Soggy Sneakers highly recommend the use of The Official State Highway Map and US National Forest maps with the descriptions in this book. Virtually all of the write-ups were written under the assumption that the reader has at least one or the other.

As a final tip, always remember to carry a couple of bucks worth of quarters for phone calls, keep your gas tank at least half full, and never, ever, believe a local who tells you, "you can't miss it"...

Appendix F. The Next Edition of The Soggy Sneakers.

Offprints of River Descriptions

Are there more rivers in Oregon that are runnable by raft, canoe or kayak that don't appear in this book? You bet your sprayskirt there are! The Willamette Kayak and Canoe Club has a number of river write-ups that do not appear in this book but that are available to the public.

Some of these descriptions are ones that came in after our printing deadline, others are exotic, eccentric or kamikaze runs. Many of these runs will probably appear in a future edition of "Soggy Sneakers," but for fifty cents per description, you can get copies now. For a free current listing of river descriptions available and an order form, please send a self-addressed and stamped envelope to:

WKCC - Offprints
PO Box 1062
Corvallis, OR 97339

How YOU can be an Author

"Soggy Sneakers" editors are still soliciting descriptions of rivers that do not appear in this guide and are within (or almost within) the State of Oregon. If you have a favorite run that's not in the book, write it up and send it to us. Take a look at the section entitled "How to Use This Book" and observe the format of descriptions in this book for a guide to what your description should include. Please make sure that you include information on gauge, gradient, scenery and season. Additionally, please check and recheck your shuttle description to make sure it is concise and correct. Finally, don't forget to include your address and telephone number so that we can contact you. Send your river descriptions to:

WKCC - Write-ups
PO Box 1062
Corvallis, OR 97339

After your description has been edited and returned to you for your approval, it will become part of the "Soggy Sneakers" offprint library. It is very likely that you'll be one of the lucky boaters to have your favorite run appear in the next edition of "Soggy Sneakers Guide to Oregon Rivers."

How YOU can be an Honorary Editor

We realize that we are not perfect, and even if we were, river conditions change. Therefore we solicit your help in keeping "Soggy Sneakers" as correct and up-to-date as possible. We shall be happy to hear from you, through the address given above, if you find anything in the book which is out of date or otherwise incorrect. Corrections will be maintained in the offprint library.

Appendix G. Whitewater Boating Organizations

Grande Ronde Whitewater Boaters Club
1610 Cedar
LaGrande, OR 97850

Lower Columbia Canoe Club
P.O. Box 5284
Portland, OR 97240

Northwest Rafters Association
P.O. Box 19008
Portland, OR 97219

Oregon Kayak and Canoe Club
P.O. Box 692
Portland, OR 97207

Southern Oregon Area Kayakers
P.O. Box 462
Rogue River, OR 97537

Washington Kayak Club
P.O. Box 24264
Seattle, WA 98124

Willamette Kayak and Canoe Club
P.O. Box 1062
Corvallis, OR 97339

Oregon Ocean Paddlers Society
P.O. Box
Portland, OR

Alphabetical Index of Rivers and Surf Locations